NETSCAPE ADVENTURES
Step-By-Step Guide To Netscape Navigator And The World Wide Web

by
Cynthia B. Leshin

Illustrated by Bob McLaughlin

Prentice Hall
Upper Saddle River, New Jersey   Columbus, Ohio

Library of Congress Cataloging-in-Publication Data

Leshin, Cynthia B.
    Netscape adventures: step-by-step guide to Netscape Navigator and the World Wide Web / by
Cynthia B. Leshin : illustrated by Bob McLaughlin
        p.   cm.
    Includes bibliographical references and index.
    ISBN 0-13-267089-5. -- ISBN 0-13-255092-X (pbk.)
    1. Netscape.   2. World Wide Web (Information retrieval system)
    3. Internet (Computer network)   I. Title.
    TK5105.883.N48L475   1997
    005.7' 1369--dc20

                                                                96-18106
                                                                CIP

Cover art: Bob McLaughlin
Editor: Charles E. Stewart, Jr.
Production Editor: JoEllen Gohr
Cover Designer: Julia Zonneveld Van Hook
Production Manager: Patricia A. Tonneman
Marketing Manager: Debbie Yarnell

This book was printed and bound by Courier/Kendallville, Inc. The cover was printed by Phoenix Color
Corp.

© 1997 by Prentice-Hall, Inc.
Simon & Schuster/A Viacom Company
Upper Saddle River, New Jersey 07458

Printed in the United States of America
10 9 8 7 6 5 4 3 2

ISBN: 0-13-255092-X

Prentice-Hall International (UK) Limited, *London*
Prentice-Hall of Australia Pty. Limited, *Sydney*
Prentice-Hall Canada Inc., *Toronto*
Prentice-Hall Hispanoamericana, S. A., *Mexico*
Prentice-Hall of India Private Limited, *New Delhi*
Prentice-Hall of Japan, Inc., *Tokyo*
Simon & Schuster Asia Pte. Ltd., *Singapore*
Editora Prentice-Hall do Brasil, Ltda., *Rio de Janeiro*

DISCLAIMER

While a great deal of care has been taken to provide accurate and current information, the Internet is a dynamic and rapidly changing environment. Information may be in one place today and either gone or in a new location tomorrow. New sites come up daily; others disappear. Some sites provide forwarding address information; others will not. The publisher and author assume no responsibility for errors or omissions. Neither is any liability assumed for damages resulting from the use of this information.

As you travel the information superhighway and find that a resource you are looking for can no longer be found at a given Internet address, there are several steps you can take:

1. Check for a new Internet address or link, often provided on the site of the old address.

2. Use one of the search engines described in Chapter 6 with the title of the Internet resource as keywords.

3. Explore Internet databases such as Yahoo, Magellan, Infoseek, Galaxy or the World Wide Web Virtual Library, which have large directories of Internet resources on Web sites.

4. As you travel gopherspace and find that a resource you are looking for cannot be found in the given path, search other menus on the server to which you are connected. Many times you will find these resources have been relocated.

5. Visit the **XPLORA** home page on the World Wide Web. Follow the link to Internet Adventures books where you will find updated information on Internet sites in this book that may have changed. The URL for XPLORA is: **http://www.xplora/xplora/**

The author welcomes readers' feedback, correction of inaccuracies, and suggestions for improvements in subsequent editions. Cynthia Leshin can be contacted by e-mail at: **cleshin@xplora.com**

Dedicated To Steve....
my best friend and partner who shares this very exciting adventure with me.

Acknowledgments

The author would like to thank many people for making this book possible.

To Charles E. Stewart, Jr. for seeing the value of this book and for helping to transform dreams into reality.

I am most grateful to Bob McLaughlin for his illustrations. His creative talents have brought to life my creative visions for this book.

Michael Moses, my copyeditor, has added many important and useful suggestions to my writing. His understanding of the Internet has provided me with valuable feedback to help improve the clarity of my work.

To Marjorie Barrows for her assistance in checking and updating Internet links.

To Richard Altman and Communication Design for providing the technical resources for the art work.

To Carrie Brandon, JoEllen Gohr, and all the others at Simon and Schuster who have made this adventure possible.

To all the Native American artists such as R. Carlos Nakai, Peter Kater, Coyote Oldeman, Tokeya Inajin, and Dean Evenson for their music that has inspired my writing.

Thanks also to all those who have created the Internet and who continue to crusade for freedom of speech. Your vision, dreams, creativity, and generosity have given us a marvelous gift.

I hope this book opens many new doors to students, professors, and anyone interested in learning about the Internet as a powerful tool for communication, information access and sharing.

Preface

Welcome to *Netscape Adventures: Step-By-Step Guide To Netscape Navigator And The World Wide Web!* While there are many books available on the Internet, this book was designed to make your experience worthwhile and meaningful. Beyond enjoying the fun of the Internet, there are practical and valuable resources for almost anyone. This book was also designed to help make your learning journey more fun, more interesting, and easier to understand. Step-by-step, easy-to-follow practical information helps you to begin exploring and using the Internet in just 15 minutes. There is no techie talk—just simple explanations of all those "weird" Internet terms.

Netscape Adventures meets the needs of professors, students, and others interested in learning how to use the Internet as a valuable tool for finding information and resources. This book is also for the entrepreneur and those who are interested in using the Internet in business or for finding a job or an employee.

Pertinent sections include:

■ What the Internet is;

■ How to get connected to the Internet;

■ How to use Eudora for communicating with electronic mail;

■ How to travel the information superhighway using Netscape Navigator 2.0;

■ How to communicate with others with similar interests using listserv mailing, lists, Usenet newsgroups, bulletin boards, on-line chats, and virtual reality environments;

■ How to use search tools for finding information and locating electronic resources;

■ How to use gopher, File Transfer Protocol (FTP), and telnet;

■ Business on the Internet;

■ How to design a World Wide Web page.

In addition this book provides Guided Tours to introduce you to Internet tools and resources and hands-on practice using these tools. You will find addresses for many of the best Internet sites.

TRIP ITINERARY

CHAPTER 4 — Netscape Navigator & The World Wide Web   93

CHAPTER 5 — Finding Information On The Internet 191

CHAPTER 6 — Gopher, FTP, Telnet   **221**

CHAPTER 7 — Business On The Net   **261**

CHAPTER 8 — Designing A Web Site 283

NETIQUETTE

References 304

Index 308

Chapter One

WEBVILLE TRAVEL AGENCY

TOURIST INFORMATION CENTER
Welcome To Webville...

In this book you will learn how to travel easily along the information superhighway. You will visit virtual communities and interact with people all over the world. You will take virtual field trips and find that viewing multimedia resources on a topic is as easy as pointing and clicking your mouse. Most importantly, you will quickly learn how to use the Internet as a tool for finding information and resources that interest you.

As you travel, you will learn how to use navigational tools such as Eudora for communicating using electronic mail (e-mail) and Netscape Navigator 2.0 for sending files and electronic mail, and for Internet navigation. You will learn about the following Internet resources:

- electronic mail
- listserv mailing lists
- World Wide Web
- gopher
- File Transfer Protocol (FTP)
- telnet
- Usenet newsgroups
- Free-Nets
- search engines
- chat

Additionally, you will learn:

- How to find valuable information and resources
- How businesses are using the Internet
- How to design a Web page

About This Internet Travel Guide

This book uses a travel metaphor to help make your journey more fun, more interesting, and easier to understand. It is for anyone interested in quickly learning how to navigate the Internet and make it a valuable tool for finding information and resources.

You will use the following aids:

Tourist Information Center

The Tourist Information Center provides basic and essential information on the Internet tools and Web resources.

Guided Tour

In the Guided Tour sections, your Internet Travel Guide will show you how to use Internet tools and resources and how to find valuable information.

Guided Walks

Each Guided Walk provides hands-on practice using Internet tools and resources.

Expedition Experience

The Expedition Experience provides opportunities for you to communicate with e-mail and listserv mailing lists and to explore the World Wide Web, gopher, FTP, and Usenet newsgroup resources using Netscape Navigator. You will also visit the best Web sites to learn how businesses are using the Internet and how a Web site attracts Net users attention.

Locator Maps

Locator maps help you to find information and resources on the Internet.

Foreign Language Center

Every foreign country has its own vocabulary and language. In the Foreign Language Center you will find definitions for new words and terms.

What Is The Internet?

in•ter•net n.
1. world's largest information network 2. global
web of computer networks 3. inter-network of many
networks all running the TCP/IP protocol
4. powerful communication tool 5. giant highway
system connecting computers and the regional
and local networks that connect these computers
syn. **information superhighway, infobahn,
data highway, electronic highway, Net,
cyberspace**

The analogy most frequently used to refer to the Internet is "information superhighway." This superhighway consists of a vast network of computers connecting people and resources around the world. The Internet is accessible to anyone with a computer and a modem.

The Internet began in 1969 when a collection of computer networks was first sponsored by the United States Department of Defense in response to a need for military institutions and universities to share their research. In the 1970s, government and university networks continued to develop and many other organizations and companies began to build private computer networks. During the late 1980s, the National Science Foundation (NSF) created a network of five supercomputer centers at major universities which is the foundation of the Internet today.

Computer networks were initially established to share information among institutions that were physically separate. Throughout the years these networks have grown, and the volume and type of information made available to people outside these institutions has also continued to evolve and grow. Today we can exchange electronic mail, conduct research, or look at and obtain files that contain text information, graphics, sound, and video. The Internet is constantly changing and growing as more schools, universities, organizations, and institutions make new resources available through our computer networks. These networks make it possible for us to be globally interconnected with each other and to this wealth of information.

What Does It Mean To "Be On The Internet?"

"Being on the Internet" means having full access to all Internet services. Any commercial service or institution that has full Internet access provides the following:

- Electronic mail (e-mail)
- Telnet
- File Transfer Protocol (FTP)
- World Wide Web

Electronic Mail

Electronic mail is the most basic, easiest to use, and, for many people, the most useful Internet service. E-mail services allow you to send, forward, and receive messages from people all over the world, usually at no additional charge. You can then easily reply to, save, file, and categorize received messages.

Electronic mail also makes it possible to participate in electronic conferences and discussions. You can use e-mail to request information from individuals, universities, and institutions.

Telnet

Telnet provides the capability to login to a remote computer and to work interactively with it. When you run a telnet session, your computer is remotely connected to a computer at another location, but will act as if it were directly connected to that computer.

File Transfer Protocol (FTP)

File Transfer Protocol is a method that allows you to move files and data from one computer to another. File Transfer Protocol, most commonly referred to as FTP, enables you to download magazines, books, documents, free software, music, graphics, and much more.

World Wide Web

The World Wide Web is a collection of standards and protocols used to access information available on the Internet. World Wide Web users can easily access text documents, images, video, and sound.

The Web And The Internet

The World Wide Web (WWW or Web) is a collection of documents linked together in what is called a *hypermedia system*. Links can point to any location on the Internet that can contain information in the form of text, graphics, video, or sound files.

Using the World Wide Web requires *browsers* to view Web documents and navigate through the intricate link structure. Currently there are between 30-40 different Web browsers. You will learn how to use the premier Web browser—Netscape Navigator. Netscape combines a point and click interface design with an open architecture that is capable of integrating other Internet tools such as electronic mail, FTP, gopher, WAIS, and Usenet newsgroups. This architecture makes it relatively easy to incorporate images, video, and sound into text documents.

The World Wide Web was developed at the European Particle Physics Laboratory (CERN) in Geneva, Switzerland. Originally it was developed as a means for physicists to share papers and data easily. Today it has evolved into a sophisticated technology that links hypertext and hypermedia documents.

The Web and the Internet are not synonymous. The World Wide Web is a collection of standards and protocols used to access information available on the Internet. The Internet is the network used to transport information.

The Web uses three standards:
- URLs (Uniform Resource Locators);
- HTTP (Hypertext Transfer Protocol);
- HTML (Hypertext Markup Language).

These standards provide a mechanism for WWW servers and clients to locate and display information available through other protocols such as gopher, FTP, and telnet.

URLs (Uniform Resource Locators)
URLs are a standard format for identifying locations on the Internet. They also allow an addressing system for other Internet protocols such as access to gopher menus, FTP file retrieval, and Usenet

newsgroups. URLs specify three types of information needed to retrieve a document

- the protocol to be used,
- the server address and port to which to connect, and
- the path to the information.

The format for a URL is **protocol//server-name/path**

Sample URLs

World Wide Web URL:	http://home.netscape.com/home/welcome.html
Document from a secure server:	https://netscape.com/
Gopher URL:	gopher://umslvma.umsl.edu/Library/
FTP URL:	ftp://nic.umass.edu/
Telnet URL:	telnet://geophys.washington.edu/
Usenet URL:	news:rec.humor.funny

NOTE

The URL for newsgroups omits the two slashes. The two slashes designate the beginning of a server name. Since you are using your Internet provider's local news server, you do not need to designate a news server by adding the slashes. In Chapter 4 you will learn how to configure Netscape for your news server.

URL TIPS..

Do not capitalize the protocol string. For example, the HTTP protocol should be **http://** not **HTTP://**. Some browsers such as Netscape correct these errors. Others do not.

If you have trouble connecting to a Web site, check your URL and be sure you have typed in the address correctly.

You do not need to add a slash (/) at the end of a URL such as **http://home.netscape.com** A slash indicates that there is another path to follow.

HTTP (Hypertext Transfer Protocol)

HTTP is a protocol used to transfer information within the World Wide Web. Web site URLs begin with the http protocol

http://

This Web URL connects you to Netscape's Home Page.

http://home.netscape.com

HTML (Hypertext Markup Language)

HTML is the programming language used to create a Web page. It formats the text of the document, describes its structure, and specifies links to other documents. HTML also includes programming to access and display different media such as images, video, and sound.

What Do I Need To Pack?

Now that you know more about the Internet and the World Wide Web, it is time to prepare for your journey.

You need the following resources to use Netscape to navigate the Internet:

- a telephone connection,
- a computer,
- a communication modem,
- a SLIP/PPP Internet connection, and
- Internet software
    - TCP/IP software
    - Netscape Navigator or other Internet browser
    - Eudora or another TCP/IP e-mail software program

Computer

Netscape Navigator supports the following platforms:

- Macintosh System 7
- Windows 3.1 or later
- Most UNIX/X Window System platforms, including Sun Sparc (Solaris, SunOS), Silicon Graphics (IRIX), Digital Equipment Corp. Alpha (OSF/1), Hewlett-Packard 700-series (HP-UX)

Communication Modem

A modem changes computer signals into signals that can be transmitted over telephone lines. The speed at which the signals are transferred is referred to as the baud rate. The higher the baud rate, the faster the signals move. You will want to select the fastest modem that can be supported by the Internet connection you are using. Netscape is optimized to run smoothly over 14.4 kilobit/second modems, as well as at higher speeds.

Direct Internet Connection

In order to "be on the Internet" your computer must have software that can send and receive data using the TCP/IP (Transport Control Protocol/Internet Protocol) communication protocols. TCP/IP are two separate protocols that work together and make it possible for different computer networks and computers to talk to each other (whether it be DOS/Windows, Macintosh, or UNIX). TCP/IP are the communication protocols upon which the Internet is built.

In order to support the transfer of data with TCP/IP you will need either a SLIP (Serial Line Internet Protocol) or PPP (Point-to-Point) account. Both SLIP and PPP are communication protocols that support an Internet connection. PPP is a newer protocol that performs exactly the function as SLIP. Some people prefer PPP over SLIP. However, most Internet users find very little difference in performance between them. PPP is likely to become better supported than SLIP in the future.

You can get a SLIP or PPP connection through an Internet service provider in your area or from your college, school, or business. The cost for service should be between $20 to $35 per month for at least 120-150 or more hours per month. The service provider gives you an e-mail account and access to Usenet newsgroups. Some Internet providers also make space available on their server for you to create a World Wide Web page.

There are several ways to find an Internet service provider:

- Contact a local computer-users group and ask for their recommendation.

- Contact a local college or university. Many universities offer free or low cost Internet accounts.

 If a friend has access to the World Wide Web, visit the following Web site to find Internet access providers by local area codes:

http://www.thelist.com/

 If a friend has access to Usenet newsgroups, the *alt.internet.services* group is the online version of Consumer Reports for evaluating Internet service providers.

ISDN (Integrated Services Digital Network)

Integrated Services Digital Network (ISDN) is a telephone service established over a decade ago that is rapidly becoming a cost-effective solution to the slow transfer of information such as graphics and multimedia files over the Internet. ISDN lines transfer data five to six times faster than 28.8 kilobit-per-second (kbps) modems. Regional telephone companies are offering the service in many locations. Additionally, the companies that make the required hardware are responding to the need and producing products at lower prices with easier installation.

The advantage of ISDN over traditional voice, fax, and modem communication that use standard phone lines is its digital nature. Currently most information is carried in analog form.

If your are interested in learning more about ISDN check with your phone company for availability and rates. Some phone companies have specially trained ISDN service reps who can offer help on the hardware you will need. You also need to check with your Internet access provider to see if they offer ISDN access in your area and find the cost for this service. For more information call the toll-free national ISDN hot line at 800-992-4736 or visit these Web sites:

http://www.alumni.caltech.edu/~dank/isdn

http://www.bellcore.com/ISDN/ISDN.html

Connecting To The Internet

There are three ways to connect to the Internet

- a network
- an on-line service
- a SLIP/PPP connection

Network Connection

Network connections are most often found in colleges, schools, businesses, or government agencies and use dedicated lines to provide fast access to all Internet resources. Special hardware such as routers may be required at the local site. Prices depend on bandwidth and the speed of the connection.

On-line Services

Examples of on-line services include America Online, CompuServe, Prodigy, Delphi, and GEnie. On-line services are virtual communities that provide services to their subscribers including electronic mail, discussion forums on topics of interest, real time chats, business and advertising opportunities, software libraries, stock quotes, on-line newspapers, and Internet resources (gopher, FTP, newsgroups). There are both advantages and disadvantages to these online services.

Advantages

The advantages to on-line services include:

- easy to install and use,
- content offered by provider,
- easy to find and download software,
- easy to use e-mail, and
- virtual community of resources and people.

Commercial on-line services are excellent places to begin exploring and learning about the use of e-mail and access to networked information and resources.

Disadvantages

The disadvantages to online services include:

- expensive to use,
- do not always access all Internet resources such as gopher, FTP, and telnet, and
- must use the on-line service's e-mail program and Internet browser.

On-line services charge an average of $9.95 per month for 5 hours of on on-line time. Additional on-line time is billed at rates of $2.95 to $5.95 per hour. Some services charge more for being on-line at peak hours such as during the day.

In comparison an Internet access provider may charge $15-30 per month for 100 to unlimited hours of online time. Prices vary depending on your locality and the Internet access provider.

SLIP/PPP Connection

Internet access providers offer SLIP (Serial Line Interface Protocol) or PPP (Point-to-Point Protocol) connections (SLIP/PPP). This service is referred to as *Dial-Up-Networking* and makes it possible for your PC to dial into their server and communicate with other computers on the Internet. Once you have established a PPP, SLIP, or direct Internet connection, you can use any software that speaks the Internet language called TCP/IP. There are several TCP/IP software applications including Eudora and Netscape Navigator.

Internet service providers should provide you with the required TCP/IP software to get you connected to the Internet. Additionally, many will provide Internet applications such as Eudora and Netscape. Prices are usually based on hours of usage, bandwidth, and locality.

TCP/IP and SLIP/PPP Software

Macintosh Software

TCP/IP software for the Macintosh is called MacTCP and is supplied by Apple. Two popular software choices necessary to implement either SLIP or PPP are MacPPP or MacSLIP. Using one of these programs with MacTCP creates a direct Internet connection.

Your Internet access provider should give you software that has already been configured for connecting your Mac to the Internet.

Windows Users

The most popular program available for Windows 3.1 users is *Trumpet Winsock*. Winsock combines all you need in one software package to create a direct Internet connection. Most Internet service providers will have configured your Trumpet Winsock software so you can immediately connect your PC to their server and access the Internet.

Windows 95

If you are using Windows 95 you have the option of connecting to the Internet using all three types of Internet connections: network, on-line service, and SLIP/PPP connection.

Microsoft Network (MSN) is an alternative to other online services such as American Online or a complete Internet access provider. After Windows 95 is installed a Microsoft Network icon is placed on your desktop. To explore MSN, just double-click on the Microsoft Network icon. Windows 95 dials up MSN and downloads the latest products and MSN phone numbers. Before you can explore MSN you must register by entering your name, method of payment, and read the rules. After you have completed the required information you will be assigned a member ID. When you first sign onto MSN you select a password. MSN offers e-mail, access to the Internet and other Microsoft services.

Figure 1.1
Microsoft Network sign-up

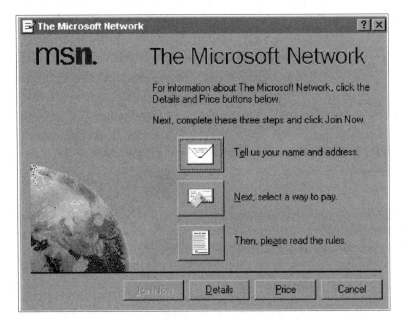

Internet Explorer makes it possible for you to use its built-in support for TCP/IP to connect to the Internet using your Internet access provider (see Figure 1.2). After you have completed the Internet set-up for Windows 95 you will be able to use any TCP/IP Internet applications such as Eudora, Netscape, or Microsoft's 32-bit Internet browser designed for Windows 95 (Internet Explorer).

Three steps are involved to connect Windows 95 to the Internet:

1. Install Dial-up Networking
2. Install TCP/IP
3. Make the connection

Before you proceed with these steps you will need information from your Internet access provider. You will need to know the following:

- Your provider's Domain Naming System (DNS) IP address.
- The dial-up telephone number for your provider.
- Your provider's host name and domain name.
- Your login ID (username) and password.

Unlike Trumpet Winsock that has already been configured with this information, Windows 95 makes it initially more difficult to connect to the Internet. However, once you have completed these three set-up steps, accessing the Internet and using your choice of Internet applications is very easy. If you need help setting up your TCP/IP software and have access to the Web on another system, visit this site for help with Windows 95 Internet set-up
http://www.windows95.com/

SUGGESTION
Ask your Internet provider for information on how to install Windows 95 TCP/IP for their Internet service. If you have installed Microsoft Plus, use Microsoft's Internet Set-up Wizard to assist you with the set-up. To find the Internet Set-up Wizard

1. Go to the Start menu, choose Programs
2. Select and open the Accessories folder
3. Select and open Internet Tools
4. Double-click on Internet Set-up Wizard

Figure 1.2
Internet Set-up Wizard allowing you to choose your own Internet provider.

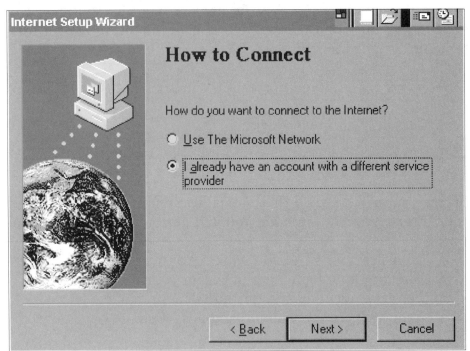

Figure 1.3
Internet Set-up wizard requesting your Internet Provider's Domain Name data.

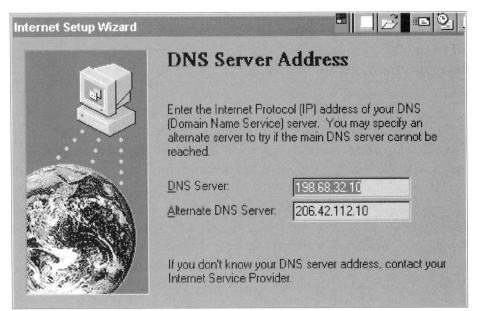

The Adventure Begins...

Once you have installed your Internet software, connecting to the Internet is easy. You will need the following:

- Electronic mail software (Eudora is recommended. See Chapter 2 on acquiring and using Eudora.)

- An Internet browser (Netscape Navigator is recommended. See Chapter 4 on acquiring and using Netscape.)

- Your e-mail address. (Check with your Internet provider if you are not sure of your e-mail address.)

- Your Internet account username and password. (Check with your Internet provider if you are not sure of your username and password.)

- The mail server address for your Internet access provider. This information will be necessary when you use Netscape Navigator. The mailserver typically appears as

    mailserver.providername.com

- The news server address for your Internet access provider. This information is necessary to access Usenet newsgroups from within Netscape Navigator. The news server address appears as

    news.providername.com

Getting Started...

1. Turn on your computer and modem.
2. Open your SLIP/PPP application.
3. Your modem dials the number for your Internet access provider.
4. Their modem answers.
5. You will be asked for your username and password.
   When the Internet access provider has verified your account, you will be connected.
6. After the connection is established, open your Internet software (Netscape Navigator or your e-mail program).

Using An Internet Navigational Suite

Internet front-end navigational suites are complete packages of tools that make it easier for you to connect to the Internet. In the past these suites provided separate software applications packaged together. The newer versions offer integrated software programs that are simple and save time. Every aspect of the Internet is easier including your initial Internet set-up, Internet navigation, and downloading files using the File Transfer Protocol (FTP).

All of the front-end packages include the following:

- A configuration utility for establishing your Internet service
- E-mail software
- A graphical Web browser
- A newsgroup reader, and
- An FTP utility.

The configuration utility assists you with dialing up a service provider and opening an account. The service providers listed in the software are usually limited to several large companies.

NOTE

- The cost for an Internet connection provided by the companies listed in front-end suites may be more expensive than the cost of using a local Internet provider.

- Integrated software packages may not allow you to use other e-mail programs or Web browsers.

Suggested Internet Navigational Suites
- Netscape Navigator Personal Edition: (415) 528-2555
- Internet In A Box: (800) 557-9614 or (800) 777-9638
- EXPLORE Internet: (800) 863-4548
- IBM Internet Connection For Windows: (800) 354-3222
- Internet Chameleon: (408) 973-7171
- Internet Anywhere: (519) 888-9910
- SuperHighway Access: (800) 929-3054

Chapter Two

ELECTRONIC MAIL (E-Mail)

TOURIST INFORMATION CENTER

What Is E-Mail?

Electronic mail, or e-mail, is the most widely used Internet service. E-mail makes it possible for you to:

- communicate with friends who have e-mail accounts,
- meet and interact with people all over the world,
- participate in electronic conferences and discussions on an unlimited range of topics,
- subscribe to electronic services,
- get answers to technical questions,
- take online workshops or classes, or
- mail electronic text and graphics to anyone with an e-mail address.

Using e-mail is like sending a letter to someone. However, your electronic letter will be created and sent by the computer. You will be sending a file rather than a piece of paper. The file or message you send will go to the electronic mailbox of the person you address. You will also have your own electronic mailbox to receive any mail that comes into your Internet account.

Most mail messages are composed of pure ASCII (see Foreign Language Center) or standard text files. This means that:

- your message can be read by users of any type of computer.
- no fancy formatting of the file is possible.
- no graphics may be transmitted.
- no special characters can be accommodated within the message.

In addition to sending a text message, most electronic mail software supports the following:

- Mail messages can be printed on paper.
- Files or messages can be attached to a message that you are sending.
- Messages can be sent to multiple recipients (courtesy copies).
- Messages can be filed and stored in folders that you create.
- Messages can be replied to or forwarded to another person.
- Messages can be read at your convenience.

The Internet Post Office... E-Mail Addresses

The best analogy for understanding how e-mail works is the U.S. Postal Service. When you write a letter and use the Postal Service to deliver it, you probably follow these steps:

1. Write the letter.
2. Put the letter in an envelope.
3. Address the envelope.
4. Give your letter to the Postal Service.

The letter is picked up by a postal truck, taken to the post office, grouped with other letters going to the same zip code, then forwarded to another place that handles that zip code. When the letters arrive at their destination, they are sorted by address, picked up by a mail carrier, and delivered to the recipient's mailbox.

A very similar process occurs when you use electronic mail to send a letter. You will follow these three steps.

1. Address your e-mail envelope on the computer.
2. Write your letter.
3. Send your e-mail message.

Two things must happen before you can use electronic mail.

1. You must have an electronic mail account and know your e-mail address.

2. You must know the e-mail address of the person to whom you are sending your message.

An electronic mail account may be obtained from several places including

- your school, college, or university;
- a commercial Internet provider; or
- your state or local network.

Your Internet E-Mail Address

All individuals who use the Internet must have their own Internet addresses. Each Internet address follows the standard format

username@host.domain

My e-mail address is: cleshin@xplora.com

My username is: cleshin
The host is: xplora
The domain is: com (commercial)

There are many variations of this format. You will frequently see addresses that include subdomains in order to indicate the department or sublocation where the host is to be found, the actual location of the host (state, country), or other information about the host's identity.

username@host.subdomain.domain

My other e-mail addresses illustrate the variation in format.

cleshin@azedlink.state.az.us
(Account with the State of Arizona, AZEDLINK project.)

cleshin@aol.com
(Account at America OnLine.)

ICCBL@ASUVM.INRE.ASU.EDU
(Account at Arizona State University.)

NOTE
The username of an e-mail account may be a number or a series of letters as in my address at Arizona State University.

> **Internet addresses include:**
> - your account name (also referred to as username, userid, or login name),
> - the "at" (@) symbol that follows your account name,
> - the name of the host for your e-mail account,
> - a dot or period (.) that separates each part of the address, and
> - domain name (type of organization that hosts this Internet account).

Organizational Domains

In the United States most Internet sites have domain names that fall into one of these categories.

edu	for educational institution
com	for commercial organization
mil	for military
gov	for government
org	for non-profit organizations
net	for networking organization
int	for international organization

Geographical Domains

Outside of the United States it is more common to use geographic zone names.

at	for Austria
au	for Australia
ca	for Canada
ch	Switzerland
de	Germany (Deutschland)
dk	Denmark
es	Spain
fr	France
gr	Greece
ie	Republic of Ireland
jp	Japan
nz	New Zealand
uk	United Kingdom
us	United States

E-Mail Travel — General Information...

Electronic-mail programs will differ slightly in the type of symbol or icon used to indicate an e-mail function. For example, your electronic mail box may be represented by an envelope icon, a mail box icon, or just a symbol that says "mail."

Figure 2.1
(a) America Online's mail icon.

(b) Eudora's e-mail icon.

YOU HAVE MAIL

Each e-mail capability will be represented by some icon that represents a command to do something. Usually the command is typed under the icon. The documentation that is supplied with your e-mail program provides more specific information.

Here are some examples of how different e-mail systems appear.

Note
Electronic mail software differs in its screen appearance, but the basic operations will be the same: send mail, read, reply, save, and print mail. In most cases, the captions for the icons or program symbols will show the e-mail function.

Figure 2.2
America Online's e-mail screen.

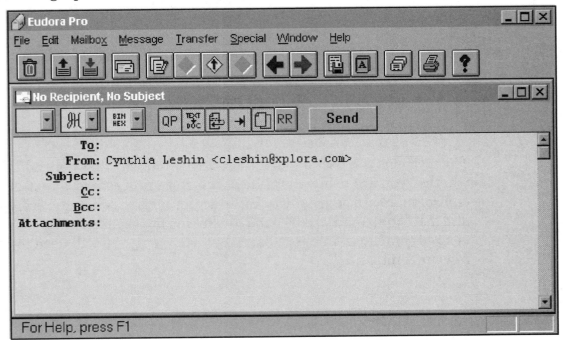

Notice the icons or program symbols that indicate the e-mail functions.

Figure 2.3
Eudora's graphical e-mail interface (Windows version).

Documentation is available for Eudora to help you understand each icon function. Eudora is one of the best e-mail programs and is available as freeware for use with SLIP and PPP Internet accounts.

America Online and Eudora are examples of graphical interface electronic mail systems that provide symbols or icons for sending and receiving mail, as well as space for your address and message.

Here is an example of a text-based e-mail program called Pine.

Figure 2.4
Text-based e-mail program.

```
 PINE 3.90   MAIN MENU                    Folder: INBOX  2 Messages


        ?     HELP              -  Get help using Pine

        C     COMPOSE MESSAGE   -  Compose and send a message

        I     FOLDER INDEX      -  View messages in current folder

        L     FOLDER LIST       -  Select a folder to view

        A     ADDRESS BOOK      -  Update address book

   I  S     SETUP             -  Configure or update Pine

        Q     QUIT              -  Exit the Pine program



   Copyright 1989-1994.  PINE is a trademark of the University of Washington.
                    [Folder "INBOX" opened with 2 messages]
  ? Help                      P PrevCmd                 R RelNotes
  O OTHER CMDS  [ListFldrs] N NextCmd                 K KBLock
```

The methods you use to send and receive mail will vary depending on whether you are using a graphical interface program or a text-based environment. In a graphical interface program, sending, receiving, and managing mail will be done by clicking on a symbol or icon for the desired command. In a text-based environment, you will need to type in your commands.

GUIDED WALKS

Electronic-Mail

Hands-On Practice

In this section you will find Guided Walks for using the Eudora electronic mail program for the Macintosh and Windows. Eudora is a freeware program (software available at no cost) and considered to be one of the best e-mail programs available. Eudora by QUALCOMM is the commercial version of the Eudora software. It is currently available from the QUEST (QUALCOMM Enterprise Software Technologies). Most Internet access providers make Eudora available to subscribers.

Eudora by QUALCOMM differs significantly from the Eudora freeware in three significant areas: features, documentation, and support.

Obtaining Freeware Eudora

The current versions of the Eudora freeware for Macintosh and Windows are available via File Transfer Protocol (FTP) and e-mail (list server). If you have a friend who has access to the Internet and understands FTP, they can login to **ftp.qualcomm.com** as anonymous and retrieve the application file from the **/quest/mac/ eudora/1.5** or **/quest/windows/eudora/1.4** directory.

To obtain the Macintosh freeware via e-mail (370k file), send a message to **majordomo@qualcomm.com** with the body text as follows:

> **get freeware Mac/Eudora.hqx**

Alternatively, if you want the Power Macintosh version of the freeware (650k file), use the following message:

> **get freeware Mac/Eudora/fat.hqx**

To obtain the Windows freeware via e-mail (290k file), send a message to **majordomo@qualcomm.com** with the body text as follows:

> **get freeware Win/Eudora.hqx**

The application files will be delivered to you as message attachments. Be aware that, due to the file sizes, the transfer may take some time on slower connections.

Note

The best way to obtain a copy of Eudora is from your Internet provider.

Both the Macintosh and Windows version of freeware have a 100 page manual. You will receive information regarding how to obtain a copy when you receive your freeware program.

Obtaining Commercial Eudora

Eudora Pro for Macintosh and Windows can be ordered from Qualcomm by calling 1-800-2-EUDORA. The retail price is $65.

Other Electronic Mail Programs

If you have chosen another e-mail program to use, follow along with the guided practice in this section. You will find that many of the functions for sending, receiving, or managing your e-mail will be similar. If you are using another graphical e-mail program, look for the icon or symbol that represents the function you are asking the computer to perform.

> **NOTE**
>
> Netscape Navigator 2.0 has a built-in electronic mail program. See Chapter 4 for information on how to use Netscape for e-mail.

In this section you will learn about and practice

- addressing your mail;
- composing and sending your message;
- receiving, reading, and replying to a message;
- managing your e-mail by deleting, saving, and filing messages;
- forwarding a messages;
- sending courtesy copies of your message;
- printing a message;
- creating an address book;
- creating a personal signature;
- attaching a file or document to your e-mail message.

Before You Begin...

Before you can use electronic mail you will need to have a personal Internet account (username and password). E-mail addresses are assigned to individuals when they receive an Internet account.

> ### NOTE
>
> All figures in this section are for the Macintosh version of Eudora. Macintosh and Windows versions are very similar. If differences are significant, an illustration will be included for the Windows version.

GUIDED WALK 1

Sending A Message

In this Guided Walk you will practice using the following e-mail functions:

- logging in to your personal account,
- addressing your mail,
- composing your message, and
- sending your message.

Practice using the Eudora e-mail program by sending a message to yourself.

1. **Login to your account**
   Before you can begin using electronic mail, you must establish contact with your Internet account. Your Internet provider will give you a local dial-up number. If you have a SLIP/PPP account, open your TCP/IP Software.

   - for Windows 3.1, open Trumpet Winsock;
   - for Windows 95 open your TCP/IP software;
   - for the Macintosh, open your PPP software such as MacPPP.

After your modem has connected with the Internet provider, you will be prompted to login. The login process consists of two parts.

a. You will be prompted for your username.

> login: ***type your username*** and press <RETURN>

b. You will be asked (prompted) for your password.

> password: ***type in your password*** and press <RETURN>

Figure 2.5
An example of a login to an Internet account.

Password Authentication Protocol (PAP)
Auth. ID: `Pxplora`
Password:
Cancel   OK

2. **Open your electronic mail software program.**
   Double-click on the icon for your e-mail program. In this case, double-click on the Eudora icon.

Figure 2.6
When you double-click on Eudora you will see this screen.

(a) Macintosh Version of Eudora.

```
  File  Edit  Mailbox  Message  Transfer  Special  Window
                  «No Recipient», «No Subject»
  [][BIN][HEX]  ✓QP  []  ✓[]  ✓[]  []  RR  [ Send ]
          To:
        From: cleshin@xplora.com (Cynthia Leshin)
     Subject:
          Cc:
         Bcc:
  Attachments:
```

(b) Windows Version of Eudora.

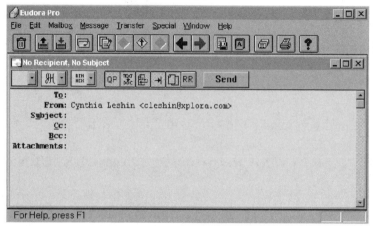

3. Create an outgoing message.

To write and send a message, click on the **Message** pull-down menu. Select, **New Message.**

Figure 2.7
Eudora Message pull-down menu.

A composition window
for writing your electronic
message will be displayed.

Message	Transfer	Spe
New Message		⌘N
Reply		⌘R
Forward		
Redirect		
Send Again		
New Message To		▶
Reply To		▶
Forward To		▶
Redirect To		▶
Send Message Now		⌘E
Attach Document...		⌘H
Change		▶
Delete		⌘D

Figure 2.8
Eudora's composition window.

4. Address your mail.

The electronic mail envelope includes

To: (electronic mail address for the person to whom you are sending the message)

From: (your e-mail address)

Subject: (topic of your message)

When you address your e-mail envelope you will need to know the address of the person who is to receive your message. It is very important to know the recipient's exact address.

a. Look up the address of the intended recipient of your message. In this case it will be yourself.

b. The place where you will enter the address will usually be a text box marked "To": Type your address, then press the TAB key or RETURN.

c. Next you will see a flashing insertion point at the "Subject" box.

Type your subject. Press TAB or RETURN.

NOTE
Your e-mail address will automatically be entered into the *From* field by the e-mail program.

Figure 2.9
An example of completed e-mail address information.

```
┌──────────────────────────────────────────────────┐
│ ▓  cleshin@autobaun.com, «No Subject»            │
├──────────────────────────────────────────────────┤
│ □ |ℬℋ|BIN  ✓QP   ▤   ✓⊞  ✓⇥   ▯   RR  [ Send ]  │
│    HEX                                            │
├──────────────────────────────────────────────────┤
│         To: cleshin@autobaun.com                 │
│       From: xplora@autobaun.com (Cynthia Leshin) │
│    Subject: practice message                     │
│         Cc:                                      │
│        Bcc:                                      │
│ Attachments:                                     │
└──────────────────────────────────────────────────┘
```

5. **Compose the message.**
    Place your cursor in the box or space provided to enter your message. Type your message. Reread your message and make any changes.

Figure 2.10
Eudora's Composition window with e-mail address, subject, and completed message.

```
┌─────────────────────────────────────────────────────────────────┐
│ ▣   cleshin@alpha.autobaun.com, practice message            ▣   │
├─────────────────────────────────────────────────────────────────┤
│ □ |📧|BIN│ ✓ QP    │📄│  ✓ 🔲   ✓ →|    🗇    RR  [ Send ]        │
│      HEX                                                          │
├─────────────────────────────────────────────────────────────────┤
│        To: xplora@alpha.autobaun.com                        ⇧    │
│      From: xplora@autobaun.com (Cynthia Leshin)                  │
│   Subject: practice message                                      │
│        Cc:                                                        │
│       Bcc:                                                        │
│ Attachments:                                                     │
│ ─────────────────────────────────────────────────────────────   │
│ This is a practice message.                                      │
│                                                                  │
│                                                             ⇩    │
└─────────────────────────────────────────────────────────────────┘
```

6. **Send your message.**
    Click on the icon that says "Send."

Traveling Hint

• When writing Internet addresses, use small (lowercase) letters.

• If you see some addresses that have both upper-and lowercase letters, it is safe to change all letters to lowercase.

If you do decide to change the address to lowercase be aware that occasionally the userid is case sensitive, and you may have to keep this part of the address in capital letters.

Examples: INFO.delphi.com
            JSMITH.aol.com

GUIDED WALK 2

Receiving, Reading, & Replying To Your Messages

This Guided Walk provides the opportunity to practice

- receiving a message,
- reading a message, and
- replying to a message.

1.   Receive your messages.

After you logon to your Internet account, open your Eudora e-mail program by double-clicking on the application icon. You will now be asked for your e-mail password.

Figure 2.11

Eudora's request for your e-mail password.

```
┌─────────────────────────────────────────────┐
│  Please enter the xplora@alpha.autobaun.com  │
│  password:                                   │
│                                              │
│              Password: │•••••••│             │
│                                              │
│  ┌──┐                    ┌────────┐ ┌──────┐ │
│  │≡ │                    │ Cancel │ │  OK  │ │
│  └──┘                    └────────┘ └──────┘ │
└─────────────────────────────────────────────┘
```

After you enter your password, click on OK. Eudora will automatically check for e-mail messages. If you have messages you will receive this mail alert.

Figure 2.12

Eudora's mail message.

If you do not have mail, Eudora displays this message.

Figure 2.13
Eudora's no mail message.

In either case, click on OK. If you have mail, your electronic mailbox will look like Figure 2.14.

Figure 2.14
New messages in Eudora.

		Who	Date		K	Subject
		Marc Siegel – NAS	9/27/95		4	LFS #12: This week's flights (Sept 25-29
		Marc Siegel – NAS	10/2/95		12	LFS newsletter – Oct 2, 1995
		Marc Siegel – NAS	Thursday		16	JUP #2: Preparing the probe, propulsion .
		newaccounts@wired	5/14/95		7	Welcome to HotWired!

In

4/37K/0K

2. **Read your message.**
   To read a message, double-click on the one that you would like to read. To move up or down the message list, use the up and down arrow keys on your keyboard or click on the desired message.

NOTE

After you read one message, Eudora will automatically display the next message in the list.

3. **Reply to your message.**

If you want to reply to a message you have received, you can do so by clicking on **Message** in the main menu, then click on **Reply** in the pull-down menu.

Figure 2.15

Eudora's **Message** pull-down menu with the **Reply** command option.

Message	Transfer	Spec
New Message		⌘N
Reply		⌘R
Forward		
Redirect		
Send Again		
New Message To		▶
Reply To		▶
Forward To		▶
Redirect To		▶
Send Message Now		⌘E
Attach Document...		⌘H
Change		▶
Delete		⌘D

A new message window will appear with the original e-mail sender's address already in the recipient or "To" box and the original subject in the "Subject" box preceded by "Re." Type your message in the composition box.

Figure 2.16

Eudora's **Reply** to a message composition box.

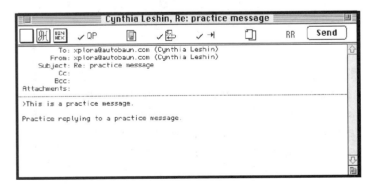

4. **Send your reply.**

Press the "Send" button to send the message.

37

GUIDED WALK 3
Managing Your E-Mail

Guided Walk 3 provides practice

- deleting a message,
- storing a message,
- using stored messages,
- printing a message,
- forwarding a message,
- sending courtesy copies of your message,
- putting e-mail addresses in your Address Book,
- creating an electronic signature, and
- working with attachments.

All incoming electronic mail is stored on your Internet host in a mailbox area shared by all users. Try to minimize the amount of space your mail takes up by deleting or filing your mail. Your e-mail software may also run faster if your mailbox is not full of messages. When you begin to receive electronic mail, practice using these functions.

Deleting A Message

Messages you no longer want should be deleted.

1. Open your **In** box that shows your messages.

2. Select, or highlight, the message you want to delete.

3. Click on **Message** in the main menu and select **Delete** from the pull-down menu.

> **NOTE**
>
> Eudora does not delete messages immediately. Deleted messages are stored in the **Trash** mailbox until you exit the program. If you realize that you did not want to delete a message, you can retrieve the message by opening the **Trash** mailbox.

Storing A Message

Messages you want to save can be stored in electronic file folders. In Eudora these file folders are referred to as **Mailboxes**. Before you begin saving messages, you may want to create categories for your file folders. For example, a file folder may be created for a student's projects that are e-mailed to a professor. Other file folders, or Mailboxes, might include, *Student's Correspondence*, *Letters Received*, and *Business* e-mail messages.

The procedure for creating **Mailboxes** and for saving messages consists of three steps.

1. Organize your mail.
2. Create a mailbox.
3. Transfer a message to your mailbox.

1. Organize your mail.
   Organize your mail by defining a set of categories. Each category will be made into a personal folder or Mailbox. Think of this as being similar to a filing system that you may use in an office.

2. Create a Mailbox.

   a. To create a Mailbox, select **New** from the **Mailbox** pull-down menu.

Figure 2.17
Eudora Mailbox menu.

Mailbox	Message	Tran
In		⌘I
Out		
Trash		
New...		
Other...		
XPLORA		
BOOK		▶
BUSINESS		▶

b. Type in the new mailbox name and click **OK**.

Figure 2.18
Eudora's dialog box for creating a new mailbox.

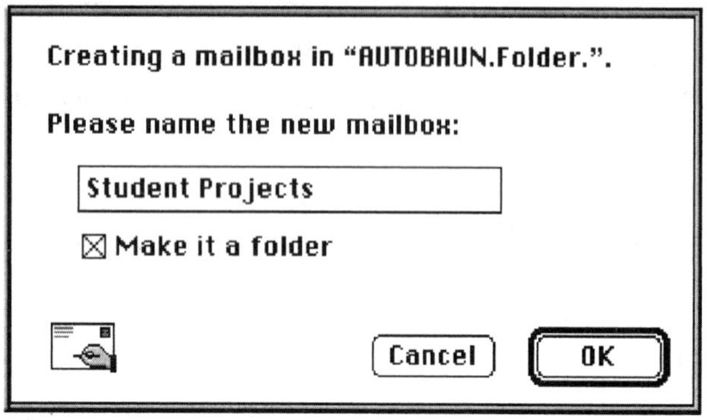

Select **Make It A Folder** if you want to have other file folders within the newly created folder.

c. To create other file folders inside your newly created Mailbox folder, select that folder from the **Mailbox** menu and choose **New** from the submenu that is displayed.

Figure 2.19
Creating a folder within a **Mailbox** folder.

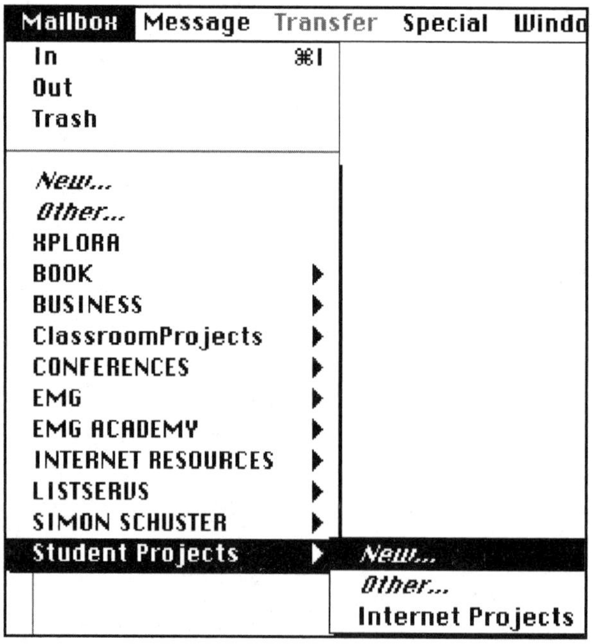

d. Type in the name of the new mailbox.

Figure 2.20
Dialog box for creating a new folder within the Student Projects folder.

e. To view your mailboxes, click on the **Window** pull-down menu and select Mailboxes.

Figures 2.21
Window pull-down menu.

Window	
Filters	
Mailboxes	
Nicknames	⌘L
Ph	⌘U
Signature	
Alternate Signature	
Send to Back	⌘B

(a) Macintosh version.

Window Help	
Cascade	Shift+F5
Tile Horizontal	Shift+F4
Tile Vertical	
Arrange Icons	
Send To Back	Ctrl+F6
Filters	
Mailboxes	
Nicknames	Ctrl+L
Ph	Ctrl+U
Signature	
Alternate Signature	
✓ 1 In	

(b) Windows version.

3. Transfer a message to your mailbox.
   To transfer an e-mail message to your Mailbox folder, click on the **Transfer** pull-down menu and select the **Mailbox** to which the message should be transferred.

Figure 2.22
Transfer pull-down menu.

Using Stored Messages

The Mailbox window provides the means for reading, transferring, and printing your filed e-mail messages. This window also provides the option for removing, renaming, or creating new Mailboxes.

Figures 2.23
Mailboxes you have created.

(a) Macintosh Mailboxes.

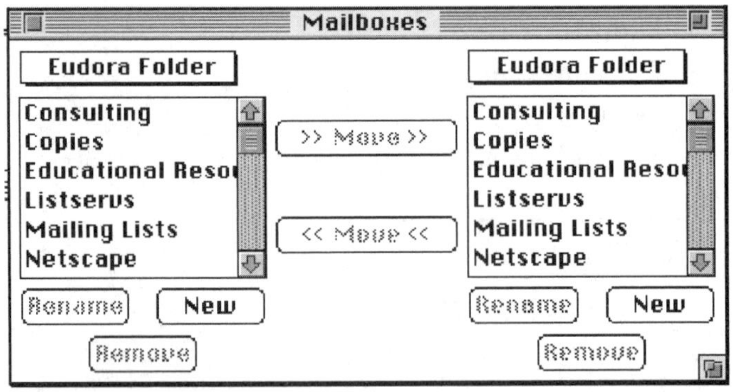

(b) Windows Mailboxes.

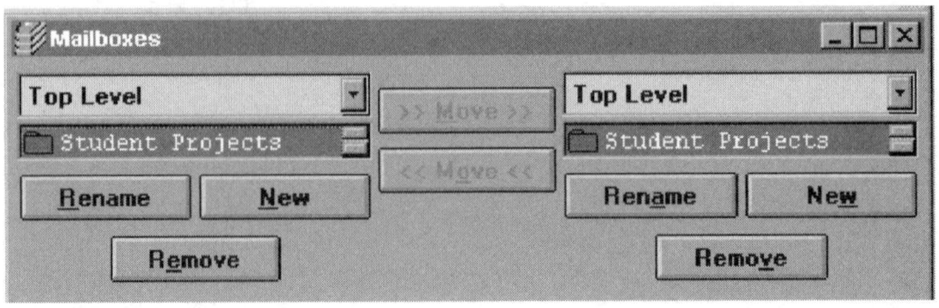

1. Reading stored messages.
   a. Click on the **Window** pull-down menu and select **Mailboxes**.

   b. From your **Mailbox** window, double-click on the Mailbox folder where the e-mail message is stored.

   c. When you locate your e-mail file, double-click on the message to open and read it.

2. Printing a stored message.
   a. Open the e-mail message.

   b. Go to the **File** pull-down menu and select **Print**.

3. Transferring a message from one folder to another.
   a. Locate the message you want to move in the list on the left and click once on it.

   b. In the other list on the right select the destination Mailbox folder so that its name and the mail messages are displayed.

   c. Click on the **Move** button that points from one folder to the other.

Figure 2.24
Transfer an e-mail message between folders.

		Mailboxes			
Student Projects			**INTERNET RESOURCE**		

Internet Projects		≫ Move ≫	Research	
			Subscriptions	
		≪ Move ≪	WWW	

| [Rename] [New] | | | [Rename] [New] | |
| [Remove] | | | [Remove] | |

Internet Projects

		Who	Date	K	Subject
R		Cynthia Leshin	Tuesday	1	practice message

1/0K/0K

Printing A Message

You can print your electronic messages either at the time you read them or a later time.

1. Select the message by either clicking and highlighting it or by opening it to read.

2. Click the **File** pull-down menu and select **Print**.

Forwarding A Message

Sometimes you may wish to send all or part of a received message to another person.

1. Select **Forward** from the **Message** menu.

2. A message sender window will appear with your address automatically placed in the **From** field. The text of the message is also automatically placed in the message box.

   Enter the e-mail address of the recipient of your forwarded message. You may also want to enter a message in the body to the recipient with information about the forwarded message.

3. Send the message.

Sending Courtesy Copies Of Your Message

Copies of your message can be sent to multiple addresses by one of two methods.

- To send your message to several people, type their address in the **To** field following the address of the primary recipient. Separate each e-mail address by a comma and a space.

- You may also use the **Carbon Copy (Cc)** or **Blind Carbon Copy (Bcc)** command. When addressing your e-mail, use the Tab key to move to the **Cc** (Carbon Copy) field. Enter the addresses of the additional recipients. Again, separate each e-mail address by a comma and a space.

Blind Carbon Copy means that a copy is sent to a recipient, without their e-mail address showing on the message to the original e-mail receiver.

Figure 2.25
Message with multiple recipients.

```
┌─────────────────────────────────────────────────────────────────┐
│▤▤ johnj@aol.com, Susans@aol.com, LFS #8: Web available, flying teac ▤▤│
├─────────────────────────────────────────────────────────────────┤
│ □ 〠H BIN ✓QP    🔲   ✓⊞  ✓→|    ⟦⟧    RR  │ Send │        │
│      HEX                                                          │
├─────────────────────────────────────────────────────────────────┤
│         To: johnj@aol.com, Susans@aol.com                      ⬆ │
│       From: xplora@autobaun.com (Cynthia Leshin)               ▓ │
│    Subject: LFS #8: Web available, flying teachers and natural lasers │
│         Cc: Internet Class                                        │
│        Bcc:                                                       │
│Attachments:                                                       │
│- - - - - - - - - - - - - - - - - - - - - - - - - - - - - - - - - │
│>Date: Fri, 1 Sep 1995 04:18:15 -0700                            │
│>From: marc@quest.arc.nasa.gov (Marc Siegel - NASA K-12 IITA Program) │
│>To: updates-lfs@quest.arc.nasa.gov                              │
│>Subject: LFS #8: Web available, flying teachers and natural lasers │
│>Cc: marc@quest.arc.nasa.gov                                      │
│>Sender: owner-updates-lfs@quest.arc.nasa.gov                    │
│>Precedence: bulk                                                 │
│>Reply-To: reply-updates-lfs@quest.arc.nasa.gov                  │
│>                                                                 │
│>"LIVE FROM THE STRATOSPHERE"      P R O J E C T  U P D A T E     │
│>                                                                 │
│>PART 1: LFS teacher resources: Web site available, $10 kit at printers │
│>PART 2: Successful test of communications to aircraft in-flight │
│>PART 3: Texas teachers Roger and Todd prepare to fly          ⬇ │
│>PART 4: Roger and Todd do science in the stratosphere         ▓ │
│>PART 5: NASA Press Release: KAO discovers natural laser       ▣ │
└─────────────────────────────────────────────────────────────────┘
```

Creating An Address Book

Electronic mail programs provide the option to save e-mail addresses for individuals with whom you frequently correspond. In Eudora, the address book is referred to as **Nicknames**. A *nickname* is used to replace a full user name and consists of an easily remembered shorter substitute for an actual e-mail address or a group of addresses. Nicknames can be used in the **To**, **Cc**, or **Bcc** fields when addressing your messages.

There are two ways to create a Nickname:

1. Create a new Nickname from within an e-mail message;

2. Add a Nickname.

Creating A Nickname From Within An E-mail Message

1. Select **Nickname** under the **Window** pull-down menu.

Figures 2.26
Creating a Nickname from within an e-mail message.

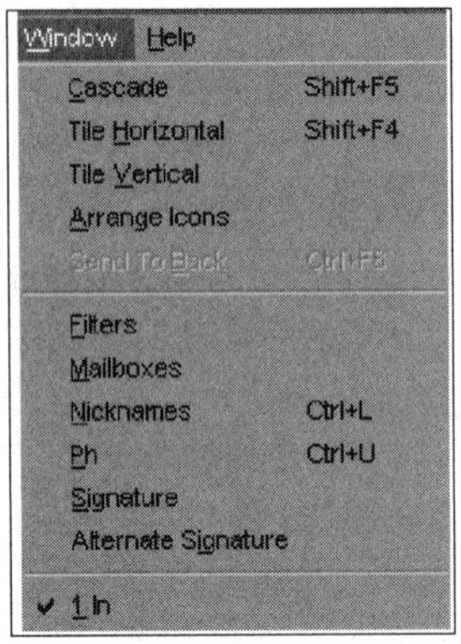

(a) Macintosh Nicknames.   (b) Windows Nicknames.

2. Enter the nickname (abbreviation to replace the full user name) and click **OK**.

Figure 2.27
New nickname
dialog box.

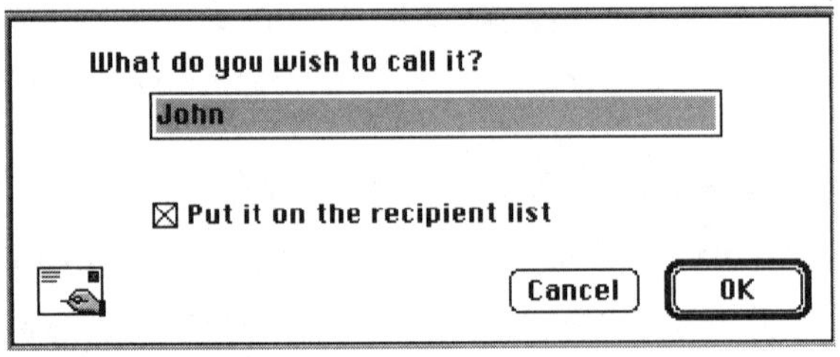

3. Check your nickname and address by selecting **Nicknames** under the **Window** menu.

Figure 2.28
The newly entered
nickname and
e-mail address.

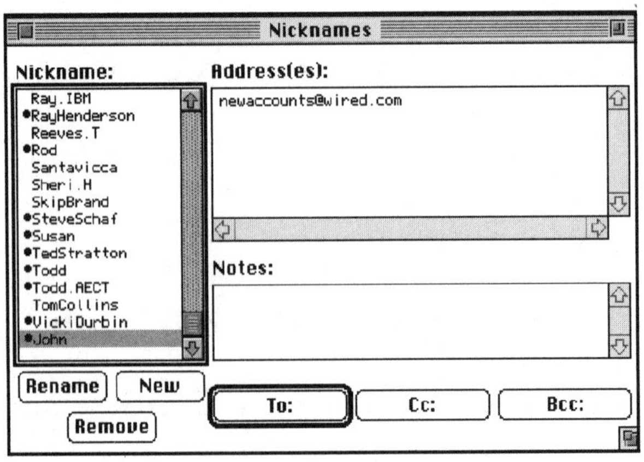

Adding New Nicknames

To add a new nickname to your address book, follow these steps.

1. Select **Nicknames** from the **Window** menu.

2. Click on the **New** button.

3. Type the new nickname. If you want this nickname to be added to your Quick Recipient list, check the box, **Put it on the recipient list.**

4. Enter the e-mail address for the new recipient in the Address(es) dialog box.

Figure 2.29
Adding a new nickname to your address book.

```
┌──────────────────────── Nicknames ────────────────────────┐
│ Nickname:              Address(es):                         │
│ ●RayHenderson  ⇧       tomc@emg.com                    ⇧   │
│  Reeves.T                                                   │
│ ●Rod                                                        │
│  Santavicca                                                 │
│  Sheri.H                                                    │
│  SkipBrand                                             ⇩   │
│ ●SteveSchaf           ⇦                            ⇨      │
│ ●Susan                                                      │
│ ●TedStratton          Notes:                                │
│ ●Todd                                                       │
│ ●Todd.AECT                                            ⇧   │
│  TomCollins                                                 │
│ ●VickiDurbin                                                │
│ ●John                                                       │
│ ●Tom          ⇩                                       ⇩   │
│ ┌────────┐ ┌──────┐  ┌──────┐ ┌──────┐ ┌──────┐           │
│ │ Rename │ │ New  │  │ To:  │ │ Cc:  │ │ Bcc: │           │
│ └────────┘ └──────┘  └──────┘ └──────┘ └──────┘           │
│    ┌────────┐                                               │
│    │ Remove │                                               │
│    └────────┘                                               │
└─────────────────────────────────────────────────────────────┘
```

Creating A Signature

A *signature* is a message added by Eudora at the end of your e-mail messages. A signature usually consists of information about the sender such as their full name and e-mail address. Additional information might include their mailing address, phone, or fax number.

Eudora supports a primary signature and an alternate signature. To create a primary signature, follow these steps.

1. Select **Signature** from the **Window** menu.

2. Type your signature text.

Figure 2.30
Signature text.

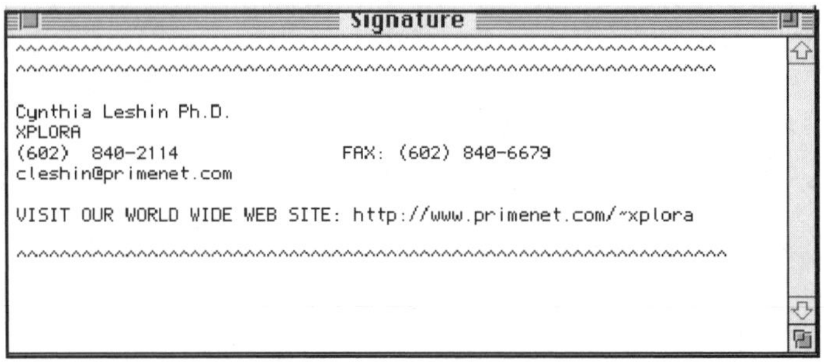

```
~~~~~~~~~~~~~~~~~~~~~~~~~~~~~~~~~~~~~~~~~~~~~~~~~~~~~~~~~~~~~~~~~~
~~~~~~~~~~~~~~~~~~~~~~~~~~~~~~~~~~~~~~~~~~~~~~~~~~~~~~~~~~~~~~~~~~

Cynthia Leshin Ph.D.
XPLORA
(602) 840-2114            FAX: (602) 840-6679
cleshin@primenet.com

VISIT OUR WORLD WIDE WEB SITE: http://www.primenet.com/~xplora

~~~~~~~~~~~~~~~~~~~~~~~~~~~~~~~~~~~~~~~~~~~~~~~~~~~~~~~~~~~~~~~~~~
```

To activate your signature on an outgoing message, select **Signature** or **Alternate Signature** from the Signature icon.

Figure 2.31
Signature Icon within Eudora.

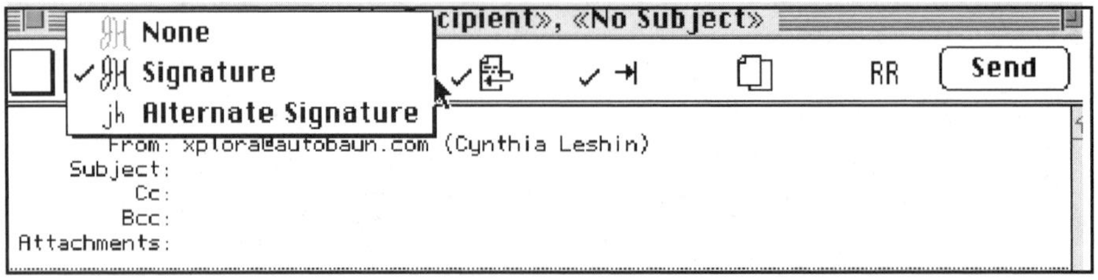

```
                      cipient», «No Subject»
     None
  ✓  Signature               ✓         ✓  ⇥      RR   Send
  jh Alternate Signature
        From: xplora@autobaun.com (Cynthia Leshin)
   Subject:
        Cc:
        Bcc:
Attachments:
```

Your signature will be displayed on your outgoing message.

Figure 2.32

An e-mail message with the signature added.

```
┌─────────────────────────────────────────────────────────────────────┐
│ ▦▦▦  Cynthia Leshin,12:05 PM -0700,Practice Message For Signatures ▦│
├─────────────────────────────────────────────────────────────────────┤
│ ┌──┐ BLAH                                                          ◗◖│
│ │  │ BLAH  Subject:  Practice Message For Signatures                │
│ └──┘ BLAH                                                           │
├─────────────────────────────────────────────────────────────────────┤
│ X-Sender: xplora@alpha.autobaun.com (Unverified)                   ⇑│
│ Mime-Version: 1.0                                                    │
│ Date: Thu, 2 Nov 1995 12:05:18 -0700                                │
│ To: xplora@alpha.autobaun.com                                       │
│ From: xplora@autobaun.com (Cynthia Leshin)                          │
│ Subject: Practice Message For Signatures                            │
│                                                                      │
│ This is a practice message to see how a signature is inserted at the end of │
│ an e-mail message.                                                   │
│                                                                      │
│                                                                      │
│ ^^^^^^^^^^^^^^^^^^^^^^^^^^^^^^^^^^^^^^^^^^^^^^^^^^^^^^^^^^^^^^^       │
│ ^^^^^^^^^^^^^^^^^^^^^^^^^^^^^^^^^^^^^^^^^^^^^^^^^^^^^^^^^^^^^^^       │
│                                                                      │
│ Cynthia Leshin Ph.D.                                                 │
│ XPLORA                                                               │
│ (602) 840-2114              FAX: (602) 840-6679                      │
│ cleshin@primenet.com                                                 │
│                                                                      │
│ VISIT OUR WORLD WIDE WEB SITE: http://www.primenet.com/~xplora       │
│                                                                      │
│ ^^^^^^^^^^^^^^^^^^^^^^^^^^^^^^^^^^^^^^^^^^^^^^^^^^^^^^^^^^^^^^^      ⇓│
└─────────────────────────────────────────────────────────────────────┘
```

Working With Attachments

Any file can be attached and sent with a Eudora message. For example, you may want to send a word processing document or a graphic file to a friend, professor, or associate. Eudora allows you to send any type of document through the mail. To attach a document or a file to an outgoing e-mail message, follow these steps for adding an attachment.

1. Select **Attach File** from the **Message** menu.

Figure 2.33

Attaching a document to an e-mail message.

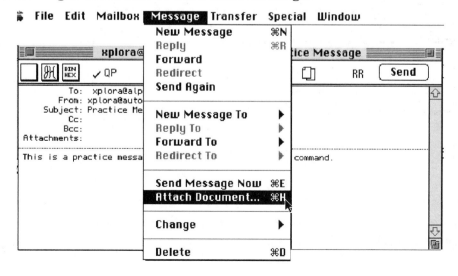

2. Locate the desired document or file. Then click on the **Open** button.

Figure 2.34
Finding the desired document on your hard drive.

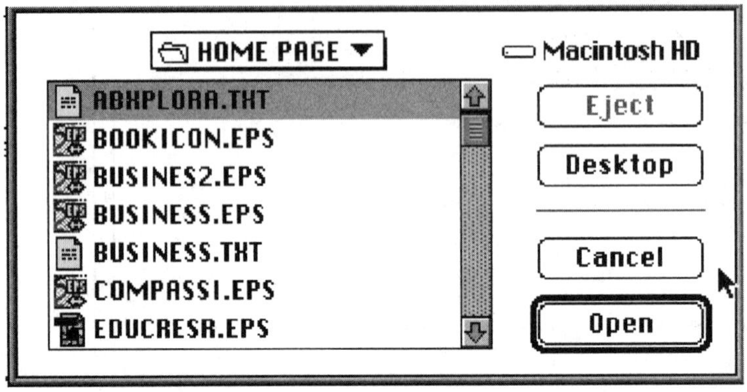

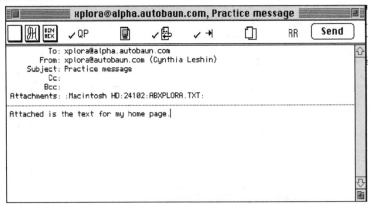

Eudora displays the name of the attached document in your e-mail message.

NOTE... For Windows Users Only
Eudora supports a "drag and drop" feature for attaching files to a message. Simply, find your file and drag the file icon inside your mail message.

Figure 2.35
An outgoing e-mail message with the information on the attached document.

The formatting you selected in your original document will be preserved with the sent message.

Receiving An Attachment

Attachments that you receive are automatically put in your Eudora directory unless you specify a different attachment directory. To specify an Attachment directory, follow these steps.

1. Select **Settings** from the **Special** menu. Scroll down to the **Attachments** option and click on the Attachment Folder or Attachment Directory.

Figure 2.36
The Settings option for designating an attachment directory.

```
┌─────────────────────────────────────────────────────────┐
│                        Settings                          │
├─────────────────────────────────────────────────────────┤
│  ┌──────────────┐ ⇧   Attachments                        │
│  │      ▱       │ ▒                                       │
│  │   Attachments│ ▒   Encoding Method:                    │
│  │      A       │     ○ AppleDouble                       │
│  │ Fonts & Display│    ○ AppleSingle                      │
│  │      ⚠       │     ● BinHex                            │
│  │Getting Attention│  ○ Uuencode                          │
│  │     Re:      │     ☐ Always include Macintosh          │
│  │   Replying   │ ⇩        information.                   │
│  └──────────────┘     Attachment Folder:                 │
│  ┌──┐                 ┌──────────────────────────────┐   │
│  │✉ │                 │      EUDORA Attachments       │   │
│  └──┘                 └──────────────────────────────┘   │
│                       ☐ Trash attachments with messages. │
│                       TEXT files belong to:  ┌──────────┐│
│                                              │ TeachText ││
│                                              └──────────┘│
│                              ( Cancel )  ┌──── OK ────┐  │
└─────────────────────────────────────────────────────────┘
```

2. Select the folder where you want your Attachments to be placed. Double-click on the name of the folder to select it. Then, click on the **Use Folder** or **Use Directory** button.

Figure 2.37
Newly identified Attachment Folder.

```
┌────────────────────────────────────────┐
│  ┌─ DOCUMENTS ▼ ─┐                      │
│  ┌──────────────────┐ ⇧  ▱ Macintosh HD │
│  │ ▱ CLASSES        │ ▒                 │
│  │ ▱ EMG            │ ▒   ┌──────────┐   │
│  │ ▱ EUDORA Attachments│ ▒ │  Eject   │   │
│  │ ▱ FILEMAKER PRO FILES│ │  Desktop │   │
│  │ ▱ IBM            │ ▒   └──────────┘   │
│  │ ▱ INTERNET       │     ┌──────────┐   │
│  │ ▱ MISCL.         │ ⇩   │Use Folder│   │
│  └──────────────────┘     └──────────┘   │
│                           ┌──────────┐   │
│                           │  Cancel  │   │
│                           └──────────┘   │
│  Move until the folder you want is shown in the │
│  small rectangle at the top, above the list of files │
│  and folders. Then click "Use Folder".   │
└────────────────────────────────────────┘
```

Tourist Information Tips

Tip 1... Save messages to be read later

Occasionally you may want to reread a message before you send it. In Eudora, messages are saved in the OUT box until you have clicked on the Send button. To find your saved messages, select OUT from the Message menu.

Tip 2... Creating mailing lists of groups

You may want to create mailing lists of groups of people who should always receive the same type of messages. For example, if you are on a committee you might want a mailing list of all the members of the committee to receive the minutes of meetings or to announce meeting dates. Mailing lists can be created in your Address Book.

- In the field where you would ordinarily enter the name of a single person, enter the name of your group or mailing list.

- In the field where you would normally enter the address of one person, enter the multiple addresses of your group. Remember, separate each address with a comma and a space.

Tip 3... Save e-mail file folders to a floppy disk

If your saved messages have been saved on your hard drive and not on a file server at your college or university, then you will want to make a back-up copy. For the same reason that you make copies of your work, you should back up saved messages and files.

Tip 4... Use mixed case lettering

UPPERCASE LETTERING IS MORE DIFFICULT TO READ AND SHOULD ONLY BE USED EMPHASIS. Uppercase lettering is often perceived as SHOUTING.

Tip 5...Do not use special formatting

Don't use bold, italics, fancy lettering, or special formatting such as tabs and indents. E-mail programs do not recognize special formatting.

Tip 6... Use your Eudora spell checker

As you use electronic mail you will find how informal this method of communication is. You will receive messages with typos, poor grammar, and other errors that are unforgivable in a normal letter. Think about how you view the sender of a message with many typos. Do you want to be this informal?

Tip 7... Request a return receipt

If you want to be notified when mail you have sent has been read, click on the "Return Receipt" command icon or box. Look carefully for this box. Many mail programs will notify you the instant when your message has been read.

Tip 8... Replying to the correct person.

When replying to a message check to see who received copies of the original message. The message header will usually display the names of all the addresses who received the same message. If you only want to reply to the sender of the message, you may have several options.

- Send a new message and address it only to the sender of the message.

- Check your e-mail program to see if one reply option replies only to the sender of the message.

RULES OF THE ROAD — E-MAIL

Electronic mail is very different from regular mail or from talking on the phone. You may have to use e-mail for awhile before you appreciate this difference.

- Never write anything in your e-mail message that you wouldn't want to be public knowledge. It is very easy to forward or copy your message to other people or to a distribution list.

- Never send a note that you would not want to be seen one year from now. It is easy to save mail messages in an electronic file that can be accessed months or years later.

- Do not assume that your mail is private. The message sent to you may have been copied to others.

- Be careful about the tone of voice in your writing.

- If you are responding to an e-mail message that is offensive or makes you feel angry, resist the temptation to respond immediately. If you do feel a need to write a reply immediately, wait a day or two before you send your message. Read it later that day or the next day and then determine if you want to send it or make changes. Once your message is mailed, there is no way to retrieve it.

- Be very careful with jokes or sarcasm. What you may perceive as being funny may be taken as obnoxious and offensive. Subtle sarcasm is almost impossible to use on e-mail and usually comes across as annoying or irritating.

EXPEDITION EXPERIENCE

Electronic Mail

Exploring E-Mail

Now that you have practiced sending e-mail to yourself, you are ready to begin meeting other people and to gather information available through electronic mail. Follow the same steps as you did in your Guided Walk.

EXPEDITIONS...

EDUPAGE

EDUPAGE is available free via electronic mail as a service of Educom—a consortium of leading colleges and universities seeking to transform education through the use of technology. After you subscribe you will be sent a summary of news items on information technology three times a week. The summary is sent to your e-mail box. You can cancel your subscription at any time.

To subscribe:

1. Send a message to this address:

   listproc@educom.unc.edu

2. Leave the subject line blank or enter a period (.) if your software requires you to make an entry.

3. Where you would normally compose your message, type the following:

   subscribe edupage <your name>

My message would look like this:

   subscribe edupage Cynthia Leshin

The White House

The White House is wired. You can send an electronic message to the President and Vice President. Your mail will be processed through the cubicles of the Executive Office Building and months from now you will receive a response. You will find several e-mail addresses for the President and Vice President.

President Clinton's e-mail address:
PRESIDENT@WHITEHOUSE.GOV

Vice President Gore's e-mail address:
VICE.PRESIDENT@WHITEHOUSE.GOV

Using E-Mail For Retrieving Information

E-mail can be used to access almost any Internet resource such as gopher, FTP (File Transfer Protocol), Usenet newsgroups, and the World Wide Web. You also can use e-mail to search for information using Archie and Veronica. To find out more information on ways to use e-mail to do this and much more:

1. Send a message to this address:
   listserv@ubvm.cc.buffalo.edu

2. Leave the subject line blank or enter a period (.) if your software requires you to make an entry.

3. Where you would normally compose your message, type the following:
   GET INTERNET BY-EMAIL NETTRAIN F=MAIL

Figure 2.38
Example of a request for information.

```
┌──────────────────────────────────────────────────────────┐
│ ▥  listserv@ubvm.cc.buffalo.edu, «No Subject»         ▣ │
├──────────────────────────────────────────────────────────┤
│ ⬜ ▨ ▨  ✓QP    ▣  ✓▣  ✓→⎸    ▯    RR  │ Send │        │
├──────────────────────────────────────────────────────────┤
│        To: listserv@ubvm.cc.buffalo.edu                 ⬆ │
│      From: xplora@autobaun.com (Cynthia Leshin)           │
│   Subject:                                                │
│        Cc:                                                │
│       Bcc:                                                │
│ Attachments:                                              │
│ ·········································                   │
│ GET INTERNET BY-EMAIL NETTRAIN F=MAIL                     │
│                                                           │
│                                                         ⬇ │
└──────────────────────────────────────────────────────────┘
```

Using E-Mail To Retrieve World Wide Web Pages

E-mail can be used to retrieve the text of a World Wide Web page.

1. Send a message to this address:
   webmail@www.ucc.ie

2. Leave the subject line blank or enter a period (.) if your software requires you to make an entry.

3. Where you would normally compose your message, type the following and include the URL for the desired World Wide Web page.
   get *URL address*

Figure 2.39
An example of an e-mail message to receive the Home Page from NASA (URL: **http://www.gsfc.nasa.gov NASA_homepage. html**).

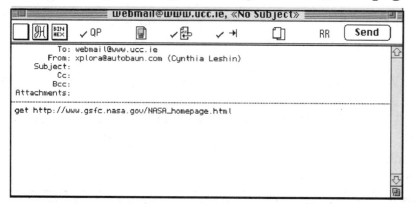

Finding Out More About Information Available Via E-mail

To find out more about services such as weather updates and almanacs, available by e-mail write to Infomania.

1. Send a message to this address:
   infobot@infomania.com

2. Where you would normally compose your message, type the following command:
   HELP

FOREIGN LANGUAGE CENTER

Electronic Mail

Electronic Mail

Some of the words and terms found in the Foreign Language Center do not appear in the Travel Guide. However, you may encounter some or all of these words as you go on discovery and adventure trips. The terms have been included to assist with your questions and understanding as you encounter them on your journey. You will need to go to other sources for additional information.

address: An Internet address consists of a userid or username and the domain of the host computer. The form of this address is:
userid@host.subdomain.domain.

ASCII(American Standard Code for Information Interchange): A standard developed by the American National Standards Institute describing how characters can be represented on a computer. The ASCII character set consists of 128 characters numbered from 0-127. Most personal computers use a form of ASCII characters. Using ASCII makes it possible for text to be read by any computer.

BBS (Bulletin Board System): On-line systems where dial-up users can download software, exchange information, or leave messages for other users. Currently there are more than 65,000 BBSs in the United States.

Bitnet (Because It's Time Network): An academic and research network with powerful mail distribution features that hosts many mailing lists. Bitnet uses a different protocol (not TCP/IP) for connecting its computer networks. Because the communication protocol is different, Bitnet is not technically the Internet. Many countries have Bitnet connections, but do not have Internet capabilities (FTP and telnet services).

client: A software program used to view information from remote computers. Clients function in a Client-Server information exchange model. This term may also be loosely applied to the computer that is used to request information from the server. (see Server)

computer network: A network that makes it possible for a group of computers to be connected so they can communicate with each other and share resources. Computers may be connected by high capacity telephone lines, fiber optics, microwaves, or satellites. A network may connect the computer users in a school, university, or company. These

smaller computer networks may connect to a larger, more global network, the Internet.

CPU (central processing unit): The term for the microprocessor chip that powers a personal computer. The term is also used to refer to the case that houses the chip. An example of a CPU is the Intel Pentium chip.

direct Internet connection: Supports the transfer of data with TCP/IP (Transport Control Protocol/Internet Protocol) communication protocols using either a SLIP (Serial Line Internet Protocol) or a PPP (Point-to-Point) protocol. A SLIP or PPP account makes it possible for you to navigate the Internet using graphical software programs such as Eudora and Netscape Navigator.

domain: Hosts and local area networks are grouped together in domains. For example, all of the computer users (hosts) of a commercial Internet provider such as CompuServe (which has many local area networks) make up a domain. CompuServe is a commercial domain.

FTP (File Transfer Protocol): This Internet protocol allows files to be transferred between computers on the Internet.

global network: Computers from different countries that talk to each other do so by satellite and special telephone connections. These networked computers form a global network.

global commercial networks: Networks such as America Online, CompuServe, and Prodigy are owned by commercial companies and charge their users for computer networking services.

gopher: Is a format structure and resource for providing information on the Internet. It was created at the University of Minnesota.

header summary: The information displayed about each mail message. This information includes: a symbol (>) for the current mail message; a letter to represent the current message status (U for unread, P for read but not deleted, or N for new); the number of the message; the username, the date and time; two numbers separated by a slash (The first number indicates the number of lines and the second indicates the number of characters); and the subject of the message.

host: Any computer that is linked to the Internet is called a host. A host may be a PC, supercomputer, giant mainframe, or a workstation. When you connect to the Internet, your personal computer will need to be connected to a host computer.

host computer: The Internet computer connected to your computer that allows you to use Internet resources.

HTML (Hypertext Markup Language): HTML is the programming language used to create World Wide Web pages. This includes the text of the document, its structure, and links to other documents. HTML also includes the programming for accessing and displaying media such as images, video, and sound.

HTTP (Hypertext Transfer Protocol): HTTP is a protocol used to transfer information within the World Wide Web. Web documents begin with the http protocol **http://**

Internet: The global network used to transport information among computers.

ISDN (Integrated Services Digital Network): A telephone service that provides superior dial-up connections for transferring information. ISDN supports data transfer rates of 128 kilobits per second (Kbps), compared with 14.4 Kbps and 28.8 Kbps for the fastest modems. This digital communication system is geared to replace the world's analog telephone system. Special hardware and set-up is required.

LAN (local area network): A computer network that is in one physical location such as one building in a school or one floor in an office building. Schools, universities, and companies may have several LANs that are connected together so that the users can share resources and information on their network.

login: Signing onto a computer and accessing your personal account.

login name: The name you use with your Internet account.

logout: Signing off from your host computer.

MacTCP: Software for the Macintosh used to connect Macs to the Internet.

modem: A device that translates computer signals into telephone signals and telephone signals into computer signals. This electronic device makes it possible for a computer to link to a computer over a phone line.

Mosaic: Graphical interface software that allows Internet browsing by pointing and clicking on icons and pull-down menus.

Netscape: Netscape is one of the newest and most impressive network navigational tools for exploring the Internet. Navigate the Net by pointing and clicking on icons and pull-down menus.

password: A word that you use when you login to verify who you are.

PPP (Point-to-Point Protocol): Allows you to establish a full Internet connection over a telephone line. PPP and SLIP connections make it possible to browse the World Wide Web with programs such as Mosaic or Netscape Navigator.

protocol: A special computer language that allows computers to talk to each other.

router: A special machine on the intersection of Internet networks that determines which path or route will be most efficient for data to travel on in its journey to another destination.

server: A software program used to provide, or serve, information to remote computers. Servers function in a Client-Server information exchange model. This term may also be loosely applied to the computer that is used to serve the information.

SLIP (Serial Line Internet Protocol): Allows you to establish a full Internet connection over a telephone line.

signature: This is an optional feature of electronic mail systems that allows you to sign your e-mail messages with information about yourself. A signature may include your name, address, phone, fax, and e-mail address. You will also see quotes, witty sayings, jokes, and drawings in e-mail signatures. To see some bizarre signatures try the alt.fan.warlord newsgroup.

smileys: Creative message writers frequently use combinations of different keyboard punctuation marks to create smiling faces, sad faces, animals, impersonations of people, or whatever creative image they can make. Smileys are at times used to help make the tone of a message more humorous or to portray a mood or feeling of the message sender. This is a happy smiley   :-}   This is a sad smiley   :-{

TCP/IP: TCP (Transmission Control Protocol) and IP (Internet Protocol) are special protocols that allow computers to communicate with each other on the Internet. Data sent from a computer is broken up into small packets by TCP. Addressing information on where these packets are to go is provided by IP. Packets may travel different routes to get to the same destination. There is a computer waiting at the intended destination to assemble all of the packets for the intended computer or Internet user.

telnet: Allows users to login to other computers on the Internet. Once the connection has been established, the computer will act as if it is directly connected to the remote computer.

userid (computer English): User identification or user name that identifies a person on the account of a host computer.

URL (Uniform Resource Locator): URLs are a standard for locating Internet documents. They allow an addressing system for other Internet protocols such as access to gopher menus, FTP file retrieval, and Usenet newsgroups. URLs specify three pieces of information needed to retrieve a document: the protocol to be used; the server address and port to which to connect; and the path to the information.

WAN (wide area network): local area networks that are connected to other local networks by high speed telephone lines. These local area networks may be in various cities or states.

World Wide Web (WWW): The World Wide Web is a browsing system that allows point and click navigation around the Internet. World Wide Web users can easily access text documents, images, video, and sound.

Chapter Three

LISTSERV MAILING LISTS

TOURIST INFORMATION CENTER

With so much attention on the World Wide Web, many new Internet users miss learning about electronic mailing lists (also referred to as lists, listservs, or discussion groups) as an Internet resource for finding and sharing information. Electronic mailing lists began in the 1960s when scientists and educators used the Internet to share information and research. Early programs, known as *listservs*, ran on mainframe computers and used e-mail to send reports or studies to a large group of users.

Today, listservs perform the same function—the sharing of information. There are hundreds of special interest lists where individuals can join a virtual community to share and discuss topics of mutual interest.

Now that you have learned to use electronic mail, you are ready to join some of the Internet's most popular mailing lists. You can also search for mailing lists on topics of personal interest.

Cool Listserv Mailing Lists

- David Letterman's Top-10 List (over 10,000 subscribers)

- The Internet TOURBUS—virtual tour of cyberspace

- Wall Street Journal—Announcement list

- ROOTS-L—a genealogy list

- HUMOR—UGA Humor list

- WMST-L—Woman's Studies list

- KIDLINK—a list for parents

- JOBPLACE—Self-directed job search techniques

- WIN95-L—a list for Windows 95 users

- TIDBITS—a newsletter for Mac users

What Is A Listserv Mailing List?

A *listserv* is the automated system that distributes electronic mail. E-mail is used to participate in electronic mailing lists. Listservs perform two functions.

- Distributing text documents stored on them to those that request them, and

- Managing interactive mailing lists.

Listservs and text documents

A listserv can be used to distribute information, in the form of text documents, to others. For example, on-line workshops may make their course materials available via a listserv. The listserv is set up to distribute the materials to participants at designated times. Other examples of documents available via a listserv include: a listing of all available electronic mailing lists, Usenet newsgroups, electronic journals, and books.

Interactive mailing lists

Interactive mailing lists provide a forum where individuals who share interest can exchange ideas and information. Any member of the group may participate in the resulting discussion. This is no longer a one-to-one communication like your e-mail, but rather a one-to-many communication.

Electronic mail written in the form of a report, article, abstract, reaction, or comment is received at a central site and then distributed to the members of the list.

How Does A Mailing List Work?

The mailing list is hosted by a college, university, or institution. The hosting institution uses its computer system to manage the mailing list. Here are a few of the management functions of a listserv:

- receiving requests for subscription to the list;
- placing subscribers' e-mail addresses on the list;
- sending out notification that the name has been added to the list;
- receiving messages from subscribers;

- sending messages to all subscribers;
- keeping a record (archive) of activity of the list;
- sending out information requested by subscribers to the list (i.e., help, the names and e-mail addresses of subscribers to the list).

Mailing lists have administrators that may be either a human or a computer program. One function of the administrator is to handle subscription requests. If the administrator is human, you can join the mailing list by communicating in English via an e-mail message. The administrator in turn has the option of either accepting or rejecting your subscription request. Frequently lists administered by a human are available only to a select group of individuals. For example, an executive board of an organization may restrict its list to its members.

Mailing lists administered by computer programs called listservs usually allow all applicants to subscribe to the list. You must communicate with these computer administrators in listserv commands. For the computer administrator to accept your request, you must use the exact format required. The administrative address and how to subscribe should be included in the information provided about a list.

Electronic mailing lists may be moderated or unmoderated. A moderator may do any of the following:

- redistribute to the list only a selected portion of the incoming messages;
- summarize critical points to decrease the amount of mail;
- make comments and suggestions to list participants;
- facilitate discussions by posing questions, making comments, or by distributing abstracts or short articles;
- answer individual's questions without posting the message to the entire list;
- remove individuals from a list.

Unmoderated lists simply pass along all incoming mail.

How To Receive Documents From A Listserv

E-mail is used to request text documents distributed by a listserv. The e-mail is addressed to the listserv *administrative address*. In the body of the message a command is written to request the document. The most common command used to request a document is "send" or "get." The command is then followed by the name of the document that you wish to receive. A command to request a list of interesting mailing lists might look like this:

"get" or "send" <name of document>
or
get new-list TOP TEN

How to Join A Listserv Mailing List

To join an interactive mailing list on a topic of interest, send an e-mail message to the list administrator and ask to join the list. Subscribing to an electronic mailing list is like subscribing to a journal or magazine.

- You mail a message to the journal with a request for subscription.

- You need the address of the journal and your address to which the journal will be mailed.

All electronic mailing lists work in the same way.

- E-mail your request to the list administrator at the address assigned by the hosting organization.

- Place your request to participate in the body of your e-mail where you usually write your messages.

- Your return address will accompany your request in the header of your message.

- Your subscription will be acknowledged by the hosting organization or the moderator.

- You will then receive all discussions distributed by the listserv.

- You can send in your own comments and reactions.

- You can unsubscribe (cancel your subscription).

The command to subscribe to a mailing lists looks like this.

subscribe <name of list> *<your name>*
or
subscribe EDUPAGE Cynthia Leshin

The unsubscribe command is similar to the subscribe command.

unsubscribe <name of list> *<your name>*

Very active lists may have 50-100 messages from list participants each day. Other less active mailing lists may have several messages per week or per month. If you find that you are receiving too much mail or the discussions on the list do not interest you, you can unsubscribe just as easily as you subscribed. If you are going away, you can send a message to the list to hold your mail until further notice.

> **NOTE**
> Once you subscribe to a mailing list, be sure to check your mail regularly.

GUIDED WALKS

Listserv Mailing Lists

Hands-On Practice

Guided Walks for listserv mailing lists provide you with the opportunity to

- subscribe to an electronic mailing list.
- receive e-mail notification that your subscription has been accepted.
- receive mail from the mailing list.
- send mail to the mailing list.
- request help from the mailing list.
- learn how to access the mailing list archives.

Before You Begin It Is Important To Remember...

Mailing lists have two different addresses.

1. An *administrative address* that you will use when you:

   - subscribe to the list;
   - unsubscribe from the list;
   - request information or help.

2. A *submission address* used to send your messages to the list.

The Administrative Mail Address

Most listserv mailing lists use software such as listserv, majordomo, or listproc that automatically processes users' requests to subscribe or unsubscribe. Some examples of administrative addresses used for subscribing and unsubscribing are:

listserv@uga.cc.uga.edu
majordomo@gsn.org
listproc@educom.unc.edu

NOTE

Requests for subscriptions are usually processed by computers, therefore, type the commands without any changes. Be sure to enter the exact address that you have received, duplicating spacing and upper-and lowercase letters. Do not add any other information in the body of your message. If your e-mail package adds a signature, be sure to take it off before sending your request.

After you join a listserv mailing list, you will usually receive notification of your subscription request and an electronic welcome. This message will provide you with information such as the purpose of the list, the names of the listserv's owners, how to subscribe and unsubscribe, and other commands to use for the list.

> **NOTE**
>
> Save a copy of this listserv welcome message. Later you may want to refer to it for information on how to unsubscribe or perform other operations related to the list.

The Submission Mail Address

Mail sent to the submission address is read by all of the subscribers to the list. This address will be different and should not be used for communicating with the list administrator. Here is an example of an address for sending your messages to the mailing list participants:

itforum@uga.cc.uga.edu

For this mailing list, the first word is the name of the list, *itforum* (instructional technology forum). Any mail sent to this address will be sent to all subscribers to the list. This is the address used to communicate with subscribers to the list.

GUIDED WALK 1

Subscribing To And Receiving Mail From A List

To subscribe to a mailing list you must know the exact commands required. Information about a mailing list will include the commands needed to subscribe. When you receive notification of your acceptance to the list you will receive additional information about the commands needed to participate and interact with the list.

Steps To Subscribe

1. Find the address and information for subscribing to the mailing list.

In this Guided Walk, you will subscribe to EDUPAGE. EDUPAGE was among the recipients of the Global Network Navigators' "Best of the Net" awards recognizing some of the best destinations on the Internet. EDUPAGE is a summary of news items about information technology and is distributed three times each week.

Here is information on subscribing to EDUPAGE.

📬 Send a message "**To**":

> **listproc@educom.unc.edu**

📬 Leave the "**Subject**" field blank. No subject line is necessary.

📬 In the "**Body**" of the message type:

> **subscribe edupage *<your Firstname Lastname>***

NOTE
Listserv subscription commands will usually include:
> *a subscribe command — name of the list — your name*

Figure 3.1
A subscription request.

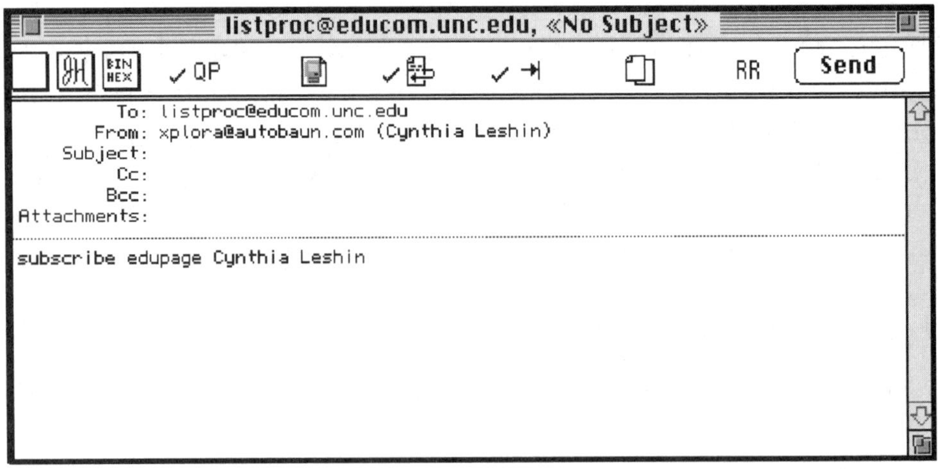

```
┌──────────── listproc@educom.unc.edu, «No Subject» ──────────────┐
│  [ ] [HH] [BIN] ✓ QP    [ ]   ✓ [ ]   ✓ ⇥    [ ]    RR  [ Send ] │
│         To: listproc@educom.unc.edu                              │
│       From: xplora@autobaun.com (Cynthia Leshin)                 │
│    Subject:                                                      │
│         Cc:                                                      │
│        Bcc:                                                      │
│ Attachments:                                                    │
│ ...............................................................  │
│ subscribe edupage Cynthia Leshin                                │
│                                                                 │
└─────────────────────────────────────────────────────────────────┘
```

Now, let's login to your account and join the EDUPAGE mailing list.

2. Login to your Internet account.

3. Open your e-mail program.

4. Address your e-mail:

   To: **listproc@educom.unc.edu**

   Subject: It is not necessary to enter a subject. If your e-mail program requires you to make an entry into the "Subject" field use a period (.).

5. Enter the subscription request where you would normally type your message.

   subscribe edupage <*your Firstname Lastname*>

   Example: **subscribe edupage John Smith**

6. Send your mail.

Your subscription request has now been sent to the EDUPAGE administrator.

Receiving Notification Of Your Subscription

▣ Check your e-mail about 30 minutes after sending the request. You will probably find an e-mail message notifying you that your name has been added to the list. This message may include a welcome or you may receive a separate welcome message.

▣ Read the other information about commands to use when interacting with the list. Most list notifications will include information about how to

- submit a comment to the list.
- view the list's archives.
- communicate with the list.

- get help.
- unsubscribe from the list.

> **NOTE**
> The EDUPAGE list will not have information about how to submit messages. This list is just a news summary and has no provisions for interaction with other subscribers. In Guided Walk 3 you will join a list that provides information about how to submit comments.

You will find many lists that have been set up to provide you with information rather than to foster discussion. There are no provisions for interaction on these lists other than an address for communication with the moderator or administrator.

Your First Mailing List Messages

After you have subscribed you will begin receiving mail from the list. The list that you just subscribed to, EDUPAGE, sends out news summaries three times a week. When the next summary is available you will receive a copy in your electronic mail box.

Read the list mail in the same way that you read your other e-mail messages. When you have read or printed the mail, either delete the message or file it if you feel it is important to keep a copy. Remember, usually all of these list mailings are archived by the listserv.

GUIDED WALK 2

Unsubscribing From A Mailing List

Eventually, you may want to unsubscribe from a mailing list. You may find that the volume of mail is too high for you to keep up with or that the discussions are not of interest to you. It is as easy to unsubscribe as it is to subscribe.

To unsubscribe from the mailing list, send a message to the same address that you used to subscribe to the list. REMEMBER... the administration address for subscribing and unsubscribing is the same.

1. Check the information that you received from the list when you joined it to see the correct message to send to unsubscribe. Many lists will use the command "unsubscribe" or "unsub." Others might use "signoff." The unsubscribe message will usually include:

    unsubscribe command — name of list — your Firstname Lastname

> **NOTE**
> Some listservs ask for your e-mail address rather than your name.

Figure 3.2
This is what an unsubscribe message looks like.

```
▣  listproc@educom.unc.edu, «No Subject»  ▣

□ ⌘H BIN    ✓ QP      ▣    ✓ ⊞    ✓ ⇥     ⬜     RR    [ Send ]
    HEX

         To: listproc@educom.unc.edu
       From: xplora@autobaun.com (Cynthia Leshin)
    Subject:
         Cc:
        Bcc:
Attachments:
..........................................................................
unsubscribe edupage Cynthia Leshin
```

2. Login to your Internet account.

3. Open your e-mail program.

4. Address your e-mail to the mailing list's administrative address:

   To: **listproc@educom.unc.edu**

   Subject: leave blank or type in a period (.).

5. Enter the unsubscribe request where you would normally type your message.

   unsubscribe edupage *<your Firstname Lastname>*

   Example: **unsubscribe edupage John Smith**

6. Send the message.

Tourist Information Tips
Tip 1...

After you subscribe to a list, don't send anything to it until you have read the messages for at least one week. This will give you an opportunity to observe the tone of the list and the type of messages that people are sending. Newcomers to lists often ask questions that were discussed at length several days or weeks ago.

Tip 2...

Remember that everything you send to the list goes to every subscriber on the list. Some lists have thousands of members. Before you reply or post a message read and review what you have written. Is your message readable, free from errors and typos? THINK BEFORE YOU SEND.

Tip 3...

The proper etiquette for a list is to not clog other people's mailboxes with mail not relevant to them. If you want to respond to mail on the list, determine whether you want your response

to go only to the individual who posted the mail or you want your response to go to all the list's subscribers. The person's name and e-mail address will be somewhere in the message. For example, a list participant may request information or help. If you can provide the information it might be more appropriate to send it directly to the person who made the request at the individual's e-mail address.

Tip 4...

The general rule for posting a message to a list is to keep it short and to the point. Most subscribers do not appreciate multiple page postings.

Tip 5...

If your e-mail program allows you to quote the message you are replying to, do so. You need not copy the entire message, only the portion that you are responding to. List members may need to be reminded of the content of the original posting.

Tip 6...

When you are sending administrative requests to the list be sure to use the administrative address. Failure to do this is the second most common mistake made by new list subscribers. Examples of administrative matters include unsubscribing, requests for help, archived files, or review of list subscribers. Remember, there are two addresses for all lists: an administrative address and a submission address.

Tip 7...

When you begin to explore mailing lists, subscribe to only a few. Limit yourself to only five or six groups at the most. Mailing lists can generate many messages that will fill your mailbox and may become overwhelming to read and manage.

Tip 8...

If you have joined an active listserv and do not have time to read your e-mail daily, consider using the list's digest features. A digest collects mail messages into one file and mails that file once a day or once a week. For information on digests see Guided Walk 3 in this chapter.

GUIDED WALK 3

Mailing List Tricks

Your journey into the land of mailing lists can be made a little easier by knowing a few tricks. Guided Walk 3 introduces you to several useful listserv commands. You can send several commands in the same message.

> **NOTE**
>
> When you are submitting an administrative request, you must use the administrative address. Therefore, if you are going to use any of these commands, address your mail to the same address as you used to subscribe to the list.

Requesting Help...

The first command that you may want to try is the HELP command. This will send you a summary of all the basic commands available on the list to which you have subscribed.

1. Send a message to the list administration address.
2. Leave the SUBJECT field blank.
3. In the BODY of the message type
   help

Many mailing lists archive messages that have been distributed. Use the "help" command find out about the lists archives.

TRICK 1: When you go on vacation...

If you are going to be away from your computer for an extended period, temporarily suspend mailings from the lists that you belong to or your mailbox will overflow and leave less space for other people's mail.

1. Send a message to the list administration address.
2. Leave the SUBJECT field blank.
3. In the BODY of the message send this command.
   set <listname> nomail

For example, for the list ITFORUM, the command would be
set ITFORUM nomail

When you return, you can begin to receive messages again by sending the list administrator
set <listname> mail

Example: **set ITFORUM mail**

TRICK 2: Finding out who is on a list...

Follow these steps to see the names and e-mail addresses of subscribers to the list.

1. Send a message to the list administration address.
2. Leave the SUBJECT field blank.
3. In the BODY of the message use this command format
   review <listname>

For example, for the list ITFORUM, the command would be
review ITFORUM

Some lists may not provide the option to review subscribers' names and addresses. Some may also give you the option not to have your name listed in a review. Check the information that is provided when you subscribe to see if the mailing list provides either of these two options. You can also use the HELP command.

TRICK 3: Receiving a digest...

Some mailing lists are digested. This means that over a period of time (usually a day or two) all mail messages are incorporated into one large message and mailed to you as a digest.

1. Send an e-mail request to the administration address.
2. Leave the SUBJECT field blank.
3. In the BODY where you normally write your messages, type
   set <listname> digest

Example: **set ITFORUM digest**

Guided Walk 4

Finding A Listserv Mailing List of Interest

Subscribe to several listserv mailing lists that interest you. Refer to the listing of listservs in the Expedition Experience. If you are unable to find any listservs of interest send an e-mail message to the following listserv requesting the names of lists on a topic of interest.

1. Send an e-mail message to
   LISTSERV@vm1.nodak.edu
2. Leave the SUBJECT field blank.
3. Where you would normally write your message, type
   LIST GLOBAL / *keyword*

Figure 3.3

Requesting the name of any listserv mailing list on bluegrass music.

```
╔══════════ LISTSERU@vm1.nodak.edu, «No Subject» ══════════╗
│  ☐  ⌐⌐ ⌐⌐  ✓ QP      🗎    ✓ ⌐⌐   ✓ ⇥      ⌐⌐    RR   [ Send ] │
│       HEX                                                       │
│          To: LISTSERV@vm1.nodak.edu                            │
│        From: cleshin@xplora.com (Cynthia Leshin)              │
│     Subject:                                                   │
│          Cc:                                                   │
│         Bcc:                                                   │
│ Attachments:                                                   │
│ ............................................................. │
│ LIST GLOBAL/ bluegrass music                                  │
│                                                                │
│                                                                │
│                                                                │
╚════════════════════════════════════════════════════════════╝
```

EXPEDITION EXPERIENCE
Listserv Mailing Lists

Exploring Mailing Lists

Mailing lists frequently provide useful information about the latest resources, research, and information on topics of interest to you both personally and professionally. You may have to subscribe to several mailing lists before you find one that meets your needs. You will find that some mailing lists are very busy and send you 10-50 postings a day. Other lists are moderated and provide only summary or updated information. You will have to subscribe and participate for a short period of time to determine if a particular list meets your needs or if you have the time to read all of its messages.

> **HINT**
> You do not have to read all the mail you receive. Read only the subjects that interest you. Remember, each e-mail message will list its subject. Delete messages whose subjects do not interest you.

In this section you will find a list of the most popular listservs (1000 plus subscribers).

In each of these expeditions you will be given the address to which to send your request and the subscription request format for the BODY of your message. Remember to leave the SUBJECT field blank. If your program requires you to make an entry in the SUBJECT field, insert a period (.).

The format for each listserv will be the same as in this example.

David Letterman's Top-10 list

Address:	listserv@listserv.clark.net
Body:	subscribe TOPTEN *< your name >*

```
┌─────────────────────────────────────────────────────────────┐
│          listserv@listserv.clark.net, «No Subject»            │
│  [  ] [⌘H][BIN/HEX]  ✓QP    [ ]   ✓[ ]   ✓→|    [ ]   RR  [ Send ] │
│         To: listserv@listserv.clark.net                      │
│       From: cleshin@xplora.com (Cynthia Leshin)              │
│    Subject:                                                   │
│         Cc:                                                   │
│        Bcc:                                                   │
│ Attachments:                                                 │
│                                                              │
│ subscribe TOPTEN Cynthia Leshin                              │
│                                                              │
└─────────────────────────────────────────────────────────────┘
```

The following lists can be found and subscribed to at this Web site:
http://www.thelist.com/

AFRICA-N — Africa news and information service
    Address: listserv%utoronto.bitnet@listserv.net
    Body: sub AFRICA-N < *your name* >

ARCH-L — archaeology list
    Address: listserv@tamvm1.tamu.edu
    Body: sub ARCH-L < *your name* >

BESTWEB — Best-Web-Site announcement list
    Address: listserv@vm3090.ege.edu.tr
    Body: sub BESTWEB < *your name* >

BGRASS-L — bluegrass music discussion
    Address: listserv@ukcc.uky.edu
    Body: sub BGRASS-L < *your name* >

CNN-NEWSROOM — CNN Newsroom mailing list
    Address: listserv@listserv.aol.com
    Body: sub CNN-NEWSROOM < *your name* >

David Letterman's Top-10 list
    Address: listserv@listserv.clark.net
    Body: sub TOPTEN < *your name* >

DOROTHYL — mystery literature e-conference
    Address: listserv@kentvm.kent.edu
    Body: sub DOROTHYL < *your name* >

EDRES-L — educational resources on the Internet
    Address: listserv@umbvm1.csd.unb.ca
    Body: sub EDRES-L < *your name* >

GARDENS — gardens and gardening
    Address: listserv@ukcc.uky.edu
    Body: sub GARDENS < *your name* >

HUMOR — UGA Humor list
      Address: listserv@uga.cc.uga.edu
      Body: sub HUMOR *< your name >*

ISRAEL-MIDEAST — Israel-Mideast - Israel Info Service
      Address: listserv@vm.tau.ac.il
      Body: sub ISRAEL-MIDEAST *< your name >*

JOBPLACE — self-directed job search techniques and job placement issues
      Address: listserv@news.jobweb.org
      Body: sub JOBPLACE *< your name >*

KIDLINK — list for parents and teachers
      Address: listserv@vm1.nodak.edu
      Body: sub KIDLINK *< your name >*

MACCHAT — The Mac*Chat newsletter
      Address: listserv@vm.temple.edu
      Body: sub MACCHAT *< your name >*

MEDIEV-L — medieval history
      Address: listserv@ukanvm.cc.ukans.edu
      Body: sub MEDIEV-L *< your name >*

NATIVE-L — aboriginal peoples: news and information
      Address: listserv@tamvm1.tamu.edu
      Body: sub NATIVE-L *< your name >*

NNEWS — Network news
      Address: listserv@vm1.nodak.edu
      Body: sub NNEWS *< your name >*

NEW-LIST — announcements of new listservs
      Address: listserv@vm1.nodak.edu
      Body: sub NEW-LIST *< your name >*

ROOTS-L — genealogy list
      Address: listserv@mail.eworld.com
      Body: sub ROOTS-L *< your name >*

SHAKSPER — Shakespeare electronic conference
    Address: listserv%utoronto.bitnet@listserv.net
    Body: sub SHAKSPER *< your name >*

TESLJB-L — jobs and employment issues
    Address: listserv@cunyvm.cuny.edu
    Body: sub TESLJB-L

TFTD-L — Thought For The Day
    Address: listserv@tamvm1.tamu.edu
    Body: sub TFTD-L *< your name >*

TIDBITS — a newsletter for Mac users
    Address: listserv@ricevm1.rice.edu
    Body: sub TIDBITS *< your name >*

TRDEV-L — Training and Development list
    Address: listserv@psuvm.psu.edu
    Body: sub TRDEV-L *< your name >*

TREPAN-L — weird news list
    Address: listserv@brownvm.brown.edu
    Body: sub TREPAN-L *< your name >*

TOURBUS — The Internet TourBus — A tour of cyberspace
    Address: listserv@listserv.aol.com
    Body: sub TOURBUS *< your name >*

WIN95-L — Windows 95 Give-And-Take List
    Address: listserv@peach.ease.1soft.com
    Body: sub WIN95-L *< your name >*

WMST-L — Woman's Studies List
    Address: listserv%umdd.bitnet@listserv.net
    Body: sub WMST-L *< your name >*

WSJ-ANNOUNCE: Wall Street Journal — Announcement List
    Address: listserv@peach.ease.lsoft.com
    Body: sub WSJ-ANNOUNCE *< your name >*

LOCATOR MAP...
Finding Listserv Mailing Lists

World Wide Web Site For Finding Mailing Lists

One of the best resources for helping you to find mailing lists is this World Wide Web site

http://www.tile.net/tile/listserv/index.html

This is a World Wide Web (WWW) addresses. See Chapter 6 for more information on WWW.

Gopher Site For Finding Mailing Lists

Travel to this excellent gopher server and follow the path to information on current mailing lists. You can also do a search for mailing lists by subject.

gopher:	**liberty.uc.wlu.edu**
path:	Explore Internet Resources/
	Searching for Listservs

URL: gopher://liberty.uc.wlu:70/11/internet/searchlistserv

E-Mail A Request For Listservs On A Topic

To request information on listserv mailing lists on a particular topic send an e-mail message to

LISTSERV@vm1.nodak.edu

In the message body type: **LIST GLOBAL / *keyword***

FOREIGN LANGUAGE CENTER

Listserv Mailing Lists

Listserv Mailing Lists

The terms found in this Foreign Language Center may be encountered in reading about or using listserv mailing lists.

administrative address: The mailing list address used to subscribe, unsubscribe, or send any requests or commands to the list. This address is used when communicating with the list administrator.

administrator: Mailing lists have an administrator that may be either a computer or a human. The role of the administrator is to handle subscription requests.

archive: Messages sent to a mailing list may be saved and stored in what is referred to as an archive. Information on how to access the archive is sent either via the HELP command or with the welcome message sent to new list subscribers.

BITNET: A worldwide network that connects over a thousand academic and research institutions in more than 40 countries in North America and Europe. Bitnet uses a protocol different from TCP/IP to transfer data on a network and is therefore not an official Internet domain.

Many bitnet sites are IBM mainframe computers that run VM operating systems. Bitnet addresses therefore frequently end in "vm" or include the word "bitnet." On some computer systems a bitnet address will not work because the local mail software is not set up to recognize the bitnet domain. If you have trouble sending mail to a bitnet address check to see if there is another non-bitnet address. This second address may end in "edu."

digest: A single list mailing that incorporates the main points of all the messages received during a specified period of time.

list: Another name used to refer to a mailing list.

listserv: A mailing list that is administered by a computer program.

moderated list: A list that has one or more human moderators who review all incoming mail and redistribute only selected portions to subscribers.

nomail: The message (**set *listname* nomail**) sent to the listserv administrative address to temporarily suspend your list mail. You can begin receiving messages again by sending the message:

set *listname* mail

signoff: One command used by some listservs for subscriptions to the list to be canceled.

submission address: The mailing list address used when sending a message to all subscribers of the list. Any message sent to this address will be read by all subscribers.

subscribe: The word used in the body of an e-mail message for requesting subscription to a mailing list.

unmoderated list: Lists do not screen received mail. All messages received by the listserv are sent to list subscribers.

unsubscribe: A command used by some listservs for requesting cancellation of a subscription to a mailing list.

Chapter Four

NETSCAPE & THE WORLD WIDE WEB

TOURIST INFORMATION CENTER

Netscape Navigator is a user-friendly graphical browser for the Internet. Netscape makes it possible to view and interact with multimedia resources (text, images, video, and sound) by pointing and clicking your mouse on pull-down menus and toolbar buttons.

Netscape Navigator (Version 1.0) was the premier Internet information browser in 1995. Netscape was developed in 1994 by Marc Andreeseen and others who developed the first graphical Internet browser, Mosaic, at the National Center for Supercomputing Applications (NCSA) at the University of Illinois at Urbana-Champaign. Netscape Navigator quickly became the standard for Internet browsers.

Netscape Navigator (Version 1.0)

Netscape Navigator (Version 1.0) features included the ability to

- connect to gopher, FTP, and telnet sites without using any additional software.

- read Usenet newsgroups.

- save your favorite Internet addresses (URLs) as bookmarks.

- download images, video, and sound files to your computer desktop.

- enhance Web page design with colored or patterned backgrounds.

- customize your Netscape travels.

- cut and paste text directly from the browser window.

- view, save, or print the HTML programming code for Web pages as either text or HTML source code;.

- send e-mail and Web documents to others.

- use forms for collecting information.

- use new HTML features such as customizable text fonts and inline JPEG images;.

- provide security for access to information and for secure transactions.

Netscape Navigator (Version 2.0)

Netscape Navigator 2.0 is far more than a browser. Navigator 2.0 is called a *platform* rather than a *browser* by Marc Andreessen and Netscape Communication Corporation (NCC). In addition to supporting the above features of earlier versions, Netscape 2.0 makes it possible for developers to build applications onto Netscape and to use Netscape as an e-mail program. Additional features include

- *New Usenet newsgroup reading options*: The News Reader was redesigned to provide a more concise view of the news hosts, newsgroups, and articles.

- *New Bookmark options:* Managing bookmarks is easier with the new Netscape Bookmarks window. You can now cut, copy, or paste bookmarks, create an alias, or drag and drop bookmarks and their folders to rearrange their order. Designate which folder you want a bookmark to be placed in by using the **Set to Bookmark Menu Folder** command from the **Item** menu.

- *Updating Bookmarks*: Update your bookmarks in the **What's New** menu under the **Bookmark** menu. Identify bookmarks that have changed or choose to check all bookmarks for an update of their URL.

- *Improved images and page presentation*: The presentation of Web pages has been improved with many new features such as the use of *frames*. Frames make it possible to specify multiple, independent, scrollable regions within a page. Each frame can contain a separate HTML document. For more information on frames see the Foreign Language Center. Images are now loaded smoother and faster with support for progressive JPEG images. Additionally, the quality of images is greatly improved. Choose and create new colors for your text and page links.

- *Background Images*: Netscape no longer waits for a background image to completely download before displaying Web page text or images. When the background image has been decoded, the page is redrawn to include the background.

- *Printing enhancements*: Add the title of Web pages or the URL in headers and footers using the **Page Setup** option.

- *FTP File Transfers*: Files can be uploaded and downloaded to and from FTP directories using drag-and-drop.

- *Security:* Netscape 2.0 allows you to conduct on-line financial transactions privately and securely.

- *JavaScript*: Netscape Navigator 2.0 includes a built-in scripting language called JavaScript. This new programming language extends the capabilities of Netscape adding new life with real time interactivity and animation. JavaScript is embedded in HTML documents with a SCRIPT tag.

New Possibilities For Interaction — Hot Java, VRML, & New Design Software

Marc Andreessen uses the term *live on-line applications* for the types of applications that can be built on the Netscape platform. These applications are distributed *on-line* by a network and provide users with a highly interactive or *live* environment. Data for these interactions is retrieved from databases. An example of one of the newest and most exciting applications that Netscape supports is *Java*. Java is a programming language (HotJava is the name of the software) developed by Sun Microsystems that brings animation and interaction to pages on the Web by creating *live objects*. Java makes possible a whole new level of interaction that has never been possible on the Web.

In addition to Java objects, you will see different types of audio and video formats, Macromedia Director files, virtual reality, and much more. Java combined with Virtual Reality Modeling Language (VRML) provides unlimited creative possibilities for creating a full sensory blend of the real and unreal (virtual) as you navigate Web pages with Java-enabled browsers such as Netscape 2.0.

Imagine being able to travel along ancient pathways to remote Himalayan hillside villages. Being able to virtually walk inside ancient Buddhist temples of an 18th century European-style palace. You pause and listen to the mystical sounds inside these temples and villages by just moving your mouse from one *live object* to another. Stop inside a

Tea House and chat. Hike along trails carved into the mountainside to magnificent forests of rhododendron, magnolia, and giant ferns. Stop and view the breathtaking views of Everest. Take a side trip along a gorge and sit by a quiet stream or a cascading waterfall. Listen to the different sounds in the virtual environments.

Travel in these highly interactive virtual environments is made possible with Web development tools such as Java, VRML, and 3-D design packages. These special Java programs have been named *applets*. Applets are essentially software programs that a browser such as Netscape downloads and executes. In the above example, an applet would be an animated journey into a temple or along a mountain pathway. Another applet would be the sound of the waterfall or an interactive animation in the temple. The applet enables you to interact with the environment that you have selected. Java-enabled browsers can therefore encounter animated and interactive applications and make possible real-time, realistic interactions between a Net user and the application.

Netscape has become the platform for creativity, interaction, and entrepreneurial activities. Web pages come to life as they exploit graphics, animation, and sound. The Web development tools are changing not only the Internet, but also multimedia and computing.

Netscape Travelers' Needs

Netscape Navigator requires the following:

- Windows 3.1 or Windows 95, with a 486 or later processor
- Windows NT
- Macintosh System 7
- 8 megabytes or more of RAM memory
- 18 megabytes of free hard disk space

Windows 3.1: If you are running Windows 3.1, you MUST use the 16-bit Navigator.

Windows 95: If you are running Windows 95 or Windows NT, use the 32-bit Navigator. The 16-bit Navigator will also work. **In order to run the 32-bit Navigator, you MUST have a 32-bit TCP/IP stack**. Both Windows 95 and Windows NT provide 32-bit TCP/IP stacks.

Obtaining Netscape Software

Individuals, businesses, or government organizations may evaluate Netscape free of charge for up to 90 days. Students, faculty, and staff of educational institutions and employees of charitable nonprofit organizations my use Netscape Navigator free of charge. Those using Netscape free of charge are not entitled to technical support.

There are several ways that you can obtain a copy of Netscape Navigator:

- Call Netscape Communication and order a copy for $39.00.
  (800) 528-6292.
  (415) 528-2555

  Annual subscriptions are also available for $17. Netscape will send you new versions.

- Connect to the Netscape Web page (**http://home.netscape.com**) and download an evaluation copy by just clicking your mouse on the download links. After 90 days, order a copy.

- Purchase a copy of Netscape Navigator Personal Edition from a local bookstore for $39.

- If you are an experienced user you can FTP the Netscape Navigator. There a number of FTP sites, here are several addresses for servers:

  ftp1.netscape.com   **ftp2.netscape.com**
  ftp3.netscape.com   **ftp4.netscape.com**

FTP Directions:
1. Connect via FTP to one of the above addresses.
2. At the name prompt, type **anonymous**.
3. At the password prompt, type your Internet e-mail address.
4. Use binary transfer mode. Do this by typing **bin**.
5. Type the following commands depending on your computer platform.
   - For Windows, type:
     get /netscape/windows/ns16-100.exe

   - For Macintosh users, type:
     get /netscape/mac/netscape.sea.hqx

GUIDED TOUR

Netscape Navigator 2.0
&
The World Wide Web

Cool World Wide Web Expeditions

◼ EARTH VIEWER

View either a map of the Earth showing the day and night regions at this moment, or view the Earth from the Sun, the Moon, the night side of the Earth, above any location on the planet specified by latitude, longitude and altitude, or from a satellite in Earth orbit. **http://www.fourmilab.ch/earthview/vplanet.html**

◼ ELECTRONIC POSTCARDS

Create and send a custom electronic postcard to on-line friends for all occasions. **http://buildacard.com/** or **http://postcards.www.media.mit.edu/Postcards**

◼ ESPN Sports Zone

If you are a sports fan you will enjoy up-to-date sports information, scores, states, schedules, standings, live chats, contests, A Sports Index and much more. **http://ESPNET.SportsZone.com/**

◼ JOBS

Visit America's Job Bank (**http://www.ajb.dni.us/index.html**), Career Path (**http://www.careerpath.com/**), or careerWEB (**http://www.cweb.com/**) to help find jobs or employees.

◼ NASA (National Aeronautics And Space Administration)

Visit NASA for links to amazing astronomy sites, and much more. **http://www.gsfc.nasa.gov/NASA_homepage.html**

◼ NEWS

Get the latest news on-line with publications such as New York Times, Time, USA Today, and the Wall Street Journal. **http://www.newslink.org/**

◼ PARIS

Take a virtual trip to France and visit the national monuments, museums, schools, stores shops. Take a break and stop by a sidewalk cafe to chat. Be sure to sign the Guest Book. **http://meteora.ucsd.edu:80/~norman/paris/**

◼ WHITE HOUSE

Visit the White House find links to all government information and independent agencies. **http://www.whitehouse.gov/**

The Netscape Window (page)

The World Wide Web is unique in that its architecture allows multimedia resources to be incorporated into a hypertext file or document called a *page*. A Web page or *window* may contain text, images, movies, or sound. Each multimedia resource on a page has associated information to link you to the resource. This information is called the URL.

The Netscape Navigator 2.0 window (see Figure 4.1) includes these features to assist you with your Internet travels:

- The *Window Title Bar* shows the name of the current document.

- The page display shows the content of the Netscape window. A page includes text and links to images, video, and sound files. Links include highlighted words (colored and/or underlined) or icons. Click on a highlighted word or icon to bring another page of related information into view.

- The Netscape window also includes *frames*. A frame is a segmented portion of a Netscape page that contains its own page.

- *The Progress Bar* shows what percentage of a document has been downloaded at any given time.

- The Mail Icon (the small envelope in the bottom-right corner of the Netscape, Mail, and News pages) provides you with information on the status of your mail. A question mark next to the mail envelope indicates that Netscape cannot automatically check the mail server for new e-mail messages. The exclamation point next to the envelope indicates that the server has new messages for you.

- The address location field shows the URL address of the current document.

- *Toolbar* buttons activate Netscape features and navigational aids.

- *Directory* buttons display resources for helping you browse the Internet.

- Security indicators (doorkey icon in the lower left corner of the window) indicate whether a document is secure (doorkey icon is blue) or insecure (doorkey icon is grey). A secure doorkey displayed with two teeth indicate high-grade encryption; one tooth indicates medium-grade.

The Home Page

The Home Page is the starting point for your journey using a Web browser such as Netscape Navigator. Home pages are created by Internet providers, colleges and universities, schools, businesses, individuals or anyone who has information they want to make available on the Internet. For example, a college or university may have links to information on the college and courses taught.

Figure 4.1
An example of a Home Page for Grand Canyon National Park using Netscape Navigator.

The URL for this Web page is **http://www.kbt.com/gc/**

GUIDED TOUR 1...

Navigating With Netscape

This Guided Tour introduces you to Netscape's graphical interface navigational tools.

- Hyperlinks
- Toolbar buttons,
- Pull-down menus

After you have been introduced to these navigational tools, take a Guided Walk to visit several Web pages using these tools.

Hyperlinks

When you begin Netscape you will start with a Home Page. Click on highlighted words (colored and/or underlined) to bring another page of related information to your screen.

Images will automatically load onto this page unless you have turned off the **Auto Load Images** found under the **Options** menu. If you have turned off this option you will see this icon that represents an image that can be downloaded. Internet users may turn off Auto Load Images to speed the downloading of Web pages.

If you want to view this image, click on this highlighted icon or on the **Images** button.

As you travel the World Wide Web, you will find other icons to represent movies, video, and sound. Click on these icons to download (link) you to these resources.

Navigating via Toolbar Buttons

Figure 4.2
Netcape toolbar buttons.

🔲 **Back**: Point and click on the **Back** button to go to the previous page in your history list. The history list keeps track of the pages you link to.

Forward: This button takes you to the next page of your history list.

Home: This button takes you back to the opening page. Later you will learn how to designate your home page.

Reload: Click on this button to reload the same page that you are viewing. Changes made in the source page will be shown in this new page.

Images: Clicking on this button downloads images onto your current page. Netscape provides you with an option to disable downloading of images when you access a page. This makes page downloading faster. If you have selected this option (in the **Options** menu **Auto Load Images**) and decide that you would like to view an image, just click on the **Images** button.

Open: Use this button to access a dialog box for typing in URL's for Web sites, newsgroups, gopher, FTP, or telnet.

Print: Select this button to print the current page you are viewing.

Find: If you are searching for a word in the current page you are viewing, click on the **Find** button for a dialog box to enter the word or phrase.

Stop: This button stops the downloading of Web pages.

Figure 4.3
Netscape navigational buttons for exploring the Net.

What's New?	What's Cool?	Handbook	Net Search	Net Directory	Software

What's New: Visit *What's New* to link to the best new sites.

What's Cool: Displays Netscape's selection of cool Web sites to visit.

Handbook: Links you to on-line Netscape tutorials, references, and index.

Net Search: Clicking on this button links you to available search engines that help find a particular site or document. Search engines use keywords and concepts to find information in titles or headers of documents, directories, or documents themselves.

Net Directory: Click on this button to explore Internet resources categorized by topic. Some directories cover the entire Internet; some present only what they feel is relevant; others focus on a particular field.

Software: This button connects you to information about Netscape Navigator software, subscription programs, upgrade information, and registration.

Pull-Down Menus

Nine pull-down menus offer navigational tools for your Netscape journeys: File, Edit, View, Go, Bookmarks, Options, Directory, Window, and Help (Windows only).

File Menu

Figure 4.4
Netscape **File** pull-down menu.

File	Edit	View	Go	Boo
New Web Browser				⌘N
New Mail Message				⌘M
Mail Document...				
Open Location...				⌘L
Open File...				⌘O
Close				⌘W
Save as...				
Upload File...				
Page Setup...				
Print...				⌘P
Quit				⌘Q

New Web Browser: Creates a new Netscape window. This window displays the first page you viewed when you connected to Netscape.

New Mail Message: Opens an e-mail composition box allowing you to create and send a message or attach a document to your mail message.

Mail Document (or **Mail Frame**): Lets you send an e-mail message with the Web page you are viewing attached. The page's URL will be included.

Open Location: Works the same way as the **Open** toolbar button. Enter a URL address in the dialog box.

Open File: Provides a dialog box for you to use to open a file on your computer's hard drive. For example, you can open a Web image downloaded to your hard drive without being connected to the Internet.

Close: Closes the current Netscape page. On Windows, this option exits the Netscape application when you close the last page.

Save as... (or **Save Frame as**): Creates a file to save the contents of the current Internet page you are viewing in the Netscape window. The page can be saved as plain text or in source (HTML) format.

Upload File: Click on this option to upload a file to the FTP server indicated by the current URL. You can also upload images by dragging and dropping files from the desktop to the Netscape window. **NOTE...** This command is only active when you are connected to a FTP server.

Page Setup: Click on this to specify your printing options.

Print: Click on this button to print the current page.

Print Preview (Windows only): Previews the printed page on the screen.

Exit (on Macintosh—**Quit**): Exits the Netscape application.

Edit Menu

The **Edit** menu makes it possible to cut and paste text from a Web page to your computer's clipboard. This option can be used to copy and paste text from a page to a word processing document or another application of your choice. The options under this menu are similar to what you have available to you in many of your computer software applications under their **File** menu (i.e., word processing, desktop publishing, and graphics applications).

Figure 4.5
The Netscape **Edit** menu.

Edit	View	Go	E
Can't Undo		⌘Z	
Cut		⌘X	
Copy		⌘C	
Paste		⌘V	
Clear			
Select All		⌘A	
Find...		⌘F	
Find Again		⌘G	

Undo.. (or **Can't Undo**): Reverses the last action you performed.

Cut: Removes what you have selected and places it on the clipboard.

Copy: Copies the current selection to computer's the clipboard.

Paste: Puts the current clipboard's contents in the document you are working on.

Clear (for the Macintosh only): Removes the current selection.

Select All: Selects all you have indicated by using the application's selection markers. May be used to select items before you cut, copy, or paste.

Find: Lets you search for a word or phrase within the current Web page.

Find Again: Searches for another occurrence of the word or phrase specified when you used the **Find** command.

View Menu

Figure 4.6
The **View** menu options from Netscape.

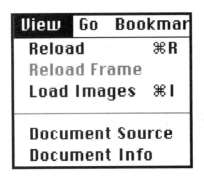

Reload: Download a new copy of the current Netscape page you are viewing to replace the one originally loaded. Netscape checks the network server to see if any changes have occurred to the page.

Reload Frame: Download a new copy of the currently selected page within a single frame on a Netscape page.

Load Images: If you have set **Auto Load Images** in your Netscape **Options** menu, images from a Web page will be automatically loaded. If this option has not been selected, choose the **Load Images** to display images for the current Netscape page.

Refresh (Windows only) **:** Downloads a new copy of the current Netscape page from local memory to replace the one originally loaded.

Document Source: Selecting this option provides you with the format of HTML (HyperText Markup Language). The HTML source text contains the programming commands used to create the page.

Document Info: Produces a page in a separate Netscape window with information on the current Web document's structure and composition, including title, location (URL), date of the last modification, character set encoding, and security status.

Go Menu

Figure 4.7
Netscape **Go** menu.

Go	Bookmarks	Options	Directory	Window	
Back					⌘[
Forward					⌘]
Home					
Stop Loading					⌘.
✓Featured Events – Livefrom HST					⌘0
NASA K-12 Internet: Live from the Hubble Space Tel...					⌘1
Web66: What's New					⌘2

Back: Takes you back to the previous page in your history list. The history list keeps track of all the pages you link to. Same as the **Back** button on the toolbar.

Forward: Takes you to the next page of your history list. Same as the **Forward** button on the toolbar.

Home: Takes you to the Home Page. Same as the **Home** button on the toolbar.

Stop Loading: Stops downloading the current page. Same as the **Stop** button on the toolbar.

History Items: A list of the titles of the places you have visited. Select menu items to display their page. To view the History list, select the **Window** menu and then choose **History.**

Bookmarks Menu

Bookmarks make it possible to save and organize your favorite Internet visits. Opening this pull-down menu allows you to quickly view and download your favorite pages.

Figure 4.8
Netscape Bookmark menu.

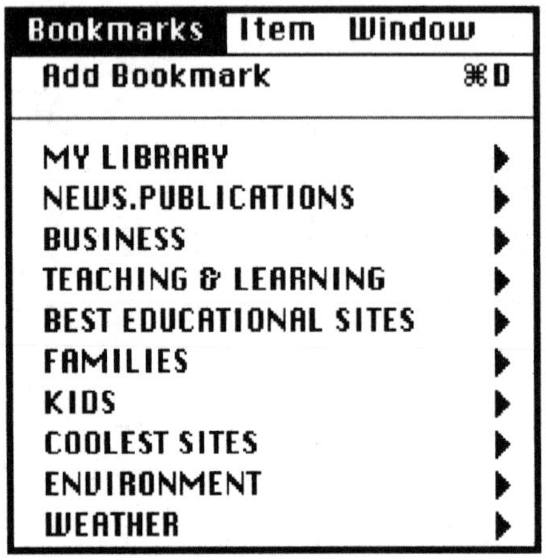

```
┌─────────────────────────────────────┐
│ Bookmarks  Item   Window            │
│ Add Bookmark                    ⌘D  │
│                                     │
│ MY LIBRARY                     ▶    │
│ NEWS.PUBLICATIONS              ▶    │
│ BUSINESS                       ▶    │
│ TEACHING & LEARNING            ▶    │
│ BEST EDUCATIONAL SITES         ▶    │
│ FAMILIES                       ▶    │
│ KIDS                           ▶    │
│ COOLEST SITES                  ▶    │
│ ENVIRONMENT                    ▶    │
│ WEATHER                        ▶    │
└─────────────────────────────────────┘
```

- **Add Bookmark**: Click on **Add Bookmark** to save this page in your bookmark list. Behind the scenes, Netscape saves the URL address so you can access this page by pointing and clicking on the item in your list.

- Bookmark Items: Below **Add Bookmarks,** you will see a list of your saved pages. Point and click on any item to bring this page to your screen.

To view your Bookmarks, add new Bookmark folders, arrange the order of your Bookmarks, or to do any editing, select the **Window** menu and choose **Bookmarks**.

Options Menu

The **Options** menu offers customization tools to personalize your use of Netscape Navigator.

- Show the toolbar buttons
- Show the URL location of a page
- Show the Directory buttons
- Automatic loading of images
- Show FTP file information
- Select styles for how your pages will appear
- Select which Home Page you want to appear when you log onto Netscape
- Select your link styles (colors)
- Select your news server to interact with Usenet newsgroups
- Set up for e-mail on Netscape

There are additional customization tools available that are more advanced. Refer to the Netscape on-line handbook for more information on Options and Preferences.

Figure 4.9
Netscape **Options** menu.

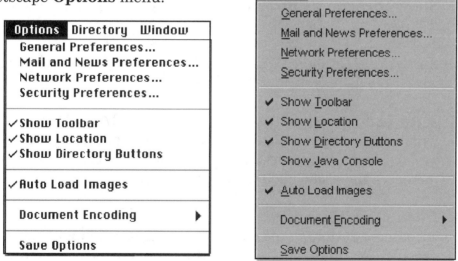

(a) Macintosh version.   (b) Windows version.

Before you can use the e-mail and Usenet newsgroup tools available in Netscape, you will need to customize the **Mail and News Preferences**.

- **General Preferences:** Presents tab buttons for selecting preferences. Each tap presents a panel for customizing Netscape's operations for your own personal needs, preferences, and interests. A detailed discussion of Preferences is discussed later in this chapter.

- **Mail and News Preferences:** Presents the panel for entering information on your mail and news server so you can use Netscape to send and receive e-mail and to participate in Usenet newsgroups.

- **Network Preferences:** Presents a panel with options for cache, network connections, and proxy configurations.

- **Security Preferences:** Displays the panel for setting security features.

- **Show Toolbar:** If selected, the Toolbar buttons are visible on the Netscape page.

- **Show Location:** If selected, the URL location for the page is displayed.

- **Show Directory Buttons**: If selected, the Directory buttons are visible.

- **Show Java Console** (Windows only): If selected, the Java Console window is displayed.

- **Auto Load Images**: If selected, images embedded into a page will be loaded automatically. If not checked, images can be loaded by clicking on the **Load Images** button. Deselecting this option increases the speed of downloading a page.

- **Document Encoding:** Lets you select which character set encoding a document uses when document encoding is either not specified or unavailable. The proportional and fixed fonts are selected using the **General Preferences/Fonts** panel.

- **Save Options:** Click on this option to save the changes you made to any of the above options.

Directory Menu

The **Directory** pull-down menu directs you to a few navigational aids to help you begin your Web exploration.

Figure 4.10
Netscape Directory menu.

Directory	Window
Netscape's Home	
What's New?	
What's Cool?	
Netscape Galleria	
Internet Directory	
Internet Search	
Internet White Pages	
About the Internet	

Netscape Home: Takes you to the Netscape Home Page.

What's New: Click on this item to see what's new on the Internet.

What's Cool: Click on this item to see Netscape's selection of interesting places to visit.

Netscape Galleria: The Galleria is a showcase of Netscape customers who have built Net sites using Netscape Server software. Visit the Galleria to learn more about how to build and maintain innovative Web sites.

Internet Directory: This is the same as the Internet Directory button on the toolbar. It links you to Internet directories for finding information and resources.

Internet Search: Connects you to many of the best on-line search engines.

Internet White Pages: Links you to tools to help you find people connected to the Internet.

About the Internet: Links to resources to help you learn more about the Internet.

Window Menu

The **Window** menu makes it possible for you to easily navigate between your e-mail, Usenet news, Bookmarks, and to see and visit places you have all ready traveled.

Figure 4.11
The **Window** menu with navigational options.

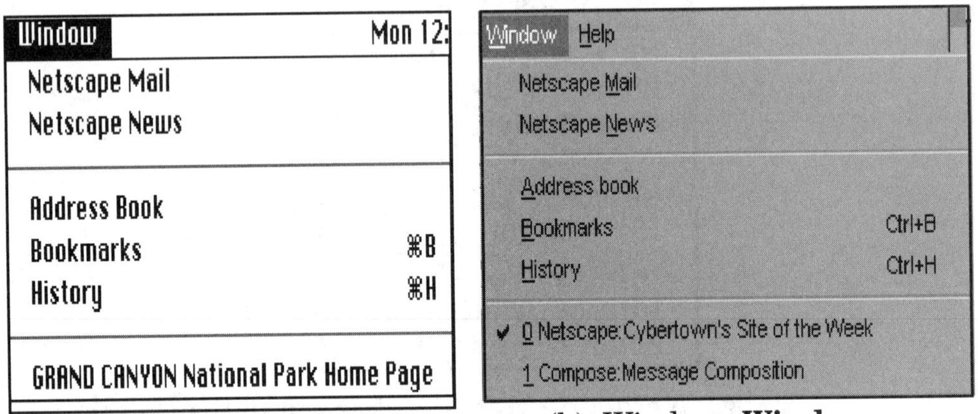

Window	Mon 12:
Netscape Mail	
Netscape News	
Address Book	
Bookmarks	⌘B
History	⌘H
GRAND CANYON National Park Home Page	

Window	Help	
Netscape Mail		
Netscape News		
Address book		
Bookmarks		Ctrl+B
History		Ctrl+H
✓ 0 Netscape:Cybertown's Site of the Week		
1 Compose:Message Composition		

(a) Macintosh **Window**   (b). Windows **Window**

- **Netscape Mail:** Click on this option to access the Netscape e-mail program.

- **Netscape News:** Click on this option to access the Usenet newsgroups.

- **Address Book:** This option displays an Address Book window for use with the e-mail program.

- **Bookmarks:** Select this option to display your bookmarks and pull-down menus for working with or editing your bookmarks.

- **History:** When selected, this option displays a history list of the pages (their titles and URLs) that you have recently viewed. Select an item and press the **Go To** button (or double-click on the item) to revisit the page.

- Below the history list is the name of the open window you are currently viewing.

Preferences Panels

The **Preferences** panels found under the **Options** menu is used for customizing your own Netscape preferences. Before you can use the Netscape e-mail program or read and interact with Usenet newsgroups you will need to find out the name of your Internet providers Mail and News servers and enter this information in the **Mail and News Preferences** panel option.

> **NOTE**
>
> If you are using Netscape Navigator on a network such as at a college, university, or school, you will not need to enter the information for Mail and News Server. This should have been done by your system administrator. If you are having trouble sending e-mail or connecting to Usenet newsgroups, then check this panel to see if the information has been added. If not, contact your system administrator.
>
> If you are using Netscape on a network, your institution would probably prefer that you do not make changes to the Preferences panel.

Figure 4.12
The **General Preferences** panel for Netscape 2.0.

```
                    Preferences: General
  ┌─────────┐
  │Appearance│ Colors  Fonts  Helpers  Images  Applications  Languages

  ┌Toolbars─────────────────────────────────────────────────┐
  │ Show Toolbar as:  ○ Pictures  ○ Text  ⦿ Pictures and Text │
  └─────────────────────────────────────────────────────────┘

  ┌Startup──────────────────────────────────────────────────┐
  │ On Startup Launch:  ⦿ Netscape Browser  ○ Netscape Mail  ○ Netscape News │
  │                                                          │
  │ Browser starts with:                                     │
  │      ○ Blank Page                                        │
  │      ⦿ Home Page Location:  http://web66.coled.umn.edu/new/new.html │
  └─────────────────────────────────────────────────────────┘

  ┌Link Styles──────────────────────────────────────────────┐
  │        Links are:  ☒ Underlined                          │
  │ Followed Links Expire:  ○ Never  ⦿ After 30 days  [ Now ]│
  └─────────────────────────────────────────────────────────┘

                        [ Cancel ]  [ Apply ]  [ OK ]
```

General Preferences

> **NOTE**
> This section will not discuss all of your **Preferences Options** (i.e., Network, Security, and Language). Knowledge of many of these Netscape options are not required for the average Internet user. Refer to the on-line Netscape Handbook for information on these and other options.

Appearance Panel

Toolbars

Your toolbar can be customized to appear in your Netscape window as **Pictures**, **Text**, or **Pictures and Text**. The default is **Pictures and Text.**

Startup

Your first option is to select one of three buttons to determine which window appears upon starting the Netscape application: **Netscape browser**, **Netscape Mail**, or **Netscape News**.

The second option is to customize which Web page you connect to when you logon and open the Netscape application. Enter in a URL for your favorite Web site in the dialog box

Link Styles

Netscape keeps track of the links you have viewed. With this option you can select how long you would like to have your links highlighted after having viewed them. Select one of two options for your followed links: **Never Expire** or **Expire After** (enter how many days). Clicking on the **Now** button determines the expiration of followed links.

Colors Panel

In the Color panel, specify your color choices for links and text. Default colors are used for unchecked boxes.

Figure 4.13
The **Preferences Color** panel.

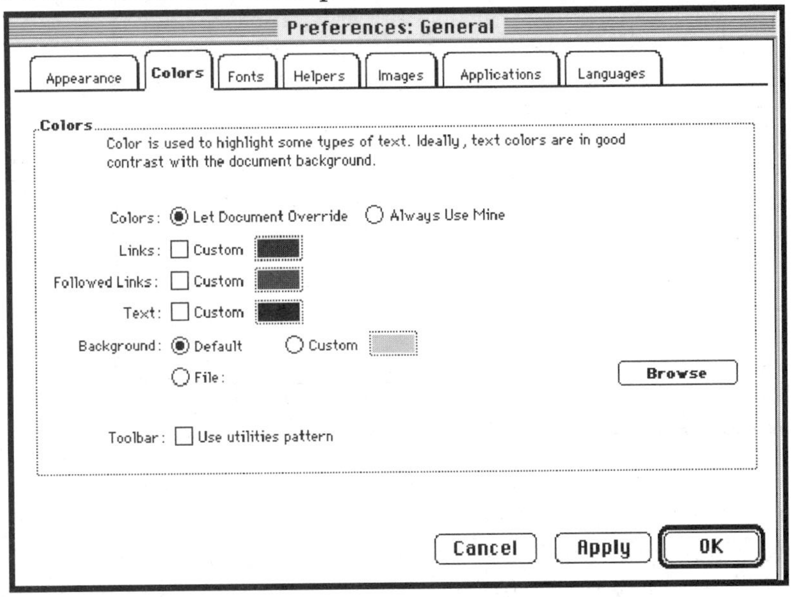
Preferences: General
Appearance
Colors
Fonts
Helpers
Images
Applications
Languages
Colors
Color is used to highlight some types of text. Ideally, text colors are in good contrast with the document background.
Colors:
Let Document Override
Always Use Mine
Links:
Custom
Followed Links:
Custom
Text:
Custom
Background:
Default
Custom
File:
Browse
Toolbar:
Use utilities pattern
Cancel
Apply
OK

- **Links and Text Colors:** Click in and select the link box to change link and text colors. Click on the color box to view the color wheel for changing colors.

- **Background:** To change the way a background of a document is presented on your Netscape page, choose one of three buttons. The **Default** button uses a standard gray background. The **Custom** button allows you to select a background color of your choice. Press **Choose Color** or click in the color box for the Macintosh. To select an image for a background, choose **File** and press the **Browse** button.

Helpers Panel

When you browse the Internet and select text, images, video, or sound files, you are downloading different file formats that require software applications to view or play these files. These applications are referred to as *helper applications*.

Figure 4.14
The **Helpers** panel.

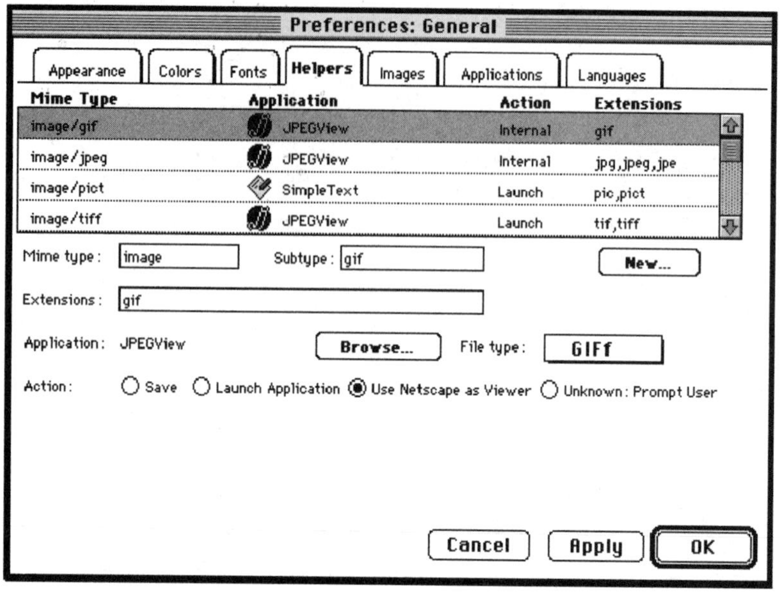

Before you can view multimedia files such as sound and video you will need to have additional software referred to as *helper applications*, *viewers*, *players*, or *sound-players*. Most of these software programs can be downloaded free from the Internet. Many Web pages will have a link to the required player software (i.e., RealAudio application. See the National Public Radio site at **http:www.npr.org**). Refer to the Expedition Experience in this chapter for Web sites where you can download free software. The Netscape Application also has information on where to obtain these Helper Applications. Choose the **Help** menu item (see Balloon Help or Apple menu on the Macintosh) and select **Frequently Asked Questions**.

Helper Applications expand Netscape's abilities. Netscape uses these applications to let you automatically decompress downloaded applications, listen to sounds, play movies, and get better display of images. For more information see Guided Walk 6, Downloading And Viewing files.

Before You Begin....

Some basic technical information and terminology will be helpful before you begin working with helper applications.

Most of the multimedia files you will find while exploring the World Wide Web are known as *MIME (Multimedia Internet Mail Extension)* type. The *MIME type* refers to the type of file: text, HTML, images, video, or sound. When Netscape retrieves a file from a server, the server provides the MIME type of the file. Netscape uses the MIME type to establish whether the file format can be read by the software's built-in capabilities or, if not, whether a suitable helper application is available to read the file. If a suitable helper application is not available, you will need to do the following:

1. Find a Web site that has the helper application you need.
2. Download the helper application.
2. Install the helper application.
3. Tell Netscape where to find this helper application.

MIME types consist of two parts: the *main type* and the *subtype*. For example, the main type for a NASA image would be *image* and the subtype might be *jpeg*. The file name extension will indicate the subtype for the file.

Configuring Netscape To Find Viewer Applications

After downloading a viewer application, check to see if there is a *Read Me* text document. Many times these documents will tell you how to install and configure your Web browser for the application.

STEP 1: Open the **Helper** panel.
STEP 2: Enter the **MIME type** and **subtype**.
STEP 3: Enter the type of extension.
STEP 4: Click on the **Launch Application** button.
STEP 5: Click on **Browse** to find where the helper application is on your hard drive.

Configuring Your Mail And News Server

Before you can use Netscape e-mail capabilities or subscribe to and participate in Usenet groups, you must do the following:

1. Obtain the name of your mail (SMTP) server and news server (NNTP server) from your Internet system administrator.

2. Configure Netscape to point to your Mail and Usenet news server.
   a. Click on the **Options** pull-down menu.
   b. Select the **Mail and News Preferences**.
   c. Click on the **Servers** panel.
   d. Enter the name of your mail server in the Outgoing Mail (SMTP) and Incoming Mail (POP) Server dialog boxes.
   e. Enter your username in the Pop User Name box.
   f. Enter the name of your News (NNTP) Server in the dialog box.

Figure 4.15

The Mail and News Servers panel.

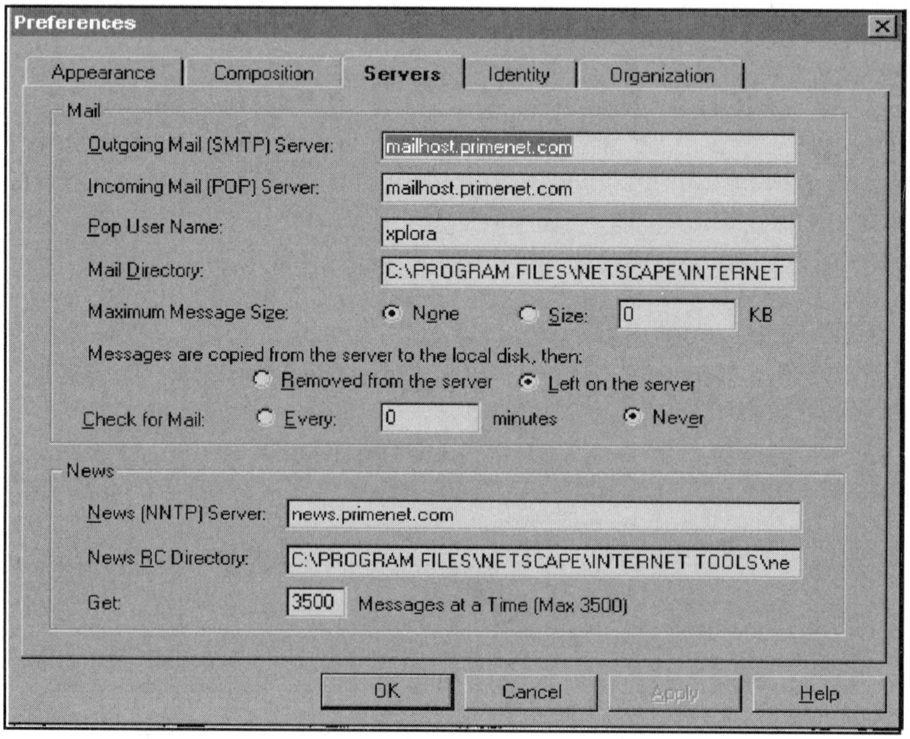

To further customize your mail and news options, select the **Identify** panel to enter in your name, e-mail address, reply-to address, organization, and the option to create a signature.

GUIDED TOUR 2 ... Using Netscape For E-Mail

Netscape 2.0 has a built-in e-mail program that makes it possible to send and receive e-mail messages, Web documents, and files (attachments). You also have options to file and store messages and create an Address Book. In Chapter 2 you learned about how to use Eudora for e-mail. With Netscape 2.0, you now have an additional e-mail program to choose from.

In this section, you will learn how to use Netscape for e-mail. Refer to Chapter 2 more a more in-depth discussion of electronic mail.

To access Netscape's e-mail program, go to the **Window** menu and select **Netscape Mail**.

Figure 4.16
The Netscape mail window.

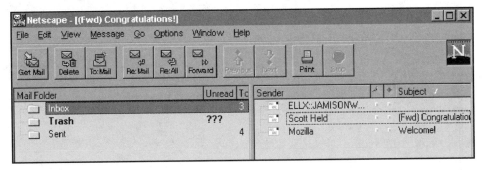

🖼 **Inbox:** Click on the **Inbox** folder and your messages will be displayed. Click on a message to read that message.

🖼 **Trash:** Drag unwanted messages that you have read to the **Trash** folder.

🖼 **Sent:** Click on the **Sent** folder to see the recent messages you have sent.

You will be using these mail toolbar buttons for e-mail functions such as getting your mail, deleting mail, replying to, forwarding, or printing messages.

Figure 4.17
Toolbar buttons for the Netscape mail program.

Sending E-Mail Messages

To send an e-mail message, click on the **To: Mail** button.

Figure 4.18
The Netscape Mail Composition window.

1. Enter in the e-mail addresses of the primary recipient and any courtesy copy recipients.

2. Enter the subject of the message.

3. Type your message.

4. Click the **Send** button to mail your message.

Receiving Your E-Mail Messages

There are three ways to download your e-mail messages.

- Click on the **Get Mail** button.

- Click on the mail envelope icon found in the lower right corner of the Netscape window. ✉?

- Go to the **File** menu and select, **Get New Mail**.

After doing one of the three, Netscape will ask you for your e-mail password.

Figure 4.19

The dialog box requesting your e-mail password.

Password Entry Dialog ✕

Password for POP3 user
xplora@mailhost.primenet.com:

[OK]

[Cancel]

After you have typed in your password, Netscape will connect to your mail server and download your e-mail messages.

Replying To E-Mail Messages

There are two ways to reply to an e-mail message that you are viewing.

- Click on the **Re:Mail** button or the **Re:All** button.

- Go to the **Message** menu and select **Reply** or **Reply to All**.

The **Re: All** or **Reply to All** options reply to any individual who was copied or listed as a recipient of the same message you received.

Managing Your E-Mail

All of your incoming messages are stored in your **Inbox** until you either delete them or create a folder to store them.

To create a new folder to store messages go to the **File** menu and select, **New Folder**.

Figure 4.20
The **mail File** menu.

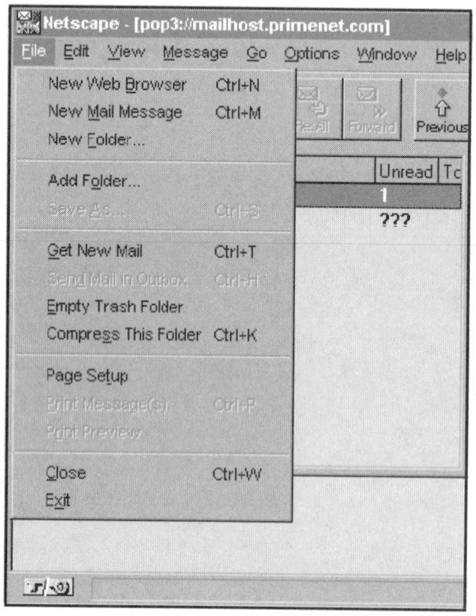

After selecting the **New Folder** option, you will see a dialog box prompting you for the name of the new mail folder.

Figure 4.21
The folder name dialog box.

After you have entered the name for the mail folder your Netscape mail window will look like this.

Figure 4.22
The new **Mail** folder window.

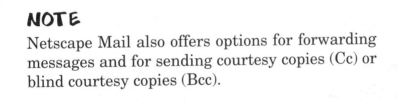

NOTE
Netscape Mail also offers options for forwarding messages and for sending courtesy copies (Cc) or blind courtesy copies (Bcc).

Creating An Address Book

Save a copy of an e-mail sender's address as you view and read your mail or create a new user in your Netscape Address Book. There are two ways to access your Address Book.

- Go to the **Window** menu and select **Address Book**.

- From within your mail composition window, click on the **Address** button.

Figure 4.23
The Mail
Composition
Address button.

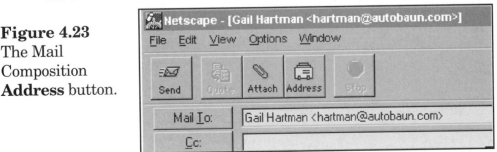

When your **Address Book** is open click on the **Item** menu and select, **New User** to add the name and e-mail address of an individual

Figure 4.24
The Netscape **Address Book** panel.

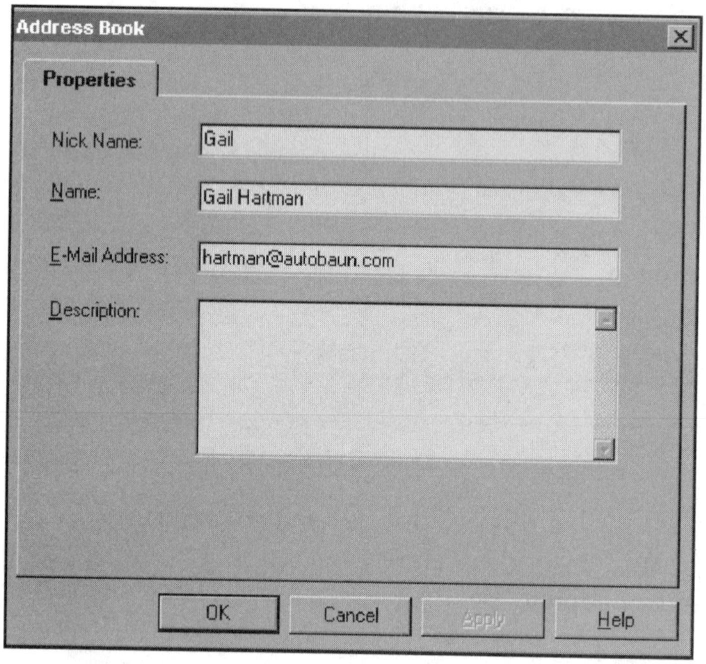

- **Nickname:** Enter a nickname for the new e-mail address.

- **Name:** Enter the name of the person.

- **E-Mail Address:** Type in the person's e-mail address

- **Description:** Enter any information that you would like to save about this individual.

To use the address of an individual in your address book, click on the **Address** button from within your mail composition window. Select either **To, CC,** or **Bcc**.

Figure 4.25
Netscape **Address Book**.

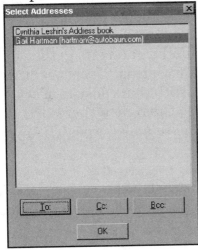

To add the e-mail address of the sender of a message you are reading, go to the **Message** menu and select **Add To Address Book**.

Attachments

Netscape has the option of adding a file, document, or the URL of a Web page to your e-mail message. (See Chapter 2 for a discussion of attachments.) To add an attachment, click on the **Attach** button from within the mail composition box. Find the file where the document is stored and click **OK**.

Figure 4.26
Netscape **Attachment** dialog box.

GUIDED TOUR 3... Netscape Newsgroups

What Are Newsgroups?

In the virtual community of the Internet, Usenet newsgroups are analogous to a cafe where people with similar interests gather from around the world to interact and exchange ideas. Usenet is a very large distributed bulletin board system (BBS) that consists of several thousand specialized discussion groups. Currently there are over 20,000 newsgroups with about 20 to 30 more added weekly. Anyone can start a newsgroup.

You can subscribe to a newsgroup, scan through the messages, read messages of interest, organize the messages, and send in your comments or questions.

Usenet groups are organized by subject and divided into major categories.

Category	Topic Area
alt.	no topic is off limit in this alternative group
comp.	computer-related topics
misc.	miscellaneous topics that don't fit into other categories
news.	happenings on the Internet
rec.	recreational activities/hobbies
sci.	scientific research and associated issues
soc.	social issues and world cultures
talk.	discussions and debates on controversial social issues

In addition to these categories there are local newsgroups with prefixes that indicate their topic or locality.

Some newsgroups are moderated and reserved for very specific articles. Articles submitted to these newsgroups are sent to a central site. If the article is approved, it is posted by the moderator. Many newsgroups have no moderator. There is no easy way to determine if a group is moderated or not. The only way to tell if a group is moderated is to submit an article. You will then be notified if your article has been mailed to the newsgroup moderator.

What Is The Difference Between A Mailing List And A Usenet Newsgroup?

One analogy for describing the difference between a listserv mailing list and a Usenet newsgroup is to compare the difference between having a few intimate friends over for dinner and conversation (a listserv) vs. going to a Super Bowl party where the entire world has been invited (newsgroups). A listserv is a smaller, more intimate place to discuss issues of interest. A Usenet newsgroup is much larger and much more open to the "everything and anything goes" mentality. This is not to say that both do not provide a place for valuable discussion. However, the size of each makes the experience very different.

A mailing list (listserv) is managed by a single site, such as a university. Subscribers to a mailing list are automatically mailed messages that are sent to the mailing list submission address.

Usenet consists of many sites that are set up by local Internet providers. When a message is sent to a Usenet site, a copy of the message that has been received is sent to other neighboring, connected Usenet sites. Each of these sites keeps a copy of the message and then forwards the message to other connected systems. Usenet can therefore handle thousands of subscribers. A listserv would find it difficult to maintain a list for thousands of people.

One advantage of Usenet groups over a mailing list is that you can quickly read postings to the newsgroup. When you connect to a Usenet newsgroup you see a list of articles. You can select only those that interest you. Unlike a mailing list, Usenet messages do not accumulate in your mailbox, forcing you to read and delete them. Usenet articles are on your local server and can be read at your convenience.

Netscape And Usenet Newsgroups

Netscape supports Usenet newsgroups. You can subscribe to a newsgroup, read articles posted to a group, and reply to articles. You can determine whether your reply is sent to the individual author of the posted article or to the entire newsgroup.

Netscape also has an additional feature. Every news article is scanned for references to other documents called URLs. These URLs are shown as active hypertext links that can be accessed by clicking on the underlined words.

Newsgroups have a URL location. These URLs are similar to, but not identical to, other pages. For example, the URL for a recreational backcountry newsgroup is **news:rec.backcountry.**
The server protocol is **news:** and the newsgroup is **rec.backcountry.** Newsgroups present articles along what is called a "thread." The thread packages the article with responses to the article. Each new response is indented one level from the original posting. A response to a response is indented another level. Newsgroups' threads, therefore, appear as an outline.

Buttons on each newsgroup page provide the reader with controls for reading and responding to articles. Netscape buttons vary depending on whether you are viewing a page of newsgroup listings or a newsgroup article.

Netscape News Window For Usenet News

To display the News window, go to the **Window** menu and select **Netscape News**.

Figure 4.27
The Netscape **News** window.

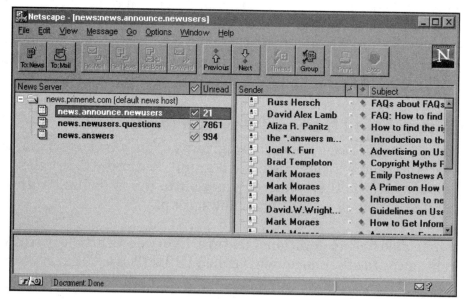

Notice that you have new options in the form of toolbar buttons and pull-down menus for receiving, reading, replying, and sending messages to newsgroups. Netscape News works in much the same way as Netscape Mail.

Figure 4.28
Netscape News window buttons.

To: News: Selecting this button displays a Message Composition window for creating a new message posting for a newsgroup.

To: Mail: This option displays a Message Composition window for creating a new mail message.

Re: Mail: Click on this button to reply to the current newsgroup message (thread) you are reading.

Re: Both: This button displays a Message Composition window for posting a reply to the current message thread for the entire newsgroup and to the sender of the news message.

Forward: Displays the Message Composition window for forwarding the current news message as an attachment. Enter the e-mail address in the **Mail To** field.

Previous: Brings the previous unread message in the thread to your screen.

Next: Brings the next unread message in the thread to your screen.

Thread: Selecting this option marks the message threads you have read.

Group: Marks all messages read.

Print: Select this button to print the message you are reading.

Stop: Stops the current transmission of messages from your news server.

Netscape News Menus
When you select Netscape News you will receive not only new toolbar buttons but also different pull-down menus for interacting with the Netscape news reader.

Figure 4.29
The Netscape News **File** menu.

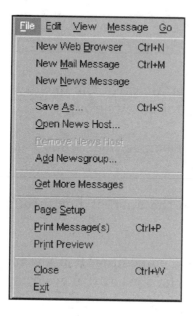

New Web Browser: Creates a new Netscape window.

New Mail Message: Displays the Message Composition window for writing a mail message.

New News Message: Displays the Message Composition window for writing a news message.

Save As... Provides an option for saving the current message as a file.

Open News Host: Provides an option for specifying the name of a news server you wish to access.

Add Newsgroup: Select this option to add a new newsgroup to your list of Usenet groups.

Page Setup: Displays the dialog box for setting up a page.

Print Message(s): Select this option to print a current message.

Close: Closes the News window.

Exit: Quits the Netscape program.

Figure 4.30

The Netscape News window **Edit** menu.

Select Thread: This option selects all messages in the current thread of messages you are reading.

Select Flagged Messages: Selects messages in the current thread that are designated in the Mark column of the message heading pane.

Select All Messages: Selects all messages in all threads.

Notice options are the standard **Edit** menu options: **Undo**, **Cut**, **Copy**, **Paste**.

Find: Searches for keywords in the text of the current message you are reading.

Cancel Message: Removes the selected message from the newsgroup.

Figure 4.31

The Netscape News window **Message** menu.

The options under the **Message** menu are similar to the toolbar buttons. Additions include the following:

Mark as Read: This option designates in the message headings field that the message being read has been viewed.

Mark as Unread: Designates that the current message has not been viewed.

Mark Thread Read: Designates in the message heading field that the messages in the current thread have been viewed.

Mark Newsgroup Read: Designates in the message heading field that all the messages in the current newsgroup have been read.

Flag Message: Marks the current message with a small icon in the flag column of the message heading field.

Unflag Message: Removes the flag icon from the current message.

Add to Address Book: Adds the e-mail address of the current message sender to your Netscape Address Book.

Figure 4.32
The Netscape News window **Go** menu.

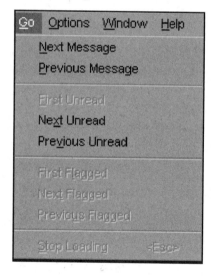

The options under the **Go** menu provide navigational tools for reading your news messages.

Figure 4.33
The Netscape News window **Options** menu.

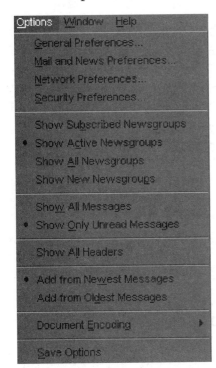

The first four options are the same as the main Netscape windows page. The added options are available for viewing newsgroups and messages.

Show Subscribed Newsgroups: Select this option to display a list of newsgroups to which you are subscribed.

Show Active Newsgroups: If selected this option displays only the newsgroups you have subscribed that have new messages waiting to be read.

Show All Newsgroups: Selecting this option displays a list of all newsgroups available on your news server.

Show New Newsgroups: This option displays only the newsgroups that have been subscribed to since you last connected to the news server.

Show All Headers: If selected this displays all the information about a news message including who the original message was from, the return path, subject, organization, content type, date, number of message lines, expiration date, and message ID.

Add From Newest Message: If selected this displays the latest messages first.

Add From Oldest Message: Selecting this option displays the earliest messages first.

Document Encoding: This option specifies the character set encoding that a document uses when the document does not specify encoding.

Reading Usenet News With Netscape Navigator

Netscape Navigator 2.0 provides four easy to access newsgroups.

- If you know the name of the newsgroup, type the URL in the location field of the Netscape main menu.

- From within the Netscape News window, go to the **File** menu and select **Add Newsgroup**. Enter the name of the newsgroup in the dialog box.

- Go to the **Options** menu and select **Show All Newsgroups**. From this list, select a newsgroup and check the **Subscribe** box beside the newsgroup name.

- From a World Wide Web site, click on a link to a newsgroup or a newsgroup message.

Finding Newsgroups With Netscape

Each newsgroup has a unique name that is written using descriptive words separated by periods. For example, the URL for a newsgroup on recreational backpacking is **news:rec.backcountry**.

- news—specifies the server protocol
- rec—category of newsgroup
- backcountry—name of the newsgroup

> **NOTE**
>
> You will be using your Internet provider's local news server for newsgroups, therefore, you do not need the two slashes to designate a server.

To find newsgroups of interest in a category, type the server protocol in the location field of the Netscape main menu, followed by the category of newsgroup in which to search for all newsgroups. For example, typing **news:rec.*** brings you a directory of the newsgroups beginning with the characters *rec*. Use an asterisk character (*) as a wildcard substitute to match all listings. To further define your search, enter a subject. For example, typing in **news:rec.backcountry*** brings you a directory of individual newsgroups with the characters **rec** and **backcountry**.

GUIDED WALKS

Netscape Navigator

&

The World Wide Web

GUIDED WALK 1
Using Your Navigational Tools

This Guided Walk demonstrates how to use Netscape Navigator to

- connect to a World Wide Web site and Home Pages.
- use pull-down menus.
- use navigational toolbar buttons.
- navigate World Wide Web sites.
- save bookmarks of your favorite pages.

1. Log onto your Internet account. When you have connected, open the Netscape Navigator application by double-clicking on the application icon.

    You will be taken to a Home Page. This Home Page may belong to Netscape Communications Corporation (**http://home.netscape.com**) or it may have been designed by the Internet provider you are using. Look at the top of the Home Page in the Title Bar to see whose Home Page you are visiting.

2. Select or enter the URL text.

    URLs are standard locations for Internet documents. Highlighted text on Netscape pages contains built-in URL information for linking you to that information. You can also type in URL text to link a page.

3. Click on the **Options** pull-down menu.

    Click on **Show Location** to select this option. When it is selected there should be a check mark before this option. You will now see the URL address of the page you are viewing in the **Location** field. If you want the URL always to be displayed on your page, click **Save Options**.

Figure 4.34
The Netscape navigational toolbar buttons.

4. Turn off the automatic loading of images if your computer is downloading images slowly. You may want to deselect the option **Auto Load Images**. Without this option, images will not be automatically downloaded and your travels will be faster. If you want to view an image, click on the **Image** button.

5. Begin exploring the World Wide Web by using Netscape's toolbar buttons and pull-down menus. Click on the **What's New** button. You will see a list of highlighted underlined links to Web sites. Click on a link. EXPLORE. . . HAVE FUN.

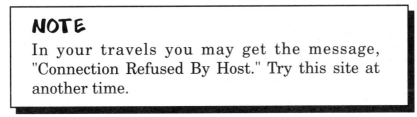

NOTE

In your travels you may get the message, "Connection Refused By Host." Try this site at another time.

6. Save your favorite pages by making a bookmark.

When you find a page that you may want to visit at a later time, click on the **Bookmark** pull-down menu. Next, click on the menu item **Add Bookmark**.

Click on the Bookmark pull-down menu again. Notice the name of the page you marked listed below the **View Bookmarks** menu item. To view this page again, select the Bookmark pull-down menu, and click on the name of the page you saved.

7. Continue your exploration by clicking on the **What's Cool** button.

8. After you have linked to several pages, click on the **Go** pull-down menu. Notice the listing of places you have most recently visited. If you want to revisit any of the pages you have already viewed, click on the name of the Web site.

9. Practice using the navigational buttons.

   • Click on the **Back** button to move to the previous page in the history list.

   • Click on the **Forward** button to move forward to the next page in your history list.

   • Click on the **Home** button to go to the Home Page.

   As you journey from page to page, notice the URL address in the **Location** box. The URL is the location information for the page you are viewing. Move your mouse pointer over highlighted words. Notice how the **Location** box displays the URL for the underlined link.

   In a later Guided Walk you will be entering URL text to travel the Internet.

10. Printing pages you want to keep.

   If you find a page that you would like to print, click on the **Print** button or open the **File** pull-down menu and select **Print**. This page will now be printed on your designated printer.

11. Quit Netscape.
   When you want to quit Netscape, click on the **File** pull-down menu, and select **Quit**.

   > **NOTE**
   >
   > If you are not using your own computer and hard drive, you will need to save the Bookmarks you made to a floppy disk. Go to the next Guided Walk to learn how to do this.

GUIDED WALK 2

Organizing and Using Bookmarks

In this Guided Walk you will learn how to organize, modify, save, and move Bookmark files.

Before you can organize and work with Bookmark files, you must access Netscape's Bookmark window. There are two ways to access the Bookmark window.

- Go to the **Bookmark** pull-down menu and select **Go To Bookmarks.**

- Go to the **Window** pull-down menu and select **Bookmarks**.

1. Organize your bookmarks.
   Before you begin saving bookmarks it is helpful to consider how to organize saved Bookmarks. Begin by thinking of categories that your Bookmarks might be filed under such as Software, Business, Education, Entertainment, or Research. Make a folder for each category. Listed below are the steps for making your Bookmark folders.

   a. Go to the **Bookmarks** menu and select **Go To Bookmarks**, or go to the **Windows** menu and select **Bookmarks**.

Figure 4.35
The Netscape Bookmark window.

Bookmarks - bookmark.htm	_ □ ×

File   Edit   Item

- Cynthia Leshin's Bookmarks
  - + BUSINESS
  - COMPUTER SUPPORT
    - Symantec Corporation Home Page
  - SHAREWARE
    - The Ultimate Collection of Winsock Software
  - MOUNTAIN BIKING
    - MOUNTAIN BIKING
    - Yahoo - Recreation:Sports:Cycling:Mountain Biking
    - The Arizona Mountain Bike Page
    - The Arizona Mountain Bike Racing Page
    - Steve's Mt. Biking Home Page
    - Moab Mountain Biking
    - Mountain Bike Links
    - Mountain Biking
    - Cannondale Home Page
    - Cycling - Mountain Bikes - BMX - Touring - Cycling News - Road Racing - Bicycle...

Netscape

Notice the Web sites saved in Bookmark folders. This Bookmark window also provides you with three new menus for working with your bookmarks: File, Edit, and Item.

    b. Create a new folder for a Bookmark category, by selecting the **Item** menu.

Figure 4.36
The **Item** menu.

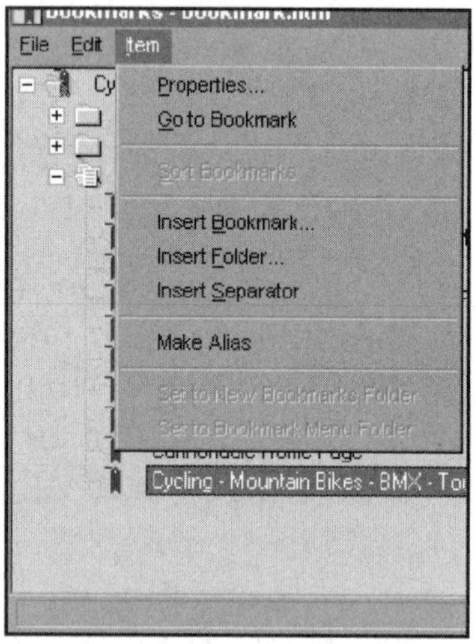

    c. Select **Insert Folder**.

Figure 4.37
The **Insert Folder** window.

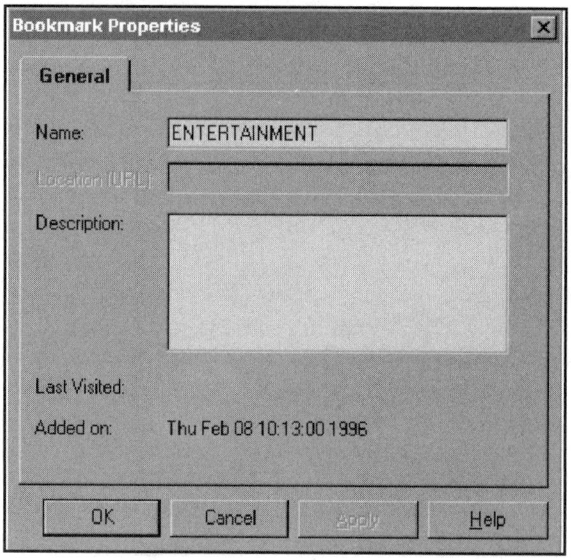

d. Type the name of your folder in the Name dialog box.

e. Enter any description of the Bookmark folder.

f. Click OK.

2. Adding Bookmarks to a folder.
   Netscape provides an option for identifying which folder you would like to select to drop your bookmarks in.

   a. Select the folder you would like to add your new bookmarks to by clicking once on the name of the folder. The folder should now be highlighted.

   b. Go to the **Item** menu and select **Set to New Bookmarks Folder**.

Figure 4.38
The Netscape Bookmark window.

Item
Properties...
Go to Bookmark
Sort Bookmarks
Insert Bookmark...
Insert Folder...
Insert Separator
Make Alias
Set to New Bookmarks Folder
Set to Bookmark Menu Folder

Go back to your Bookmark window and notice how this newly identified folder has been marked with a colored Bookmark identifier. All bookmarks that you add will be placed in this folder until you identify a new folder.

3. Modify the name of your bookmark.
   A Bookmark contains the name of the Web site and the URL. You may want to change the name of the bookmark to better indicate the information available at this site. For example, the bookmark name *STCil/HST Public Information* has very little meaning. Changing the name to Hubble Space Telescope Public Information is more helpful later when selecting Bookmarks.

   a. To change the name of a Bookmark, select the Bookmark by clicking on it once.

   b. Go to the **Item** menu from within the Bookmark window.

   c. Select **Properties**.

Figure 4.39
The **Properties** window.

d. Enter the new name for your Bookmark by either deleting the displayed text or begin typing the new name when the highlighted text is visible. Notice the URL for the Bookmark. You can also enter a description of the bookmark.

e. Click OK.

4. Make copies or your Bookmarks for adding to other folders.
Occasionally you will want to save a Bookmark in several folders.
There are two ways to do this.

- Select the Bookmark that you would like to copy. Go to the **Edit** menu from within the Bookmark window, and select **Copy**. Then select the folder where you would like to place the copy of the Bookmark. Go to the **Edit** menu and select **Paste**.

- Make an alias of your Bookmark by selecting **Make Alias** from the **Item** menu. When the alias of your bookmark has been created, move the alias Bookmark to the new folder.

> **NOTE**
> Bookmarks can be moved from one location to another by dragging an existing Bookmark to a new folder.

5. Delete a Bookmark.

   a. Select the Bookmark to be deleted by clicking on it once.

   b. Go to the **Edit** menu from within the Bookmark window.

   c. Choose either **Cut** or **Delete**.

6. Exporting and saving Bookmarks.
Netscape provides options for making copies of your Bookmarks to either save as a backup on your hard drive, to share with others, or to use on another computer.

   a. Open the **Bookmark** window.

   b. From within the **Bookmark** window, go to the the **File** menu and select **Save As**.

Figure 4.40
The Bookmark window **File** menu.

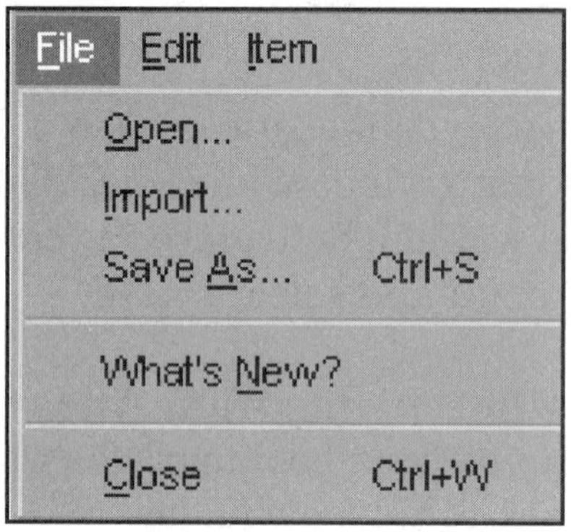

c. Designate whether you would like to save the Bookmark file on your hard drive or to a floppy disk in the **Save in** box.

Figure 4.41
The Netscape Bookmark window for saving bookmark files.

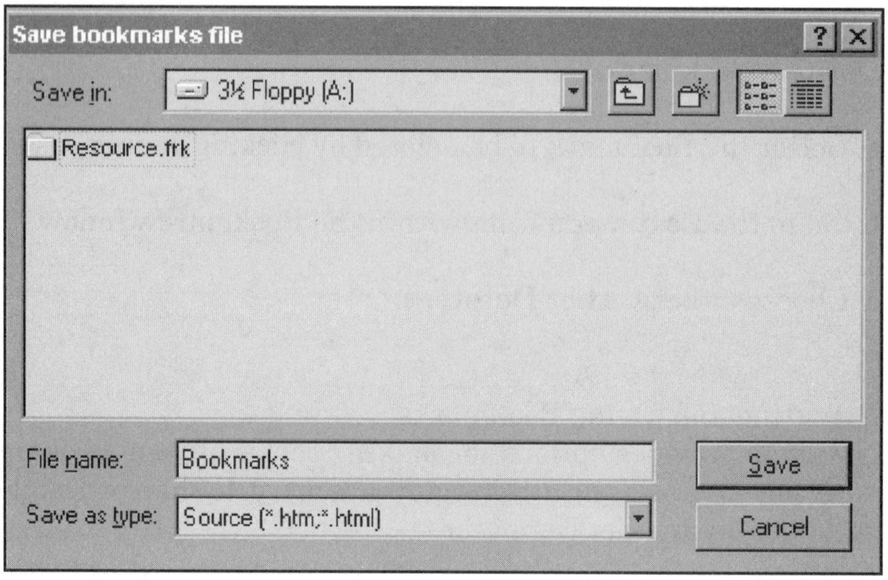

d. Enter a name for your Bookmark file in the **File name** dialog box.

e. Click **Save**.

7. Importing Bookmarks.
   Bookmarks can be imported into Netscape from a previous Netscape session or if you have a Bookmark list from another person.

   a. Insert the floppy disk with the Bookmark file into your computer.

   b. Open the Bookmark window.

   c. From within the Bookmark window, go to the **File** menu and select **Import** (see Figure 4.2).

   d. Designate where the Bookmark file is located: on a floppy disk or from your hard drive.

Figure 4.42
The **Import** bookmarks window.

Import bookmarks file	? ✕

Look in: 3½ Floppy (A:)

☐ Resource.frk

File name: _____ Open

Files of type: Source (*.htm;*.html) Cancel

   e. Click on **Open**.
   The Bookmarks will now be imported into your Netscape Bookmark list.

GUIDED WALK 3
Using Netscape To Travel The Internet

In this Guided Walk you will enter URL addresses to link to World Wide Web (WWW) sites.

There are three places in which you can type the URL.

- The **Location** text field
- The **File** menu, select **Open Location**
- The **Open** toolbar button dialog box.

1. Select one of the above locations to enter URL text.

2. Listed below are several interesting Web sites to visit. Type in their URL. EXPLORE. . . HAVE FUN. Save your favorite sites as Bookmarks.

NASA: **http://www.nasa.gov/**

Silicon Surf: **http://www.sgi.com/**

Old Sturbridge Village: **http://www.osv.org/**

Time Warner Pathfinder:
http://www.timeinc.com/pathfinder/Greet.html

Wired: **http://www.hotwired.com/**

Library of Congress: **http://www.loc.gov/**

The White House: **http://www.whitehouse.gov/**

CityNet: **http://www.city.net/**

ESPNetSportsZone: **http://espnet.sportzone.com/**

Cybertown: **http://www.cybertown.com/**

You will find more URL location information to enter and explore in the Expedition Experience in this chapter.

Guided Walk 4

Finding Information And Resources

Internet tools for helping you find information and resources are software programs called *search engines*. Netscape Navigator links you to many search engines that help find information on the Internet. Click on the **Net Search** button.

Figure 4.43
The Netscape navigation buttons.

| What's New? | What's Cool? | Handbook | Net Search | Net Directory | Software |

You now have a list of on-line search engines to aid you in finding information. Search engines use keywords or concepts to look for matching words in a title of a document, in a document, in an index or directory, or by entering a concept of what you are searching for. Each search engine provides you with guidance on how to conduct a search.

A Note about researching...

New search engines are arriving every few months. Each claims to be better than the other. Some search tools claim to be smarter; others claim to have the largest and most comprehensive database. *Internet World* tested seven Internet search engines and came to the striking conclusion that all the search engines had a long way to go before they could be relied on to deliver consistently accurate search findings. Each search engine delivered a high proportion of irrelevant information. Ultimately, the quality and quantity of search results depend on your skill at constructing queries. Before you begin using a search tool learn how to phrase a query by investigating help or advanced search options on the search engines Web page.

ACTIVITY: Determine a topic of interest (your field of study, a professional or personal interest, a topic to research, or a hobby). Use several of the search engines provided in Netscape's **Net Search. Compare** and contrast the different search engines. How do they differ in the their ability to refine and narrow your search? Which search engines are most helpful in the way their research results are provided to you? Several rank results by relevancy as matched to your request. Which search tools provide useful information? Which save you time?

Another World Wide Web site to visit to access many different search engines is the *All-In-One Search Page:***http://www.albany.net/allinone/**

Guided Walk 5

Usenet Newsgroups

In this Guided Walk, you will use Netscape Navigator to

- view articles in a newsgroup.
- find a listing of all the newsgroups available to to you.
- subscribe to a newsgroup.
- unsubscribe to a newsgroup.

1. Click on the **Window** menu and select **Netscape News**.

Figure 4.44
The Netscape News window.

Notice that Netscape has subscribed you to two newsgroups for new users: **news: announce. newusers** and **news.newusers.questions**. The first newsgroup has 21 unread messages with a total of 21 messages posted. The second newsgroup has 8131 unread messages with a total of 8131 posted messages available for reading.

2. To read the news postings in a newsgroup, double-click on the name of the newsgroup.

Figure 4.45
Netscape's news reader.

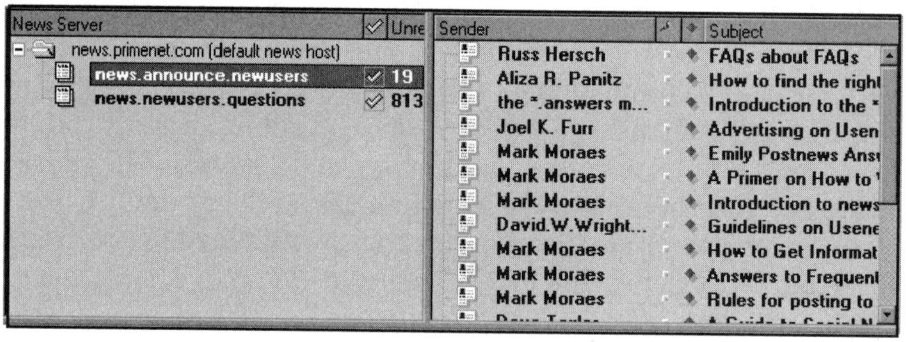

Notice that for each newsgroup posting located (in the right window) there is a category to indicate the **Sender** of the message and the **Subject** of the message.

3. To read a news message, double-click on the posting.

Figure 4.46
Emily Postnews Answers...

News Server	☑	Unre	Sender	✓	♦	Subject
⊟ 🖳 news.primenet.com (default news host)			🗐	Mark Moraes		Emily Postnews Answers
📄 news.announce.newusers	✓	18	🗐	Mark Moraes		♦ A Primer on How to
📄 news.newusers.questions	✓	813	🗐	Mark Moraes		♦ Introduction to news
			🗐	David.W.Wright...		♦ Guidelines on Usene
			🗐	Mark Moraes		♦ How to Get Informat

```
     Subject: Emily Postnews Answers Your Questions on Netiquette
        Date: Sun, 28 Jan 1996 09:00:15 GMT
        From: netannounce@deshaw.com (Mark Moraes)
    Reply-To: netannounce@deshaw.com
  Newsgroups: news.announce.newusers, news.answers
 Followup-To: news.newusers.questions

Original-author: brad@clarinet.com (Brad Templeton)
Archive-name: usenet/emily-postnews/part1
Last-change: 13 May 1995 by brad@clarinet.com (Brad Templeton)
```

NOTE

To change the size of the window viewing panels, click your mouse on the line dividing the window. You will now see your cursor become a cross. Hold down your mouse button and slide the dividing panel to enlarge or reduce a viewing window.

4. Read the newsgroup posting. Review the Newsgroup header for information such as a list of all the newsgroups to which this message is posted. Explore Netscape's news reader. Click on the news toolbar buttons to see your options.

Figure 4.47
Newsgroup toolbar buttons.

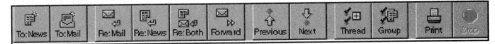

To cancel the Netscape option you are exploring (i.e., sending a reply to the posted message), close the news window. EXPLORE.... the newusers newsgroups.

5.   View all newsgroups available on your Internet provider's news server by choosing the **Options** menu and selecting **Show All Newsgroups**.

Figure 4.48
A partial list from **All Newsgroups**.

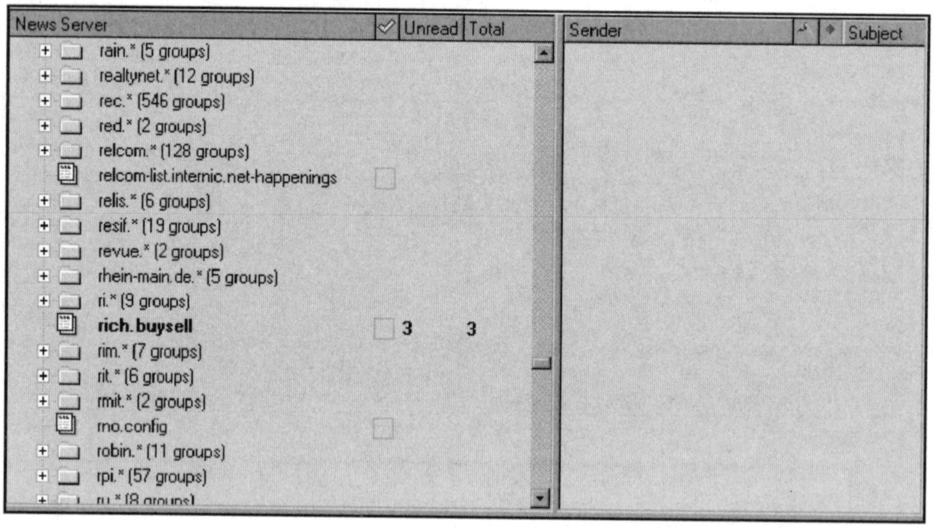

Notice that newsgroups are organized in folders according to categories. You may want to start viewing newsgroups by some of the more familiar categories described earlier. Click on a folder to see a listing of newsgroups in that category.

6.   Subscribe to a newsgroup by clicking in the box next to the group.

Figure 4.49
News server window.

News Server	✓	Unread	Total
+ ☐ rec.autos.* (22 groups)			
+ ☐ rec.aviation.* (18 groups)			
📄 **rec.backcountry**	✓	**1609**	**1609**
+ ☐ rec.bicycles.* (7 groups)			
📄 **rec.birds**	☐	**795**	**795**
📄 **rec.boats**	☐	**1023**	**1023**
+ ☐ rec.boats.* (5 groups)			
📄 **rec.climbing**	☐	**1402**	**1402**
📄 **rec.collecting**	☐	**1949**	**1949**
+ ☐ rec.collecting.* (13 groups)			
+ ☐ rec.crafts.* (16 groups)			

7. Check your new subscription by opening the **Options** menu and selecting **Show Subscribed Newsgroups**. You will now see your new newsgroup added to the list of newsgroups.

8. To see a listing of new newsgroups that have been added to your Internet provider's news server, go to the **Options** menu and select **Show New Newsgroups**.

9. To unsubscribe from a newsgroup, click once in the box with the check mark to remove the check. Go to the **Options** menu and select **Show Subscribed Newsgroups**. The newsgroup to which you unsubscribed will be removed from your list.

NOTE

If your Internet provider does not carry Usenet newsgroups you can still read and post to newsgroups by connecting to public Usenet News servers. Several public Usnet news servers include: **news.ichange.com**, **news.uwsuper.edu**, **online.magnus1.com** and **news.ak.net**.

To use these servers you will need to configure your Usenet newsreader. Suggested programs include Free Agent for Windows and News Agent for the Macintosh. For example, use **news.ichange.com** as your news (NNTP) server, then download the list of available groups.

Guided Walk 6
Using Internet Multimedia Files

The World Wide Web brings to Internet users the world of multimedia. Text on the Web is enhanced through the use of brilliant images, video clips, and sound. Netscape Navigator makes it possible for you to download Internet multimedia files to your computer's hard drive. These download files can be used outside of the Internet environment providing you are considerate of copyright issues related to the use of another's work.

In addition to these multimedia enhancements, Netscape Navigator 2.0 supports a new functionality-enhancing feature that provides a richer delivery of multimedia content by allowing users to view content with plug-ins such as Adobe Acrobat, Apple QuickTime, and Macromedia Shockwave for Director. For more information on the newest Netscape plug-in capabilities, how to receive free developer copies, and viewer applications visit the Netscape Home Page at **http://home.netscape.com/**

Before You Begin...

Before you begin downloading multimedia files, it will be helpful to learn about how Netscape and the World Wide Web make it possible for multimedia files to be viewed and downloaded to your computer. An important concept to understand is that any computer file that is going to be made available to other computers around the world needs to do two things.

1. Be in a format that can be transmitted quickly from one computer to another

2. Be in a format that can be read by all computers (i.e., Macintosh, Windows, etc.).

To understand how this is accomplished we need to understand compression and helper applications because before you can view or use many multimedia files you may have to uncompress them and/or use a helper application to see or hear them.

Compression

Large files are compressed to save disk space and to make it faster to transmit them between computers. Software applications (that is, Internet browsers, Helper Applications, and compression programs) are examples of large files that you will be downloading to your computer from remote computers. More than likely these files will be compressed. Some of these files will be *self-extracting,* which means that the program will decompress by just double-clicking on it. If the file is not self-extracting, you will need a decompression program to open them. Likewise, if you are going to send large files, use a decompression program to make them smaller. Software applications are available to make your compressed files self-extracting.

The type of compression method used on a file is indicated by an extension added to the end of the filename. For example, many compressed Macintosh files end with **.sea.** A filename compressed using this method may look like this

Eudora2.1Fat.sea

Files ending in **.sea** are self-extracting archives and can be decompressed by double-clicking on the program icon.

Files compressed for the PC also may have extensions to indicate the type of compression. The best programs for PC decompression and compression is WinZip and PKzip. Many of these compressed files will also be self-extracting.

> ### NOTE
> Most of the multimedia files that you download will not be compressed.
>
> Most compression, decompression, and self-extracting software programs can be obtained free from the Internet as a shareware or freeware program.

Macintosh Decompression

Macintosh compressed file extensions include

.hqx   (BinHex or a textual representation of binary files)
.sit   (files compressed using Stuffit)
.cpt   (files compressed using Compact Pro)

One of the most commonly used decompression programs for Macintosh is Stuffit Expander. There are many Internet sites where you can find a copy of Stuffit Expander and download it to your computer by double-clicking on the Web link. After you obtain a copy of Stuffit Expander, place a copy on your desktop. When you receive files that need to be decompressed, drop them onto the Stuffit icon.

Two World Wide Web sites you can visit to search for compression software are JUMBO and the All-In-One Search page. The URL for JUMBO is: **http://www.jumbo.com/** When you connect to this page, scroll to the bottom and click on the search button. Enter the name of the software for which you are searching.

The All-In-One Search page URL is **http://www.albany.net/allinone/** When you connect to this page, scroll down and select the **Software** option. After linking to the page of search engines for software programs, select one for your type of computer (Mac or PC) and type in the name of the software application.

PC Decompression

Most PC compression and decompression is done with a package called, PKzip. The best Web site to find free copies of PKzip and other software for your PC is TUCOWS—**http://www.tucows.com/**

After selecting the icon for Compression Utilities you will be connected to a page with several compression, decompression, and self-extracting programs. Note that the best file compression/decompression program listed is WinZip. WinZip also makes an application for creating self-extracting archives.

Check the All-In-One Search page for more software options for your PC.

Figure 4.50
The TUCOWS Web page.

Anti-Virus Scanners	Archie	Audio Applications	Bundled Applications	Compression Utilities	Control Panels
Diagnostic Tools	File Transfer Protocol	Finger & Who	Games, MUD's & MOO's	Gopher	HTML Editors
Image Viewers	Internet Tools	IRC Using Keyboard	IRC Using Voice	Mail Applications	Modem Dialers
Movie Viewers	Networking	News Readers	NFS Clients	Ping & NS-Lookup	Plug-In Modules
Printer Clients	Server Daemon	Televideo Conferencing	Telnet	Time Logs	Time Synchronizers
Utilities	VRML Viewers	WAIS	Windows 95	World Wide Web Browsers	X.500 (DUA) Clients

Helper Applications For Viewing Images

Graphics images can be saved in as many as 50 different formats. These formats are merely different ways to preserve images. However, you will find that most images have one of these extensions:

GIF, JPEG, XBM

GIF (Graphics Interchange Format) was created by CompuServe; JPEG (Joint Photographic Experts Group) is named for the group that invented it; XBM refers to X Bit Map format. Regardless of the format, images can only be seen by using an image viewer. Netscape Navigator has the built-in capability to view images saved in these formats. You can also use Netscape to view these images when you download them to your computer's hard drive.

Two popular image viewers for the Macintosh are GIFConverter and JPEGView. Obtain copies of these applications by visiting Jumbo and All-In-One sites.

There are several image viewing programs for the PC: LVview Pro, Paint Shop Pro, Thumbs Plus, and VuePrint, and WebImage. Visit the TUCOWS Web site to obtain more information and free copies **http://www.tucows.com**

> ### NOTE
> Image formats can be changed. For example, a JPEG image can be converted to an EPS, PICT, or other image format for use in your desktop applications. Many of the Image viewing programs provide options to save the image in a format of choice. Additionally, may graphics programs such as Adobe Photoshop will open these images and provide options to save in different formats.

Helper Applications For Sound & Video Files

To see a listing of helper applications required to view image, video, and sound files, go Netscape's **Option** menu, select **General Preferences** and open the panel for **Helpers**. Find the name of the helper application for viewing the desired multimedia file. Go to one of the Web sites for freeware and shareware, or use the All-In-One Search page for software to obtain your copy.

Movie viewers allow users to view and manipulate movie files such as Quicktime or MPEG. Several of the more popular movie players for the PC are QuickTime Player, VMPEG Lite, and MPEG Movie Player. QuickTime is the most widely used movie player for the Macintosh.

Many sound files are heard using RealAudio. RealAudio makes it possible to hear sound immediately after clicking on a sound link. There is little or no time used to download the sound file. Visit the Web site **http://www.realaudio.com/** for a copy of RealAudio.Visit the National Public Radio site **http://www.npr.org/** to experience RealAudio.

GUIDED WALK 7

Text, Image, Video, And Sound Files

Now that you have learned about multimedia files on the Web, practice downloading and viewing text, images, video, and sound files.

Before You Begin...

To view images from Web pages, you will need a helper application. Refer to Guided Walk 6 in this chapter.

Saving Web images

For this Guided Walk, visit the Hubble Space Telescope **http://www.stsci.edu/pubinfo/Pictures.html** or the Nine Planets site **http://seds.lpl.arizona.edu/nineplanets/nineplanets/** to find images, video, and sound files that you can download and view off-line.

1.   Open the image you wish to save.

2.   For a PC, click the right side of the mouse button. On the Macintosh, hold down the mouse button.

Figure 4.51
Netscape pop-up menu for saving images.

| Back |
Forward
View this Image
Save this Image as...
Copy this Image
Copy this Image Location
Load this Image

3. Select, **Save this Image as**...
   Designate where you want Netscape to download the image.

Figure 4.52

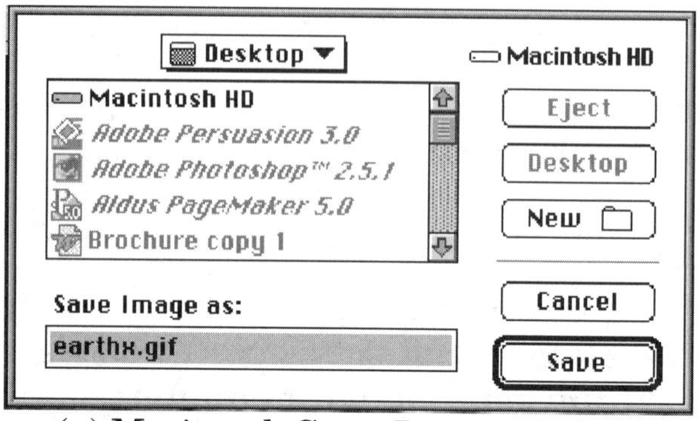

(a) Macintosh **Save Image** dialog box.

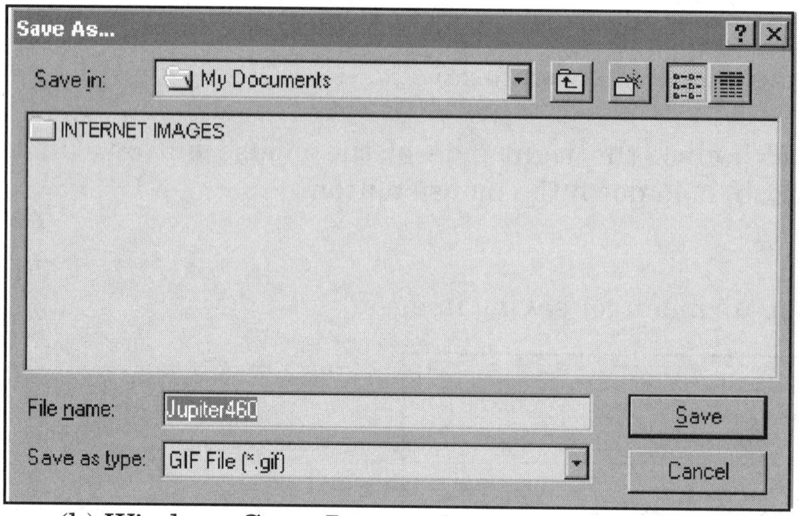

(b) Windows **Save Image** dialog box.

In the dialog box, **Save Image As** (Macintosh) or **File Name** (Windows) enter a name for your image. You may want to include the type of image (that is gif or jpeg) in the name.

4. Click Save.

Viewing Your Saved Image

There are two ways to view your saved image after downloading to your computer or floppy disk

- Use the Netscape application.
- Use a image viewer helper application.

Viewing Images Using Netscape

To view an image using your Netscape application program, go to the **File** menu and select **Open File**. Find your image. Netscape will open the file for viewing off line.

Viewing Images With An Image Viewer

Refer to Guided Walk 6 for information on viewing images with helper applications. You will need to find and download a copy of an image viewer for JPEG or GIF images.

> ### NOTE
>
> In the following example, the image viewer program is for the Macintosh and is called GIF Converter. Other image viewing programs work in similar ways. Use this as an example to help understand how to open and view images.

1. Open the image viewing application.

2. Go to the **File** menu and select **Open**. Find the location where you saved the image. Select the image and click **Open.**

Figure 4.53
GIFConverter open image dialog box.

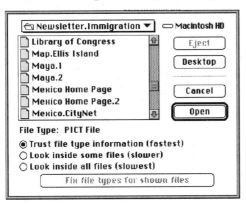

3.   When the image is displayed, go to the **File** menu and select
     Save As to save in a different file format.

Figure 4.54
GIFConverter save image dialog box

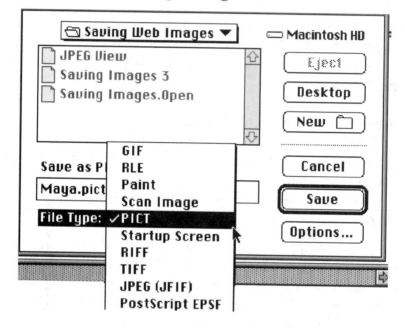

After the image is saved, it can be imported into another software
application program such as a word processing or desktop publishing
program.

> **NOTE**
>
> You can also use the **Copy** and **Paste** command
> from inside the image viewing program to copy
> the image to another software program.
>
> These images also can be opened using a graphics
> program such as PhotoShop.

Saving Audio And Video Files

Audio and video files can be downloaded and saved in the same way as images.

1. Check the URL information for the type of audio or video file.

2. Download the needed helper application.

3. Now proceed to download the sound or video file as described under **Save this Image as**...
   For movie and audio files, you will see, **Save This File as**...

Figure 4.55
Netscape's dialog box to save movie files.

```
Back
Forward
─────────────────────────
Open this Link
Add Bookmark for this Link
New Window with this Link
Save this Link as...
Copy this Link Location
```

4. Use the helper application for viewing and listening to these files.

NOTE

Although you can view and listen to video and audio files on-line, you may want to download them first to your computer and play them locally.

Listed below are several Web sites to find multimedia files to practice downloading.

Internet Resources Home Page. Select Music, Images, and Multimedia
http://www.eit.com/web/netservices.html

Film And Video Resources
http://http2.sils.umich.edu/Public/fvl/film.html

Music Resources
http://www.music.indiana.edu/misc/music_resources.html

http://pathfinder.com/@@Lm0giEF@twAAQJeO/vibe/mmm/music.html

Weather Maps and Movies
http://wxweb.msu.edu/weather

GUIDED WALK 8

Saving Web Pages

Netscape provides you with the opportunity to save a page as a file on your computer. There are three ways to save a Web page.

- **File/Save As** option
- **Save This Link As** option
- **File/Mail Document** option

File/Save As Option

This Netscape option lets you save the current Web page as a source (HTML) file or a text file on your disk. A file saved in HTML source format retains the formatting of the original page. A file saved in text format is displayed as plain text. To use this option, go to the **File** menu and select **Save As**.

Save This Link As

While pointing at a link, click on the right mouse button (On the Macintosh, hold down the mouse button.) to view the pop-up menu. Select **Save this Link as**... to save to disk rather than bringing it to your screen. The option, **Copy this Link Location**, copies the URL to the clipboard.

File Mail Document

To mail a Web document go to the **File** menu and select **Mail Document.**

Figure 4.56

Netscape's Mail Document dialog window.

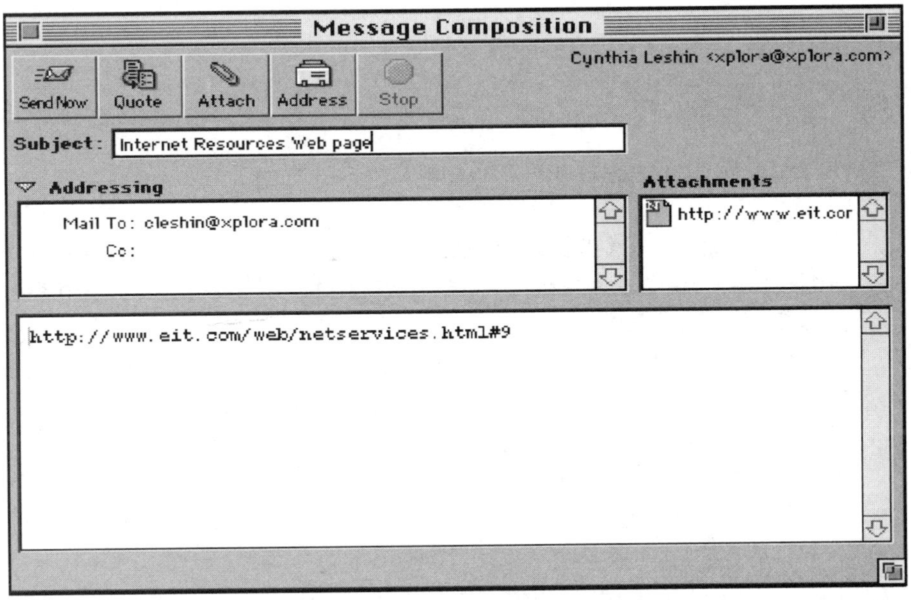

After you enter in the e-mail address Netscape mails the current page URL, along with an e-mail attachment of the page.

GUIDED WALK 9

Using Netscape E-mail

In this Guided Walk you will practice using Netscape's e-mail program.

Go to the **Windows** menu and select **Netscape Mail**.

1. Send an e-mail message to yourself.

    a. Enter your e-mail address in the **Mail To** dialog box.

    b. Enter the subject.

    c. Type a message.

    d. Click the send button.

2. Receiving your e-mail message.

    a. Click on the **Get-Mail** button, the mail envelope icon at the bottom of the Netscape page, or go to the **File** menu and select **Get New Mail**.

    b. Enter your e-mail password for your Internet account.

    c. After your mail is downloaded, read and delete it.

3. Practice creating file folders for your mail.

4. Create an address book of your most frequently used e-mail addresses.

EXPEDITION EXPERIENCE
World Wide Web

World Wide Web Expeditions

Now that you have begun to explore the Internet using Netscape, here are additional sites to explore.

Art Galleries & Museums

Archaeology – Kelsey Museum

The Kelsey Museum is an on-line resource designed to enrich your experience of the Museum. Visit the Roman and Greek galleries or the Roman site of Karanis, Egypt. You will find a large number of resources for Classics and Mediterranean Archaeology.
http://www.umich.edu/~kelseydb/

Artserv

Travel to the Australian National University to view 2,800 images and prints from the 15th through the 19th century. There are over 2,500 images of mainly classical architecture and architectural sculpture around the Mediterranean. In November, 1994, an additional 3,281 images were added from Classical, Medieval, and Renaissance architecture and sculpture.
http://rubens.anu.edu.au/

Art Source

ArtSource is a gathering point for networked resources on Art and Architecture. This site contains links to not only resources but also work submitted by librarians, artists, and art historians. This is an excellent site for finding an electronic field trip to art galleries and museums.
http://www.uky.edu/Artsource/artsourcehome.html

Art Treasures

The World Art Treasures WWW server is a collaborative venture between the J. E. Berger Foundation and the Swiss Federal Institute for Technology. Their goal is to promulgate the discovery and love of art. Visit this Web site and take a pilgrimage to ancient Egypt or discover images from China, Japan, India, Burma, Laos, Cambodia, and Thailand.
http://sgwww.epfl.ch/BERGER/index.html

Berkeley Museum Of Paleontology

Visit this rapidly growing virtual museum. Navigate through the extensive on-line exhibits using phylogeny, geology or evolutionary theory as your paradigm. Hop on the subway and travel to science resources.

http://ucmp1.berkeley.edu/welcome.html

Heard Museum — Phoenix, AZ

The mission of the Heard Museum is to promote appreciation and respect for native people and their cultural heritage. Today the museum has a collection of more than 30,000 works of art and artifacts. Visit this excellent educational resource and learn more about Native Americans.

http://hanksville.phast.umass.edu/defs/independent/Heard/Heard.html

Kaleidospace

Visit this creative site for independent artists. Here you will meet artists in an interactive arena. Visit art studios, a screening room, reading room, or newsstand. Stop by the music kiosk to browse through music and spoken word artists by genre.

http://kspace.com/

The Louvre

Jump on a virtual airplane to Paris and visit the WebLouvre. This is one of the coolest sites. Visit the gallery of famous paintings or stop by and view the medieval exhibit. When you are finished, take a tour of Paris.

http://www.cnam.fr/louvre/

Explore this other Louvre connection.

http://meteora.usce.edu:80/~norman/paris/Musees/Louvre/

Web Virtual Library

This World Wide Web Virtual Library contains links to museums all around the world.

http://www.comlab.ox.ac.uk/archive/other/museums.html

ASTRONOMY

Astroweb

Visit this Web page for links to astronomy-related information: observing resources, data resource, publication-related resources, people-related resources, organizations, software, research, lists of astronomy resources, images, and miscellaneous resources.
http://fits.cv.nrao.edu/www/astronomy.html

Hubble Space Telescope

Ride aboard the Hubble Space Telescope and view the latest images from deep space. Don't miss the dramatic images of the birth of the star, M16.
http://www.stsci.edu/

NASA's Links To Astronomy Sites

This excellent Web site provides links to sites such as the Comet Shoemaker-Levy Home Page, The Hubble Space Telescope, National Air And Space Museum, A Guide To Stars and Galaxies, The Solar System Home Page, astronomical images, and much more.
http://quest.arc.nasa.gov/lfs/other_sites.html

Welcome To The Planets

This site is maintained by the California Institute of Technology and provides an excellent collection of many of the best images from NASA's planetary exploration program. The collection has been extracted from the interactive program "Welcome to the Planets."
http://stardust.jpl.nasa.gov/planets/

Solar System

Hop into a virtual spaceship for a tour of the solar system. Visit each planet as well as all their comets and asteroids. Explore black holes and see images of the Shoemaker-Levy comet.
http://bang.lanl.gov/solarsys

World Wide Web Virtual Library — Astronomy

This sit has links to many excellent educational resources in astronomy and astrophysics.
http://www.w3.org/hypertext/DataSources/bySubject/astro/educational.html

Computer Resources

Apple

APPLE: A visit a day keeps Windows 95 away. Visit this site to learn more.

http://www.apple.com/

Compaq

Compaq's site is most informative about modern technology.
http://compaq.com/

Hewlett-Packard

Visit this well done site to learn more about Hewlett-Packard's products and services.

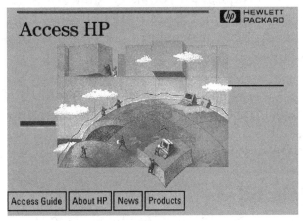

http://www.hp.com/

IBM

Sushi, planets, Greece, and fish stories from the Aegean Sea. Visit IBM's site to learn more.
http://www.ibm.com/

Microsoft

This site offers many technology toys.
http://www.microsoft.com/

http://www.microsoft.com/Windows/

Netscape Communication Corporation

Visit NCC to download the most current version of Netscape Navigator. Also learn about supported plug-ins, Java, and much more.
http://home.netscape.com/

Electronic Field Trips

Antarctica

This highly rated Web site has information on Antarctica's environment, education, science, history, tourism, and news. You can also view images and learn how to get more involved with one of the coldest places on earth.
http://icair.iac.org.nz/

Cape Town

Cape Town is known as the Fairest Cape. It is famous for beautiful mountain- and seascapes and its magnificent flora, which form one of the seven floral kingdoms in the world. It is one of South Africa's most popular tourist destinations, offering natural splendor and a cosmopolitan atmosphere. The Waterfront is a favorite venue for locals and visitors.

Visit this Web site to learn more about the Fairest Cape and to get an idea of the commercial activity in the region. Look at the page of local resources. on-line weather reports.
http://www.aztec.co.za/aztec/capetown.html

Ellis Island

Learn about immigration by visiting this Web site from PBS.
http://www.turner.com/tesi/html/migration.html

Grand Canyon National Park

This Web site offers general information on the Grand Canyon such as services, what to see and do, weather, trails and trail maps, river running, and history. You can also take a guided tour.
http://www.kbt.com/gc/

Mexico

Journey to Mexico to learn about the culture, art, and archaeological sites.
http://www.wotw.com/wow/mexico/mexico.html

Moscow Kremlin

Take an excursion to the Moscow Kremlin and view images and historical text.
http://www.kiae.su/www/wtr/kremlin/begin.html

Nepal

Travel to Nepal to trek with Scott Yost who spent six weeks visiting Nepal in the fall of 1994. Read Scott's travel journal and see his images of this beautiful country by viewing his photographic album. Follow his journey with the interactive maps.

http://enigma.phys.utk.edu/~syost/nepal/index.html
http://www.lonelyplanet.com/dest/ind/nep.htm

Paleolithic Cave Paintings in Southern France

An exceptionally important archaeological discovery was recently made in the southern France in the form of a vast underground network of caves decorated with paintings and engravings dating from the Paleolithic age (17,000-20,000 years ago). This fascinating Web site has information on the discovery as well as images from the cave walls.

http://www.culture.fr/culture/gvpda-en.htm

Paris

Take a virtual trip to France and visit the national monuments, museums, schools, stores, and shops. Take a break and stop by a sidewalk cafe to chat. Be sure to sign the Guest Book.

http://www.paris.org/ /

Polar Regions

This Web site links you to excellent resources on the Arctic, Antarctic, Alaska, and Norway. Learn about polar region animals (bears, seals, and penguins) and about the history of the regions.

http://www.stud.unit.no/~sveinw/arctic/

South Africa

Take a tour of South Africa and visit Botswana, Johannesburg, Port Elizabeth, Cape Town and other towns and regions.

http://osprey.unisa.ac.za/0/docs/south-africa.html

Old Sturbridge Village

Step Back In Time... Everywhere you look, costumed "Villagers" are going about their daily chores. The blacksmith is hammering links in a chain; the farmer is yoking his oxen; the printer's wife is baking bread in a beehive oven; and the kids are playing "rounders" near the

Common. It's just another day in a small New England community—of the 1830s!
http://www.osv.org/

Toyko

Journey to Tokyo and explore this fascinating country in either English or Japanese.
http://www.tokyo-teleport.co.jp/

Ecology — Environment

Ecology Web Environmental Links

Here is an extensive list of links to environmental-related information around the world. Sites are arranged under the following topics Alternative Energy, Communities, Democratic Arts, Eco-living, Forestry, Government, Housing, Information, Native Peoples, Peace and Justice, Search Tools, and Specific Groups/Sites.
http://www.pacific.net/~dglaser/ENVIR/LINKS/*links.html

Environment On The Internet

This page links to information on general environmental topics. Here you will find links to EcoWeb, Enviro Web, Econnet and other environmental sites.
http://www.nceet.snre.umich.edu/envlinks.html

Education

EdWeb

This excellent Web site explores the worlds of educational reform and information technology. With EdWeb, you can hunt down on-line educational resources around the world, learn about trends in education policy and information infrastructure development, examine success stories of computers in the classroom, and much, much more.
http://edweb.cnidr.org:90/

Geology

Geological Time Machine

Hop aboard the Web time machine and visit different geological time periods from Precambrian (4,500 to 544 million years ago) to Holocene (1.8 MYA to 10,000 years ago). Learn about stratigraphy, fossils, and fossil localities.
http://ucmp1.berkeley.edu/timeform.html

Music

Music On the Internet

This site maintained by Indiana University Music Library contains links to academic music sites all over the world.
http://www.music.indiana.edu/misc/music_resources.html

For something a little less academic, try the Music Kitchen.
http://www.nando.net:80/music/gm/

Rock-In-Roll Hall Of Fame

Do you know the "500 Songs That Shaped Rock and Roll?" Visit this informative site to learn more about Rock-In-Roll.
http://www.rockhall.com/

News

CNN Interactive

For the latest US and world news visit CNN Interactive.
http://www.cnn.com/

National Public Radio On-line

Listen to a five minute audio clip from NPR at this Web site.
http://www.npr.org/

New York Times On-line

Visit this site to download an electronic copy of the daily New York Times.
http://nytimesfax.com/

Newslink

This excellent site provides links to over 2,000 news sites.
http://www.newslink.org/

Newspage

With 500 information sources and 25,000 pages refreshed daily, NewsPage is the most comprehensive news site on the Web. To use NewsPage, simply select an industry and drill your way through categories and topics to today's news, hot off the virtual presses.
http://www.newspage.com/

The OTIS Index

This site helps you search the Internet to find software, on-line books, commercial sites, newsgroups, and electronic publications.
http://www.interlog.com/~gordo/otis_pubpubs.html

Pathfinder

Pathfinder is an adventure into new publishing territory with Time Warner as your guide. Time's goal is to discover innovative ways to inform and be informed, entertain and be entertained. Time publishes many magazines and books, operates a movie studio, a music company, and cable company with programming on Home Box Office. This provides many wonderful resources, many of which are currently available now at this Web site.
http://www.timeinc.com/pathfinder/Greet.html
or
http://pathfinder.com/time/daily/time/1995/latest.html

Wall Street Journal Money and Investing

This information rich site provides information from the Wall Street Journal daily paper as well as information on money and investing.
http://update.wsj.com/

Science

Aquarium – Florida

Take a virtual trip to the Florida Aquarium. Put on your waders, slap on some sunscreen and strap on your scuba gear, and please don't feed the animals.
http://www.sptimes.com/aquarium/default.html

Earth Viewer

Earth viewer makes it possible for you to view either a map of the Earth showing the day and night regions at this moment, or view the Earth from the Sun, the Moon; the night side of the Earth; above any location on the planet specified by latitude, longitude, and altitude; or from a satellite in Earth orbit. Images can be generated based on a topographical map of the Earth, up-to-date weather satellite imagery, or a composite image of cloud cover superimposed on a map of the Earth.
http://www.fourmilab.ch/earthview/vplanet.html

Exploratorium

Housed within the walls of the Palace of Fine Arts, the Exploratorium is a collage of 650 interactive exhibits in the areas of science, art, and human perception. The Exploratorium stands in the vanguard of the movement of the "museum as educational center." It provides access to, and information about, science, nature, art and technology.

Visit this site for an excellent collection of electronic exhibits and resources for teachers, students, and science enthusiasts.
http://www.exploratorium.edu/

Frog Dissection

This interactive program generates views of a frog dissection from many different directions and at major organ levels. The dissection kit is available in English, Spanish, German, French, and Dutch.
http://george.lbl.gov/ITG.hm.pg.docs/dissect/

The Great White Shark

Travel to the virtual waters of California to view movies and still images of sharks both above and under water. Doug Long, a biology graduate student, has been studying Great Whites and shares his movies. After you finish viewing the sharks, stop by the Museum of Paleontology to see the Great White Shark exhibit.
http://ucmp1.berkeley.edu/Doug/shark.html

NASA

This Web page links you to NASA resources: Ames Research Center, Dryden Flight Research Center, Goddard Space Flight Center,

Headquarters, Jet Propulsion Lab, Johnson Space Center, Kennedy Space Center, Langley Research Center, Lewis Research Center, Marshall Space Flight Center, and the Stennis Space Center. There are also links to other NASA resources.
http://mosaic.larc.nasa.gov/nasaonline/nasaonline.html
http://rubens.anu.edu.au/

The best images from NASA can be viewed and downloaded from this site. **http://stardust.jpl.nasa.gov/planets/**

Planet Earth

This excellent Web site is a good starting point to see what useful Internet resources can be found on planet earth. Visit the virtual library and use the search capabilities to do research.
http://www.nosc.mil/planet_earth/info.html

To view the extensive listing of Planet Earth resources connect to **http://www.nosc.mil/planet_earth/everything.html**

Software — Freeware & Shareware

Jumbo

The Biggest, Most Mind-Boggling, Most Eye-Popping, Most Death-Defying Conglomeration of Freeware and Shareware Programs on the Web! 24,582 PROGRAMs at this time.
http://www.jumbo.com/

MIT's HyperArchive

Search MIT's archive for software or browse by categories.
http://hyperarchive.lcs.mit.edu/HyperArchive/HyperArchive.html

TUCOWS (The Ultimate Collection Of Winsock Software)

This site has an excellent selection of Internet software for Windows 95. TUCOWS provides Windows 3.x and '95 winsock programs to facilitate PC access to the Internet.
http://www.tucows.com/

Other Sites Of Interest

Afro-American Newspaper

Get PLUGGED-IN with this well-designed, colorful, and informative Web site. Visit the virtual Black History Museum, or get information on Africa or jobs.

http://www.afroam.org/

Awesome List

Use this as a starting point to explore some awesome Web sites.

http://www.clark.net/pub/journalism/awesome.html

Card Store

This site is listed in Yahoo's Cool Web Sites. Create a greeting card that can be viewed through the Web.

http://infopages.com:80/card/

City.Net

The City Net Web page links you to community and tourist information around the globe.

http://www.city.net/

EcoWeb

This site links you to art, Buddhist studies, women's studies and activism resources, and HIV/Aids resources.

http://ecosys.drdr.virginia.edu/

Garden Net

If you love plants, you will appreciate the Guide to Gardens of the USA where you will find information on public gardens across the country as well as listings of different types of gardens and their location. Other impressive resources are being added to this new Web site.

http://www.olympus.net/gardens/welcome.html

Global Network Navigator

The world's first Internet-based hypermedia magazine and commercial resource discovery center from O'Reilly and Associates, GNN offers a

range of products and services to help find the best resources on the Net.
http://gnn.com/

Once Classified Government Documents

This page is maintained by the US. Department of Energy Office of Scientific and Technical Information. It links you to thousands of previously classified government documents including those discussing nuclear weapons and radiation, which were released on June 27, 1994.
http://www.doe.gov/

HotWired

Visit HotWired produced by WIRED magazine. Here you will find news about the Net, industry gossip, new Net journalism from around the globe, and digital galleries with sounds, videos, and pictures from artists all over the world. Visit PIAZZA to exchange information, love-letters, or business cards. Buy, sell, or trade goods and services in the COIN. HotWired is free.
http://www.hotwired.com/

I-Way 500
OVERWHELMING. That is perhaps the most apt term to describe the World Wide Web. Visit this excellent site to explore some of the best Web sites on the Internet that have been categorized. I-Way 500 ranks the 25 best sites in each of 20 categories.
http://www.cciweb.com/iway500/iway500.html

Library of Congress

Explore over 70 million documents at the Library of Congress without ever leaving your desktop. If you are interested in copyright or Capital Hill publications, this is a MUST VISIT.
http://www.loc.gov.

Mercury Site

Manipulate a robotic arm. Use blasts of air to uncover artifacts buried in the sands of the Nevada desert. Surrealism and strange virtual experiences characterize this experience.
http://www.usc.edu/dept/raiders

Myers-Briggs Personality Test

Check out what type of personality you have using the famous Myers-Briggs Personality Test. Answer the 70 multiple-choice questions online and tally your score. You also can get a list of others with a similar personality.
http://sunsite.unc.edu/jembin/mb.pl

Native Web Home Page

Welcome to NativeWeb, a project of many people. Our vision touches ancient teachings and modern technology. Our purpose is to provide a cyberplace for Earth's indigenous peoples. Information at this site is organized into some of the following categories: Nations/Peoples, Languages, Education, Literature, Newsletters & Journals, Organizations, Bibliographies, and Historical Material.
http://web.maxwell.syr.edu/nativeweb/

Oneida Indian Nation

Visit this site to learn more about the Oneida Native Americans. This site has information on "The Treaties Project," an ongoing project to restore the significance of the treaties conducted between Native American Nations and the United States. Also visit the Shako:Wi Cultural Center exhibit, or listen to audio samples of the Oneida language.
http://one-web.org/oneida/

Postcard Store

Choose an electronic postcard, write a message, and send it to a Web friend.
http://persona.www.media.mit.edu/Postcards/

The Subway

The Subway will take you to many virtual destinations throughout the Internet: Honolulu Community College Dinosaur Exhibit, Australian Botanical Gardens, Australian National University, United States Geological Survey, EXPO, Smithsonian Institution, Harvard Biodiversity Gopher, The National Science Foundation, Exploratorium and more.
http://ucmp1.berkeley.edu/subway.html

Toy Story

Visit Woody, Buzz, and the other Toy Story characters. Download icons for your computer or choose one of your favorite characters for your computer background.
http://www2.disney.com/ToyStory/?GL=H

United Nations

Avoid traffic jams in New York by taking a virtual trip to the UN. Partake in the 50th-anniversay celebration.
http://www.un.org

Virtual Travel

Take a virtual trip around the world. Stop at a Virtual Pub in the Scottish Highlands; visit St. Petersburg in Russia; explore Web resources in Nepal, China, or Brazil. Global Network Navigator's Travel Center provides an excellent place to begin your travels.
http://gnn.interpath.net/gnn/meta/travel/res/countries.html

Weather

WeatherNet is one of the Internet's premier source of weather information. Providing access to thousands of forecasts, images, and the Net's largest collection of weather links, WeatherNet is the most comprehensive and up-to-date source of weather data on the Web sponsored by The Weather Underground at the University of Michigan.
http://cirrus.sprl.umich.edu/wxnet/

Weather Satellite Images

Visit these Web sites for images collected all over the globe. Some images are only a few hours old.
http://wx3.atmos.uiuc.edu/
or
http://rs560.cl.msu.edu/weather/

White House

This White House site contains links to tours, maps, and federal agencies.
http://whitehouse.gov/

FOREIGN LANGUAGE CENTER

World Wide Web

The Internet & The World Wide Web

applets: Mini applications that a software program such as Netscape downloads and executes.

ASCII (text) files: One of the file transfer modes (binary is another mode) used when transferring files on the Internet. ASCII treats the file as a set of characters that can be read by the computer receiving the ASCII text. ASCII does not recognize text formatting such as boldface, underline, tab stops, or fonts.

binary file: Another transfer mode available for transferring Internet files. In the binary mode, files are transferred identical in appearance to the original document.

Binhex (BINary HEXadecimal): A method for converting non-text files (non-ASCII) into ASCII. Used in e-mail programs that can only handle ASCII.

Bit: A single digit number, either a 1 or a zero, that represents the smallest unit of computerized data.

bookmarks: A feature providing the user with the opportunity to mark favorite pages for fast and easy access. Netscape's bookmarks can be organized hierarchically and customized by the user through the Bookmark List dialog box.

browser: A client program that interprets and displays HTML documents.

client: A software program assisting in contacting a server somewhere on the Net for information. Examples of client software programs are Gopher, Netscape, Veronica, and Archie. An Archie client runs on a system configured to contact a specific Archie database to query for information.

compression: A process by which a file or a folder is made smaller. The three primary purposes of compression are to save disk space, to save space when doing a backup, and to speed the transmission of a file when transferring over a modem or network.

domain name: The unique name that identifies an Internet site. Names have two or more parts separated by a dot such as **xplora.com**

finger: An Internet software tool for locating people on the Internet. The most common use is to see if an individual has an account at a particular Internet site.

fire wall: A combination of hardware and software that separates a local area network into two parts for security purposes.

frames: A new feature of Netscape Navigator 2.0 that makes it possible to create multiple windows on a Netscape page. Below is an example of a Web page divided into several windows called frames.

FTP (file transfer protocol): Protocol for transferring files between computers on the Internet.

GIF (Graphic Interface Format): A format developed by CompuServe, Inc. for storing complex graphics. This format is one of two used for storing graphics in HTML documents.

Helper Applications: Programs used by Netscape to read files retrieved from the Internet. Different server protocols are used by Netscape to transfer files: HTTP, NNTP, SMTP, and FTP. Each protocol supports different file formats for text, images, video, and sound. When these files are received by Netscape, the external helper applications read, interpret, and display the file.

History List: Netscape keeps track of your Internet journeys. Sites that you visit are listed in the History List found under the GO pull-down menu. Click on an Internet site on your list, and you will be linked to that destination.

Home Page: The starting point for World Wide Web exploration. The Home Page contains highlighted words and icons that link to text, graphic, video, and sound files. Home Pages can be developed by anyone: Internet Providers, universities, businesses, and individuals. Netscape allows you to select which Home Page is displayed when you launch the program.

HTML (HyperText Markup Language): A programming language used to create a Web page. This includes the text of the document, its structure, and links to other documents. HTML also includes the programming for accessing and displaying media such as images, video, and sound.

HTTP (HyperText Transfer Protocol): One protocol used by the World Wide Web to transfer information. Web documents begin with **http://**.

hyperlinks: Links to other Web information such as a link to another page, an image, a video or sound file.

hypertext: A document containing links to another document. The linked document is displayed by clicking on a highlighted word or icon in the hypertext.

IP address: Every computer on the Internet has a unique IP address. This number is unique consisting of four parts separated by dots such as 198.68.32.1

InfoSeek: A commercial search engine that researches information in World Wide Web sites, Usenet postings, computer journals, newswires, and magazines. Accessed through Netscape's Net Search or this URL: **http://www.infoseek.com/**

live objects: Java brings life and interaction to Web pages by making it possible to create live objects. Move your mouse over an image of a house and see the lights go on. Move your mouse to a picture of a woman and hear her welcome you to her Home Page.

JavaScript: A new programming language developed by Sun Microsystems that makes it possible to incorporate mini applications *applets* onto a Web page.

JPEG (Joint Photographic Experts Group): A file format for graphics (photographs, complex images, and video stills) that uses compression.

MIME (Multimedia Internet Mail Extension): Most multimedia files on the Internet are MIME. The MIME type refers to the type of file: text, HTML, images, video, or sound. When a browser such as Netscape retrieves a file from a server, the server provides the MIME type to establish whether the file format can be read by the software's built-in capabilities or, if not, whether a suitable helper application is available to read the file.

newsgroups: Large distributed Bulletin Board Systems that consist of several thousand specialized discussion groups. Messages are posted to a Bulletin Board by e-mail for others to read.

NNTP (News Server): A server protocol used by Netscape for transferring Usenet news. Before you can read Usenet news, you must enter the name of your news server to interact with Usenet newsgroups. The news server name is entered in the Mail and News dialog box (Options pull-down menu; Preferences; Mail and News).

page: A file or document in Netscape that contains hypertext links to multimedia resources.

PKzip: PC software used to compress files.

platform: Netscape Navigator 2.0 is referred to as a platform rather than a browser. A platform program makes it possible for developers to build applications onto it.

PPP (Point-to-Point Protocol): A method by which a computer may use a high speed modem and a standard telephone line to have full Internet access. A PPP or SLIP connection is required to use graphical interfaces with the Internet such as Netscape Navigator and Eudora for e-mail. Using a PPP or SLIP connection enables you to point and click your way around the Internet.

.sea (self-extracting archives): A file name extension indicating a compression method used by Macintosh computers. Files whose names end in .sea are compressed archives that can be decompressed by double-clicking on the program icon.

Search Engine: Software programs designed for seeking information on the Internet. Some of these programs search by keyword within a document, title, index, or directory.

server: A computer running software that allows another computer (a client) to communicate with it for information exchange.

shell account: The most basic type of Internet connection. A shell account allows you to dial into the Internet at your provider's site. Your Internet software is run on the computer at that site. On a shell account your Internet interface is text-based. There are no pull-down menus, icons, or graphics. Some Internet providers offer a menu system of Internet options. Others merely provide a Unix system prompt, usually a percent sign or a dollar sign. You must know the commands to enter at the prompt to access the Internet.

SLIP (Serial Line Internet Protocol): A method by which a computer with a high speed modem may connect directly to the Internet through a standard telephone line. A SLIP account is needed to use Netscape. SLIP is currently being replaced with PPP (Point-to-Point Protocol).

SMTP (Simple Mail Transport Protocol): A protocol used by the Internet for electronic mail. Before using Netscape e-mail the host name of the Internet provider's mail server must be designated. The mail server name is entered in the Mail and News dialog box (Options pull-down menu; Preferences; Mail and News).

source file: When saved as "source" the document is preserved with its embedded HTML instructions that format the Internet page.

Stuffit Expander: One of the most widely used decompression programs for the Macintosh. It is available as freeware.

toolbar: Navigational buttons used in graphical interface applications.

TCP/IP (Transmission Control Protocol/Internet Protocol): The protocol upon which the Internet is based and which supports transmission of data.

Usenet: Developed in the 1970s for communication among computers at various universities. In the early 1980s, Usenet was being used for electronic discussions on a wide variety of topics and soon became a tool for communication. Today, Usenet groups are analogous to a cafe where people from everywhere in the world gather to discuss and share ideas on topics of common interest.

URL (Uniform Resource Locator): URLs are a standard for locating Internet documents. They use an addressing system for other Internet protocols such as access to gopher menus, FTP file retrieval, and Usenet newsgroups. The format for a URL is

protocol://server-name:port/path

URL object: Any resource accessible on the World Wide Web: text documents, sound files, movies, and images.

VERONICA (Very Easy Rodent-Oriented Net-wide Index to Computerized Archives): An Internet service offering a keyword search of most gopher server menus in the world. The result of a VERONICA search is a gopher menu customized according to the user's keywords given in the search request. Search results are immediately accessible via gopher.

viewer: Programs needed to display graphics, sound, and video. For example, pictures stored as a GIF image have the file name extension ".gif" and need a gif helper application to display the image. Netscape has the required viewers (external helper applications) built into the software. A list of programs required to view files can be found in the Helper Application menu of Netscape. Open the **Options** pull-down menu select **Preferences**, then **Helper Applications**.

VRML (Virtual Reality Modeling Language): a programming language that makes 3-dimensional virtual reality experiences possible on Web pages.

WAIS (Wide Area Information Servers): A commercial software package that indexes huge quantities of information, and then makes those indices searchable across networks. Search results are ranked according to how relevant the result is.

Winsock: The most popular Internet access software for Windows. The software combines TCP/IP and PPP in one package.

Window: A window is also know as a Web page. It may contain text and hyperlinks to images, video, and sound files.

Window Title Bar: Displays the name of the current document being viewed on the Netscape page.

World Wide Web (WWW or Web): A hypermedia system developed at the European Particle Physics Laboratory (CERN) in Geneva, Switzerland. Originally developed as a means for physicists to share papers and data easily. Today it has evolved into a sophisticated technology that links together hypertext and hypermedia documents.

YAHOO (Yet Another Hierarchically Officious Oracle): An Internet navigational directory created in April 1994 by David Filo and Jerry Yang two Stanford University electrical engineering students. On their YAHOO Home Page they listed their favorite World Wide Web sites, organized by topic. Friends began sending in their favorite sites. Soon YAHOO became the unofficial hub of the Web. In February 1985, Netscape Communications acquired YAHOO, giving it a home with more server space. Today the site has over 2.5 million hits per day.

.zip: The file extension for PC files that indicates that the file has been compressed. Most PC compression is done with PKzip.

Chapter Five

FINDING INFORMATION ON THE INTERNET

LOCATOR MAP...
Using Search Engines To Find Information And Resources

The Internet contains many tools that speed the search for information and resources. Research tools called *search engines* are extremely helpful.

How Do Search Engines Work?

Search engines periodically scan Internet sites for resources and then add them to their database. Most search engines provide options for other Web sites to submit information that is entered into the search engine's database of resources. When an Internet user requests information on a topic by entering a descriptive keyword, the search engine scans its database for items that match the keyword and returns a series of hits or links to resources.

Basic Guidelines For Finding Information

There are many different search engines available. Although each search engine has different features and capabilities, the basics for using these tools are similar.

1. Determine one or more descriptive words (keywords) for the subject you are researching. Enter your keywords into the search dialog box.

2. Determine how specific you want your search to be. Do you want it to be broad or narrow? Use available options to refine or limit your search. Some search engines permit the use of Boolean operators; others provide HELP for refining searches; still others have pull-down menus or selections to be checked for options.

3. Submit your query.

4. Review your list of search results.

5. Adjust your search based on the information returned. Did you receive too much information and need to narrow your search? Did you receive too little or no information and need to broaden your keywords?

The search engines described in this section include:

- Yahoo
- EINetGalaxy
- Magellan
- Lycos
- Excite
- Infoseek
- Savy Search
- Alta Vista
- Open Text

Yahoo

Yahoo is one of the most popular search tools available on the Internet and still considered by many to be the smartest for those who understand how to conduct an Internet search. If you are new to search engines, Yahoo is an excellent place to begin.

Yahoo can be accessed from the Netscape Search Directory button, or by entering this URL **http://www.yahoo.com/**

There are two ways to find information using Yahoo: search through the subject directory or use the built-in search engine.

Yahoo Subject Directory
When you connect to Yahoo you will see a list of subjects. Select the topic area that best fits your search needs. Follow the links until you find the information you need.

Yahoo Search Engine
Follow these steps to use Yahoo to search for information.

1. Enter a descriptive keyword for your subject. Think of words that uniquely identify or describe what you are looking for. For example, if I were researching rain forests I would enter the words **rain forests**.

Figure 5.1
Yahoo search form and subject directory.

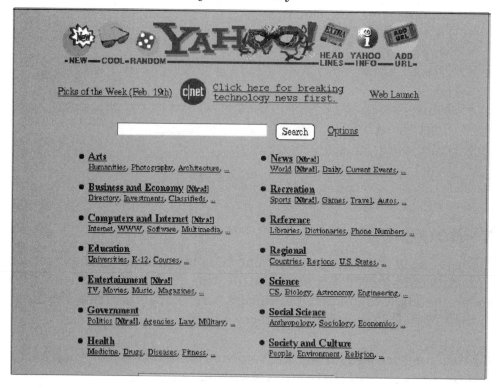

Figure 5.2
Yahoo search options.

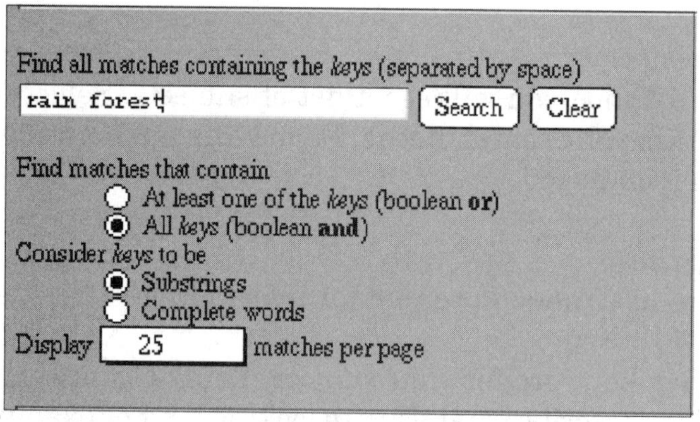

2. Determine how extensive you want your search to be. If you are using two keywords, do you want Yahoo to look for either word (boolean **or**), both keywords (boolean **and**), or each word as a individual string? For example, in the search for

rain forests I would select the boolean **and** because I want to find resources that contain both of the words *rain* and *forest*. Otherwise the search would be too broad and would find all resource that contained either of the keywords *rain* or *forest*.

3. Further limit or expand your search by selecting substrings or complete words. For example, with my *rain forest* search, I would select the search option for *complete words* or Yahoo would treat each word as a series of letters rather than a whole word. My research return using *substrings* would include words such as *rainbow, raindrops, rainfall, forester*, or *forestry*.

4. Determine how many matches you want returned for your search.

5. Submit your query.

6. Review your return list of hits and adjust your search if necessary.

7. Submit the search again.

EINet Galaxy

EINet is another popular and easy to use tool for finding information. Like Yahoo, information can be found using the subject index or the search engine. The URL for EINet Galaxy is **http://galaxy.einet.net/search.html**

Galaxy Subject Directory
To see a list of topics, click on the Galaxy link. To use the Galaxy subject directory.

1. Determine what topic area to search.

2. Navigate down the subject topic list, following links on each page until you find the information you need.

Figure 5.3
EINet subject directory.

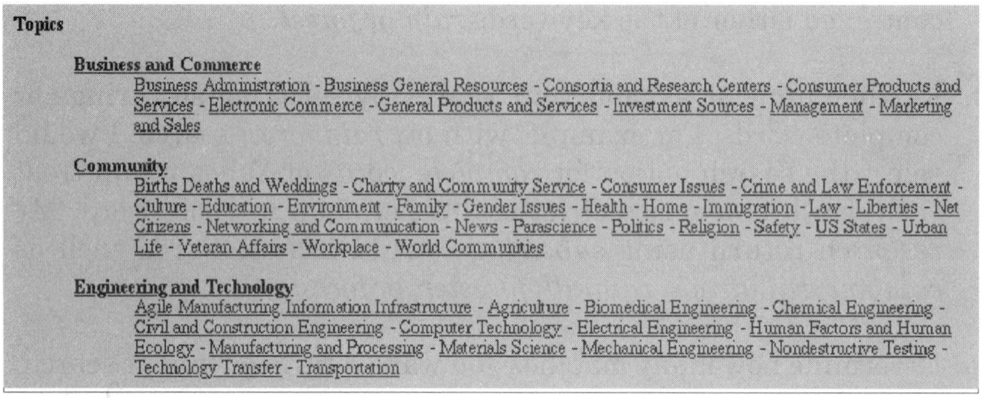

Topics

Business and Commerce
Business Administration - Business General Resources - Consortia and Research Centers - Consumer Products and Services - Electronic Commerce - General Products and Services - Investment Sources - Management - Marketing and Sales

Community
Births Deaths and Weddings - Charity and Community Service - Consumer Issues - Crime and Law Enforcement - Culture - Education - Environment - Family - Gender Issues - Health - Home - Immigration - Law - Liberties - Net Citizens - Networking and Communication - News - Parascience - Politics - Religion - Safety - US States - Urban Life - Veteran Affairs - Workplace - World Communities

Engineering and Technology
Agile Manufacturing Information Infrastructure - Agriculture - Biomedical Engineering - Chemical Engineering - Civil and Construction Engineering - Computer Technology - Electrical Engineering - Human Factors and Human Ecology - Manufacturing and Processing - Materials Science - Mechanical Engineering - Nondestructive Testing - Technology Transfer - Transportation

Galaxy Search Engine

The Galaxy search engine differs slightly from Yahoo in that it uses weighted searching. Galaxy orders the search results as they believe you wish to see them. For example, when searching for *rain forests*, Galaxy will first return all instances where both words are found followed by resources that have either word.

1. Enter a descriptive keyword or phrase for your subject. Use the selection buttons under the keyword box to specify whether **any** or **all** of the keywords should be present in the result. You can also use the boolean options of **and** or **or** to further your search. I would enter the words **rain forest** and select the box for **all** search terms.

Figure 5.4
Search form for EINet Galaxy.

Search for: `rain forest` [Search] **Need Help?**

Match ○ **any** search term, or ● **all** search terms. [Long output]

☒ Search the Web - for each document:
Search ● **all** text , ○ **title** text only, or ○ **link** text only.

Also search ☒ Galaxy Pages ☒ Gopher Titles ☐ Telnet Resources

2. The default settings search all Web pages referenced by Galaxy. Click on the **Search** button (or hit *RETURN* on your keyboard).

NOTE

Other search options available with Galaxy include:

- **search all text** — This searches all of the text on a World Wide Web page.

- **search title text** — This searches only the titles of Web pages referenced in Galaxy.

- **search link text** — This searches the text of the links found in the World Wide Web text and helps find very specific information.

Magellan

Magellan is another excellent search directory. This search tool rates many of the Web sites returned from a query by a scale of one to four stars. Magellan provides option for narrowing or expanding your search: narrow your search to sites rated with three stars or more; restrict your search to exclude sites with mature content by searching for "Green Light" sites only (see the stop light icon).
http://magellan.mckinley.com/

Lycos

Lycos from Carnegie Mellons is one of the oldest Web search sites and continues to deliver comprehensive search results. One of the best features of the Lycos search engine is that a relevant passage from each hit is displayed in the search results. This information is extremely beneficial in saving you time checking links produced in the search results. After reading the description of the Internet site, you may decide that the link is not what you wanted.

Lycos can be accessed from the Netscape Search Directory button, or by entering this URL **http://www.lycos.com/** Check out Lycos' short review of the most popular Web sites or visit their new directory.

Figure 5.5
The Lycos Web site.

If you need to expand or narrow your search, click on **Enhance your search.**

Figure 5.6
Lycos' enhanced search form.

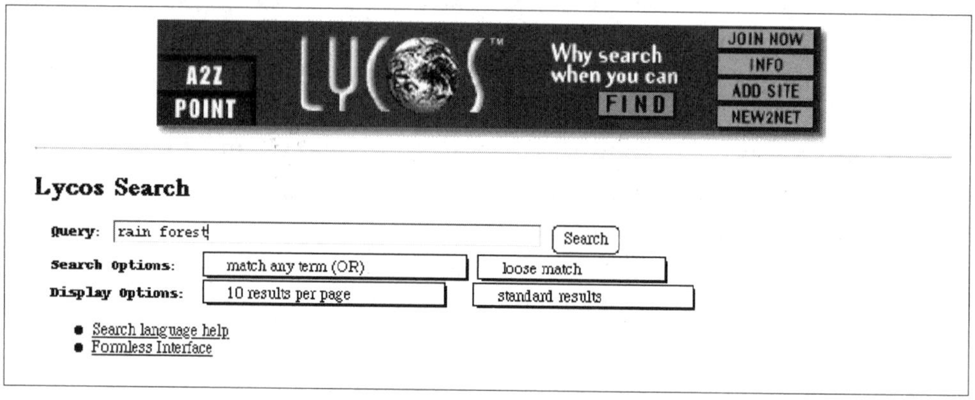

How To Search Lycos Using Search Options

By default Lycos will find all documents matching any word you type in your query (except for words like **a** or **the**). For example, if you type **rain forest** Lycos will find all documents containing either **rain OR forest**. If you want both words to be searched, select **match all terms (AND)** in the **Search Options** box.

Search Options are also used to adjust the selectivity of your search. When you select **loose match** more documents will be returned, but they will tend to be less relevant to your query. For a more selective search, change the Search Option to **close match** or a **strong match** to further refine your search.

Display Options

Lycos always makes available all of the results from your query. However, you have the control options to determine how many are displayed on a page.

Lycos also provides options for selecting the amount of information displayed for each "hit." Select either *standard*, *detailed* (all information displayed), or *summary* (the minimum amount of information is displayed).

Figure 5.7
Lycos search results with a standard display.

Lycos search: rain forest
April 6, 1996 catalog (37,643,037 unique URLs)
Found 73415 documents with the words rain (22372), rainbow (16952), forest (41748), forestry (14152), forests (14110), ...

---

1) Pura Vista S.A. - Tropical Rain Forest [1.0000, 2 of 2 terms, adj 1.0]

Outline: Pura Vista - Tropical **Rain Forest** KR007: Tropical **Rain Forest**

Abstract: Pura Vista S.A. - Tropical **Rain Forest** Pura Vista - Tropical **Rain Forest** KR007: Tropical **Rain Forest** Location This impressive parcel of tropical **rain forest** occupies 609 hectares (1,504 acres) of the southwest portion of the Osa Peninsula, near Corcovado National Park. The Osa Peninsula lowlands are the only wet **forests** still existing on the Pacific side of Central America. There is road access from San Jose which is 404 km away, including 298 km that are paved. The last 27 km from Puerto Jimenez requires 4WD vehicles during the **rainy** season (April to November). Regularly scheduled domestic air service is available on two
http://www.webcom.com/~pvsasa/listings/KR007.html (7k)

---

2) Arachnomania:Rain Forest [0.9292, 2 of 2 terms, adj 1.0]

Outline: Types of **Rain** ForestEcology:Humans and **Rain Forests**:

Abstract: Arachnomania:**Rain Forest** Jungle and **rain forest** are terms that are often used synonymously but with little precision. The more meaningful and restrictive of these terms is **rain forest**, which refers to the climax or primary **forest** in regions with high **rainfall** (greater than 1.8 m/70 in per year), chiefly but not exclusively found in the tropics. **Rain forests** are significant for their valuable timber resources, and in the tropics they afford sites for commercial crops such as rubber, tea, coffee, bananas, and sugarcane. They also include some of the
http://www.nex.com/~spider/rainforest.html (7k)

---

3) Rain Forest [0.8931, 2 of 2 terms, adj 1.0]

Outline: Rain Forest Big QuestionsPLAN

Abstract: Rain Forest Interdisciplinary Thematic Unit [Plan] [Summary] [Lesson Plans]
http://www.stuk.k12.oh.us/Docs/units/rainforest/ (3k)

Notice at the top of the search query Lycos tells you how many documents it found using your keywords. If you do not have time to explore the links, print a copy of the search results with the URLs for the Web sites.

Excite

Excite provides the fullest range of services of all the Web search sites. In addition to a Web search engine, Excite has a Web directory, daily news summary, opinion columns, cartoons, and review of Web sites. **Excite** searches scan Web pages and Usenet newsgroups for keyword matches and create summaries of each match. **Excite** consists of three services.

- **NetSearch**—comprehensive and detailed searches

- **NetReviews**—organized browsing of the Internet with site evaluations and recommendations

- **The Excite Bulletin**—an on-line newspaper with reviews of Internet resources, a newswire service from Reuters, and its own Net-related columns.

Excite provides two different types of search options: concept-based searching and keyword searching. The search engines described thus far have used keyword search options. Keyword searches are somewhat limited due to the necessity of boolean qualifiers to limit searches.

Concept-based searching goes one step beyond keyword searches and attempts to interpret what you mean and not what you say. Using the words **rain forest** a concept-based search will find not only all documents with the words **rain** and **forest** but also other documents about rain forests. Excite is available at **http://www.excite.com**

Searching with Excite

1. Type in a phrase that fits your information need.
   Be as specific as you can and use words that uniquely relate to the information you are looking for, not generally descriptive words. For example, with our rain forest search, if we are searching for information on the rain forest as an ideal ecosystem we would add the words *ideal ecosystem* to uniquely identify our search options.

Figure 5.8
Excite concept-based search.

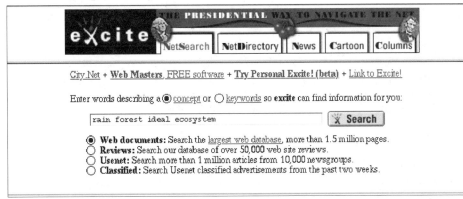

Figure 5.9
Search results for *ideal ecosystem rain forest.*

2. If certain words in your search phrase are critically important to the search, you can give them special emphasis by repeating them. For example, if I am very interested in vanishing rain forest, my search phrase might look like this

   vanishing vanishing vanishing rain forests

Figure 5.10
Excite search using critically important words.

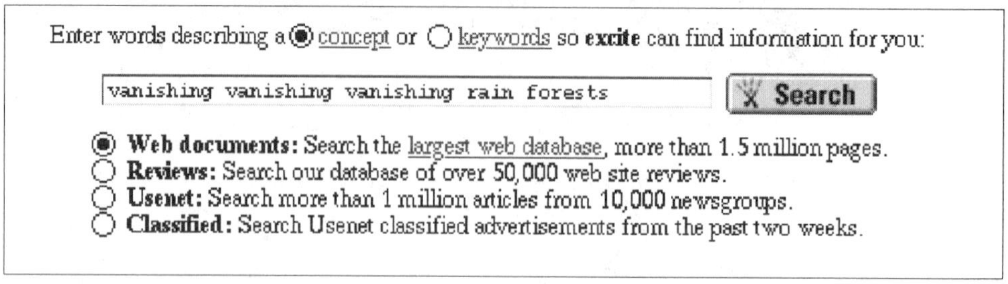

Enter words describing a ⦿ concept or ○ keywords so **excite** can find information for you:

vanishing vanishing vanishing rain forests | ✕ **Search**

⦿ **Web documents:** Search the largest web database, more than 1.5 million pages.
○ **Reviews:** Search our database of over 50,000 web site reviews.
○ **Usenet:** Search more than 1 million articles from 10,000 newsgroups.
○ **Classified:** Search Usenet classified advertisements from the past two weeks.

By adding these extra words you will be assured that the search results you get back are about vanishing rain forests and not just about rain forests.

Figure 5.11
Excite search results on vanishing rain forests.

Grouped by ⦿ **Confidence** ○ Site

Search for concept in Web Documents: **vanishing vanishing vanishing rain forests** | ✕ **New Search** | ✕ **Refine Search**

● Scores with a red icon show confidence in the match between the document and your search.
● Search for similar documents by clicking on the red or black icons next to each score.

Documents 1 to 10 (of 26) found by matching keyword prefixes and concept-based associations:

⊞ 84% Vanishing Rainforests
Summary: In conjunction with our tropical rain forest project, Dale Beasley's sixth grade class of St. Philomena School in Des Moines, Washington, has completed a project entitled, "Rainforests of the Pacific Northwest", examining a different type of rainforest right in our own country.

⊞ 78% Environment Alert!
Summary: The world's oceans are in danger from chemical pollution, garbage, toxic runoff, sewage, and overheating. Dying Oceans is a particularly strong survey of the pollution and overfishing policies which are extinguishing life in the world's oceans."

⊞ 77% /homes/sjl/froggy/frogs-disappear.txt at www.dept.cs.yale.edu
Summary: CALIFORNIA SPECIES In California, the mountain yellow-legged frog and the Yosemite toad are missing from most of the Sierra Nevada. The red-legged frog that once lived throughout Southern California is down to one remote area of Riverside County.

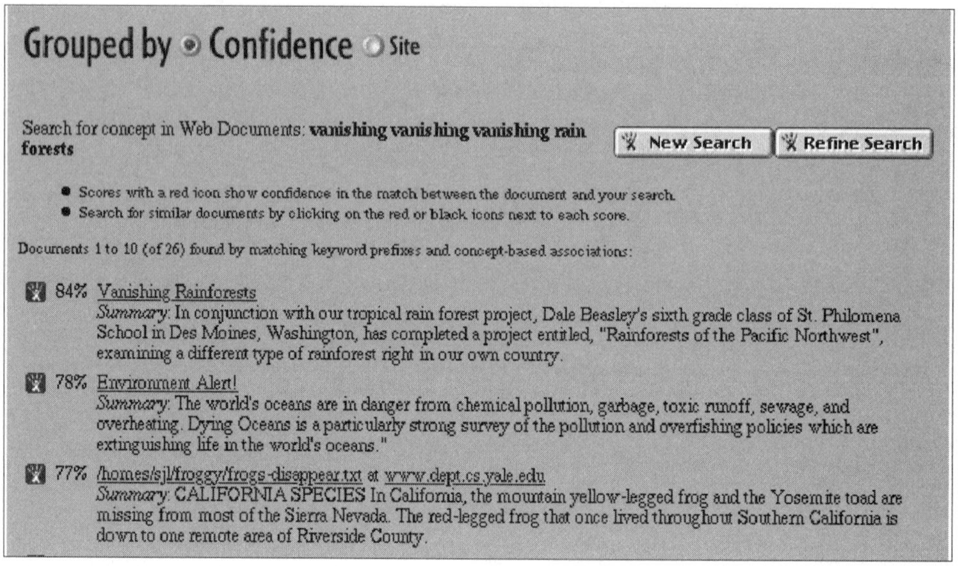

3. If you are not sure how to spell a word, type in multiple spellings in your search phrase.

4. There are two ways to have your search results displayed.

- **Grouped by confidence**—listed in the order from highest calculated relevance to lowest (see figure 5.11).

- **Grouped by site**—the physical location of your items.

Infoseek

InfoSeek is a professional service provided by InfoSeek Corporation. In 1995 InfoSeek made easy-to-use search services available for free or for a monthly subscription fee. Due to the popularity of Infoseek, the service has now been expanded and includes the Infoseek Guide and Infoseek Professional.

Infoseek Guide is the free service that integrates the latest search technology with a browsable directory of Internet resources located on World Wide Web sites, Usenet newsgroups, and other popular Internet resource sites. Users can choose to use the search engine with keywords or phrases or browse the navigational directories. Visit the InfoSeek Guide site **http://guide.infoseek.com/** and try these tools for finding Internet information and resources.

Infoseek Professional is a subscription-based service that offers individuals and business professionals comprehensive access to many Internet resources such as newswires, publications, broadcast programs, business, medical, financial, and government databases. The difference between Infoseek Guide and Infoseek Professional is the capability to conduct more comprehensive searches and to have options for refining and limiting your searches. For example, you can conduct a search query by entering in a question such as **How can I get information on ISDN?** You can also limit your query to the important words or phrases that are likely to appear in the documents you want, for example,

> information on the best "ISDN" "hardware"

By identifying the key words or phrases (ISDN and hardware) with quotes your search accuracy is greatly enhanced.

Infoseek Professional is available for a free trial period at **http://professional.infoseek.com**/ Before you perform a search, link to Infoseek's information on search queries and examples. This will save you time by learning how to perform the most efficient search.

Figure 5.12
Infoseek guide for finding information and resources.

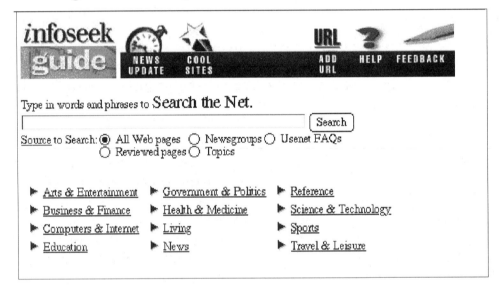

Savvy Search

Savvy Search is designed to query multiple Internet search engines simultaneously. Use the Search Form to enter your query, indicate whether you would like to search for all or any of the query terms, and indicate the number of results desired from each search engine.

While Savvy Search provides a convenient interface, you are encouraged to visit each search engine directly, as each provides a unique and powerful service.
http://guaraldi.cs.colostate.edu:2000/

Alta Vista

Digital's Alta Vista is considered one of the best search engines currently available with one of the largest Web-search databases. Alta Vista's searches are consistently more comprehensive than any of the other search tools. Although you will spend a great deal of time

browsing your search results, you will be provided with as much information as possible on a search query.
http://altavista.digital.com/

Open Text

Open Text has one of the most comprehensive collections of search tools and is one of the best designed search engines on the Internet.
http://www.opentext.com/

Open Text offers many search options.

- simple query on words;
- a power search using up to five operators between terms (*and, or, not, but not, near,* and *followed by*);
- options to create your own weighted search;
- results scored by relevancy;
- an option to show a report of where Open Text found your search matches.

Open Text produces better returns on your search if you break up a phrase into keywords. For example, when "the use of solar energy to produce electricity" was entered, Open Text reported "not matches." When the query was changed into individual search terms "solar energy" and "electricity" a large number of results were displayed.

NOTE
All-In-One Search Page
An Internet site to visit and explore for accessing most of the search engines is the All-In-One Search Page at **http://www.albany.net/allinone**

Use different search engines and see which ones you like the best. Then visit each home page and see if information is provided on how to refine your searches.

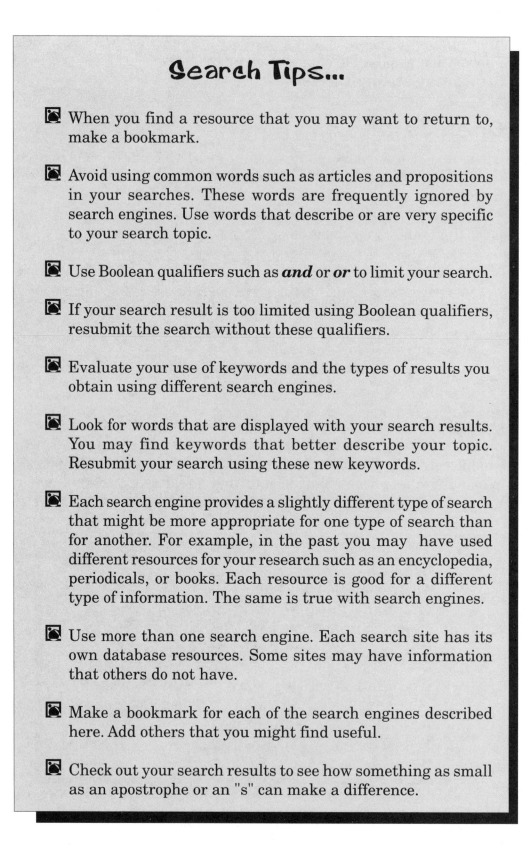

Search Tips...

- When you find a resource that you may want to return to, make a bookmark.

- Avoid using common words such as articles and propositions in your searches. These words are frequently ignored by search engines. Use words that describe or are very specific to your search topic.

- Use Boolean qualifiers such as *and* or *or* to limit your search.

- If your search result is too limited using Boolean qualifiers, resubmit the search without these qualifiers.

- Evaluate your use of keywords and the types of results you obtain using different search engines.

- Look for words that are displayed with your search results. You may find keywords that better describe your topic. Resubmit your search using these new keywords.

- Each search engine provides a slightly different type of search that might be more appropriate for one type of search than for another. For example, in the past you may have used different resources for your research such as an encyclopedia, periodicals, or books. Each resource is good for a different type of information. The same is true with search engines.

- Use more than one search engine. Each search site has its own database resources. Some sites may have information that others do not have.

- Make a bookmark for each of the search engines described here. Add others that you might find useful.

- Check out your search results to see how something as small as an apostrophe or an "s" can make a difference.

Other Resources For Finding Information

ArchiePlex
Here you can locate files (reports, documents, software etc.) on the Internet that are available for Anonymous FTP (file transfer protocol)
http://www.interlog.com/~gordo/otis_pubsearch.html

Art Source
ArtSource is a gathering point for networked resources on Art and Architecture. The content is diverse and includes pointers to resources around the net, as well as original materials submitted by librarians, artists, and art historians, and more.
http://www.uky.edu/Artsource/artsourcehome.html

Electric Library—Infonautics Corporation
Infonautics Corporation creator of Homework Helper, the on-line research service for students, now makes available The Electric Library. The Electric Library aggregates more than 150 full-text newspapers, 900 full-text magazines, two international newswires, two thousand classic books, hundreds of maps, thousands of photographs as well as major works of literature and art. Included are materials from renowned publishers such as Archive Photos, Reuters, Simon and Schuster, Gannett, Times Mirror and Compton's New Media. The Electric Library also incorporates a host of local, ethnic, and special interest publications.

Users can search quickly and simultaneously across more than 10 million pages of data by asking questions in plain English. For example, asking **Will there be peace in Bosnia?** will yield citations to a magazine article about the future of the Balkans, the full text of president Clinton's peacekeeping speech, a recent newswire photo of U.S. troops in Bosnia, the region's history from reference books, as well as hundreds of common references and allusions from newspapers and other reliable sources. Searches can also be narrowed to particular dates, authors, subjects or publications.

The cost for using these services is currently $9.95 per month for unlimited access. The Electric Library is free on a trial basis for two weeks. Visit the site and sample these research services.
http://www.elibrary.com/ or http://www.infonautics.com/

Electronic Newsstand Home Page

This Web site has links to a wide selection of articles from the world's leading magazines, newsletters, newspapers, catalogues and more: You can browse for free.

http://www.enews.com/

Indiana University Library

Visit this excellent electronic library to do research using on-line catalogs, electronic collections, and resources. Ask a librarian a question or download multimedia resources.

http://www-lib.iupui.edu/home.html

Internet Public Library

Visit this electronic library and take a tour of its services. Research information or visit the classroom, exhibit hall, or reading room.

http://ipl.sils.umich.edu/

Libraries — Finding With NetLink

Library Catalogs Sorted By Name

http://honor.uc.wlu.edu/net/catalogs/Library_Catalogs_sorted_by_Name.html

Library of Congress

This 195-year-old library has links to over 70 million documents including the U.S. Copyright Office, Congressional records, Capitol Hill publications, digitized versions of American cultural and historical documents, and much more.

http://www.loc.gov/

Tile.Net/Lists

This WWW site is a reference to all the LISTSERV discussion groups on the Internet. The data comes from the LISTSERV command "list global." Search for a list by subject or view the most popular listservs.

http://www.tile.net/tile/listserv/index.html

Newlink

This Web site links you to over 2,000 news sites including newspapers, magazines, television and radio stations, search sites, publishers, e-zines, and much more.

http://www.newslink.org

My Virtual Reference Desk
This "Cool Site Of The Day" pick contains links to weather sites, news, sports, free stuff, "cool" and "HOT" Web sites and much more.
http://www.intercom.net/user/rbdrudge/main.html

The OTIS Index
This site helps you search the Internet to find software, on-line books, commercial sites, newsgroups, and electronic publications.
http://www.interlog.com/~gordo/otis_index.html

Pangea Reference Systems—NASA
Pangea Reference Systems, Inc. developed by NASA Ames Technology Commercialization Center in Sunnyvale, California, is committed to making public domain information more easily accessible on the Internet.

The initial service, Pan*Reference, is a digital library of network news and various public e-mail lists, accessible both through their Web interface, as well as via e-mail.
http://www.reference.com/

Searching The Web
This page has a collection of references and searching services.
http://union.ncsa.uiuc.edu/HyperNews/get/www/searching.html

Time Magazine
Time Warner is one of the earliest publishers to go on-line. They offer an excellent resource for finding and researching information in the Time Warner database.
http://www.pathfinder.com/time

Find Newsgroups
This Web site has a simple tool for discovering Usenet newsgroups of interest. Enter a single string and a menu of newsgroups whose names or brief descriptions match the search string will be returned.
http://www.cen.uiuc.edu/cgi-bin/find-news

Virtual Library of Museums
These pages provide an eclectic collection of WWW services connected with museums, galleries, and archives.
http://www.comlab.ox.ac.uk/archive/other/museums.html

Web Developer's Virtual Library
This site offers links to development tools, technical sites, style guides, and Web related job listings.
http://www.enterprise.net/stars

World Wide Web Virtual Library
This site is an excellent site to visit to find information on the Internet catalogued by subject.
http://www.w3.org/hypertext/DataSources/bySubject/Overview.html

LOCATOR MAP...
Finding A Person's E-Mail Address

Now that you have learned to use e-mail, you are probably asking, "How can I find a person's e-mail address?" Finding an e-mail address is not easy. Lack of centralization, concerns about privacy, and the daily growing number of Internet users make the task of discovering an e-mail address, even of a friend, very complicated. One World Wide Web site **http://sunsite.oit.unc.edu/~masha/** makes available the best and most useful methods for finding an e-mail address.

NOTE

There is no one search method presently available, nor will there ever be, that will guarantee that you will find the person you are looking for. In fact, it will be unlikely that you will find the person in a single search session. You will most likely need to use several search tools to help find a person.

Before You Begin...

The more information you have to start with, the more likely it is that your search will be successful. The following information may be helpful in your search.

- Where is the person located? What region or country?
- Could the individual actually be on the same machine (network) as you are?
- Is the person on a network other than Internet?
- Who is the individual using for an Internet provider? An organization, business, school or university? Is the person using a commercial or local Internet provider?
- What listserv mailing lists might the individual subscribe to?
- Could the person have posted to Usenet newsgroups?
- Could the individual have a Home Page?
- Might the person be active on Internet, or serve in some position of responsibility within an organization related to the Internet?

Based on this information, use one of the search tools at this site that falls under such categories as, finding someone who

- is at university or college.
- is in another country.
- is on a network other than the Internet.
- has a home page.
- subscribes to a listserv mailing list or Usenet newsgroup.

Also available are Internet phone books, White Pages, and Internet directories. Netscape's Directory menu has a link to the Internet White Pages.

LOCATOR MAP...

Finding Jobs And Employees On The Internet

The Internet is providing new opportunities for job-seekers and companies to find good employment matches. Many companies are turning to the Internet believing that the people who keep up with the most current information and technological advances in their field are the best candidates for positions. The growing perception among employers is that they may be able to find better candidates if they search on-line.

The types of jobs offered on the Internet have changed dramatically over the last ten years. In the past, job announcements were primarily academic or in the field of science and technology. Now, thousands of positions in all fields from graphic artists to business and marketing professionals, from medical professionals to Internet surfers and Web programmers are being advertised.

Many companies realize the impact of the digital revolution on business and are searching for professionals who are already on-line cybersurfing, networking with peers, researching information, asking questions, and learning collaboratively from others around the world. The digital revolution is happening now. It is a new economy, a new counterculture, and a new politics. Many believe that tremendous wealth and power will either be gained or lost according to who most shrewdly associates themselves with the newest technologies for communication, information exchange, and entertainment.

The World Wide Web has created opportunities for new types of resumes and business cards. Those individuals who take advantage of the power of this new medium stand out as being truly technologically advanced and in touch with the future.

Net Sites For Job Seekers

There are many services available for job-seekers and for companies looking for employees. Companies usually pay to be listed; job-seekers may be allowed to post their resumes at no cost.

America's Job Bank
This on-line Employment service offers information on over 250,000 employment opportunities
http://www.ajb.dni.us/index.html

Career Mosaic
This popular on-line career center receives over 100,000 visitors per month posting jobs for companies such as Intel, USWest, and Sun Microsystems. **http://www.careermosaic.com/**

Career Path
Review employment opportunities from a number of the nation's leading daily newspapers such as the New York Times, Los Angeles Times, Boston Globe, Chicago Tribune, San Jose Mercury, and the Washington Post. **http://www.careerpath.com**

Career Resources Home Page
This Web site has links to on-line employment services including professional and university-based services.
http://www.rpi.edu/dept/cdc/homepage.html

CareerWeb
Search by job, location, employment, or keyword to find the perfect job. You can also browse employer profiles and search the Library's list of related publications. **http://www.cweb.com/**

College Grad Job Hunter
Visit this excellent Web site to learn about life after college. Learn how to start looking for your first job, how to develop a resume, and master interviews. Browse through job postings or visit employer Web sites. **http://www.collegegrad.com/**

IntelliMatch
Connect to IntelliMatch, fill out a resume and hundreds of employers will have access to your profile via the Holmes search software. Review other related services such as job-related sites and products, participating companies, and description of available jobs.
http://www.intellimatch.com/

The Internet On-line Career Center
This career center and employment database is one of the highest volume job centers with a long list of employment opportunities and resources. Post your resume in HTML format. Use multimedia (images, photographs, audio, and video) to enrich your resume.
http://www.occ.com/

The Monster Board
This unusual ad agency is a service for recruitment and provides information for job-seekers. **http://www.monster.com/home.html**

Stanford University
Stanford University's site provides listing of on-line job services such as Medsearch and the Chronicle of Higher Education. They also have links to other agencies. **http://rescomp.stanford.edu/**

Student Center
The Student Center offers an on-line questionnaire to help you determine what type of job you are best suited for. Explore resume tips and learn more about setting goals.
http://www.studentcenter.com/

Helpwanted.com
This site offers a searchable index of job openings that have paid to be listed. **http://helpwanted.com/**

Sample On-line Resumes & Home Pages
John Lockwood's Home Page
http://ipoint.vlsi.uiuc.edu/people/lockwood/lockwood.html

Mike Swartzbeck Home Page
http://myhouse.com/mikesite/

Sandra L. Dain —Web designer, author, editor
http://q.continuum.net/~shazara/resume.html

Jon Keegan—Illustrator
http://web.syr.edu/~jmkeegan/resume.html

Allan Trautman—Puppeteer and actor
http://www.smartlink.net/~trautman/

Ricardo Araiza — Student
http://pwa.acusd.edu/~ricardo/resume.html

Kenneth Morrill — Web Developer
http://webdesk.com/resumes/kjmresume.html

LOCATOR MAP...
Finding An Internet Provider

There are several Web sites to help you find an Internet access provider.

http://thelist.com/
http://www.clari.net/iap/iapcode.htm
http://www.primus.com/providers/

To find the names of providers in your area, click on the link to your area code. You will find descriptive information of providers in your area code and a description of their services.

NOTE

Note all providers that service your area will be found by the area code listing.

Tips For Finding A Provider

If your area code is not listed

There are providers who have nationwide access. Some of the Web sites provide information on these service providers.

If there is no local dial-in number

Look for service providers that are the closest to you or who have 800 dial-in access. Many of these providers are also listed on these Web sites.

Types of Internet accounts

There are several types of services that most Internet providers offer. Listed below is a description of each to assist you.

Shell: Offers a basic connection running UNIX environment. Services include electronic mail, Usenet news, FTP, telnet, gopher, IRC, etc. Most providers have a menu-driven interfaces.

SLIP: Allows you to run graphical TCP/IP software for navigating the Internet such as Netscape, Eudora, news readers, and other Web browsers such as Mosaic. You can run services such as FTP and telnet directly from a PC or Mac.

PPP: Similar to SLIP but a much better protocol.

LAN: This is for connecting a local area network to the Internet.

ISDN: High-speed network connections that are offered as dialup access via digital modems.

Leased lines: These cover the 56K through T3 speeds and are dedicated line connections that are high speed and high bandwidth.

Choosing a provider

Contact providers by phone, fax, or electronic mail. If you want to use Netscape and Eudora you will need to get a SLIP or a PPP account. Ask about the following:

- Type of Internet accounts available

- Price and hours of access: Ask how much it will cost per month for a SLIP or PPP account? How many hours of Internet access are included? An average price is $20 per month for 150 hours of graphical access.

- Technical support. Does the provider offer technical support? What are the hours (days, nights, weekends, holidays)? Is support free?

- Software: Do they provide the TCP/IP software? Is the software custom configured? Do they provide free copies of an e-mail program such as Eudora or a Web browser such as Netscape. Good Internet providers will provide custom configured TCP/IP software and the essential Internet navigation and communication software.

> **NOTE**
> If you are using Windows 95 you will need to get information for configuring your Windows 95 TCP/IP software. At the time of this printing you cannot get TCP/IP software custom configured for Windows 95.

Internet connection

Ask the provider how many users they have? What type of line are they using to connect to the Internet. Generally, you will want a provider that has a least a T1 line. Providers that have many thousands of users frequently are busy in the evenings making it impossible to get an Internet connection.

Web sites

Ask if they provide space on their server for you to have a Web page? How much drive space do they provide? What are additional costs associated with having a Web site? Do they offer services to help you design, program, or put up your Web page?

Newsgroups

What newsgroups do they offer. A good Internet provider will offer at least 10,000 newsgroups.

LOCATOR MAP...
Finding HTML Training Documents

Hypertext Markup Language (HTML) is the programming language used to create World Wide Web documents or Web pages. HTML controls how a page appears: its links, buttons, background, icons, forms, graphical presentation of content, and interaction.

HTML is a relatively simple language to learn. Most people can begin to create HTML documents within several hours of training.

Listed below are several World Wide Web sites where you can get HTML tutorials and instructions on using HTML to create a Web page. Everything that you need to learn HTML can be obtained on-line. You will need a basic text editor such as SimpleText to create HTML source code. You can download the source code for Web pages you are viewing by selecting, "Source" from the VIEW menu.

- NCSA's Beginner Guide To HTML
  http://www.ncsa.uiuc.edu/General/Internet/WWW/HTML Primer.html

- Getting Started On The World Wide Web
  http://www.wired.com/Staff/justin/dox/started.html

- HTML Crash Course
  http://www.ziff.com:8002/~eamonn/crash_course.html

- Web Communications Comprehensive Guide To HTML
  http://www.webcom.com/~webcom/html/

- HTML page icons
  http://www.yahoo.com/Computers/World_Wide_Web/ Programming/Icons/

- Daniel's Icon Archive
  http://www.jsc.nasa.gov/~mccoy/Icons/index.html

- Web Developers Virtual Library
  http://www.enterprise.net/stars

LOCATOR MAP...
Finding Listserv Mailing Lists

World Wide Web Site For Finding Mailing Lists

One of the best resources for helping you to find mailing lists is this World Wide Web site

http://www.tile.net/tile/listserv/index.html

Gopher Site For Finding Mailing Lists

Travel to this excellent gopher server and follow the path to information on current mailing lists. You can also do a search for mailing lists by subject.

gopher: **liberty.uc.wlu.edu**
path: Explore Internet Resources/
               Searching for Listservs

URL: gopher://liberty.uc.wlu:70/11/internet/searchlistserv

E-Mail A Request For Listservs On A Topic

To request information on listserv mailing lists on a particular topic send an e-mail message to:

LISTSERV@vm1.nodak.edu

In the message body type: **LIST GLOBAL / *keyword***

Chapter Six

GOPHER, FTP, TELNET

Gopher, FTP, And Telnet

You have learned that Netscape Navigator is a browser that makes it possible to access easily not only World Wide Web sites, but also Usenet newsgroups, and to communicate with electronic mail. In this chapter you will learn how to use Netscape to telnet and to access gopher and FTP servers.

Before You Begin...

Listed below are several points to remember as you begin your travels.

- The addressing information that defines the transfer protocols for accessing, viewing, and downloading information is different for each of these Internet navigational tools.

- When you access this information using Netscape, remember that you are working within the World Wide Web environment. Information and access to files, data, and directories is by use of hyperlinks. Access these informational resources by clicking on the highlighted words.

- Navigate forward and backward using the Netscape navigational tools: buttons and pull-down menus (including the history list).

- You can save bookmarks of your favorite places.

- Files that you download will automatically be saved on your hard drive.

- To travel outside the World Wide Web, just change the URL format.

For example,

| This gopher address: | **cwis.usc.edu** |
| Becomes: | **gopher://cwis.usc.edu/** |

| This FTP address: | **ftp explorer.arc.nasa.gov** |
| Becomes: | **ftp://explorer.arc.nasa.gov** |

Traveling Outside The Web—The URL

URLs are a standard for locating Internet documents. They are an addressing system for all Internet resources such as World Wide Web, gopher menus, FTP file retrieval, Usenet newsgroups, and telnet. Netscape uses the URL text to find a particular item among all the computers connected to the Internet. URLs specify three pieces of information needed to retrieve a document.

The format for a URL is
protocol://server-name/path

- The protocol to be used followed by a colon **http:**
- The server address to connect to is preceded by two slashes
  //home.netscape.com
- The path to the information preceded by only one slash
  /index.html

Sample URLs

World Wide Web URL   http://home.netscape.com/index.html

Document from a
secure Web server: https://netscape.com/
Note the "s" after **http**
to indicate security.

Gopher URL: gopher://umslvma.umsl.edu/Library/

FTP URL: ftp://ftp.netscape.com/pub/

Telnet URL: telnet://geophys.washington.edu/

Usenet URL: news:rec.humor.funny

Secure news server: snews:news.announce.newusers

Gopher—Connecting To Gopher

Gopher is a navigational tool that uses a multi-level menu system to help find information and resources on the Internet. A *client* program is needed to access gopher resources outside of the World Wide Web browser environment. Graphical software programs such as TurboGopher for the Macintosh and Gopher for Windows are most commonly used.

Notice the difference in how gopher resources appear and are accessed via a non-graphical client versus a graphical browser such as Netscape Navigator.

Figure 6.1
Gopher site without a graphical client.

```
┌─────────────────────────────────────────────────────────────┐
│           │Internet Gopher Information Client 2.0 p15│         │
│   I                                                            │
│                        gopher.tc.umn.edu                       │
│                                                                │
│  -->  1.   Information About Gopher/                           │
│       2.   Computer Information/                               │
│       3.   Discussion Groups/                                 │
│       4.   Fun & Games/                                       │
│       5.   Internet file server (ftp) sites/                  │
│       6.   Libraries/                                         │
│       7.   News/                                              │
│       8.   Other Gopher and Information Servers/              │
│       9.   Phone Books/                                       │
│      10.   Search Gopher Titles at the University of Minnesota <?>│
│      11.   Search lots of places at the University of Minnesota  <?>│
│      12.   University of Minnesota Campus Information/         │
│                                                                │
│                                                                │
│                                                                │
│                                                                │
│                                                                │
│ Press ▓ for Help, ▓ to Quit, ▓ to go up a menu    Page: 1/1   │
└─────────────────────────────────────────────────────────────┘
```

Figure 6.2
Gopher site with Netscape.

Gopher Menu

- Information About Gopher
- Computer Information
- Discussion Groups
- Fun & Games
- Internet file server (ftp) sites
- Libraries
- News
- Other Gopher and Information Servers
- Phone Books
- Search Gopher Titles at the University of Minnesota
- Search lots of places at the University of Minnesota
- University of Minnesota Campus Information

Gopher sites lack the rich formatting that you are accustomed to on the Web. Notice the menu is a list of hyperlinks. Each link is preceded by a small icon indicating the type of resource with which the link connects. Gopher links connect with

- menus,
- text files,
- images,
- indexes,
- movie and binary files.

Gopher Addresses
Before you access information at a gopher site, you need to know the gopher address which looks like this
> **gopher.tc.umn.edu** or **cwis.usc.edu**

If you are accessing gopher from an Internet shell account (text-based) or from a graphical client such as TurboGopher or Gopher for Windows, you type in an address such as **cwis.usc.edu**

To use Netscape to access this same site, change the address to
> **gopher://cwis.usc.edu/**

File Transfer Protocol (FTP)

Transferring Files With FTP

The Internet provides access to many different types of information in the form of files and data. Files may contain computer software, text, images, and sound. You will want to transfer some of these files to your computer for your personal use. For example, use Netscape to leave the Web and travel to FTP servers to download the most current versions of software such as Netscape, Eudora, or Helper Applications. Internet files are transferred using a protocol called FTP (File Transfer Protocol).

With Netscape you will be able to browse FTP sites using hyperlinks. Click on a link to view and download files. To visit the FTP site for Project Gutenberg type this URL in Netscape's **Open Location** field
ftp://uiarchive.cso.uiuc.edu

Figure 6.3
Netscape link to an FTP site.

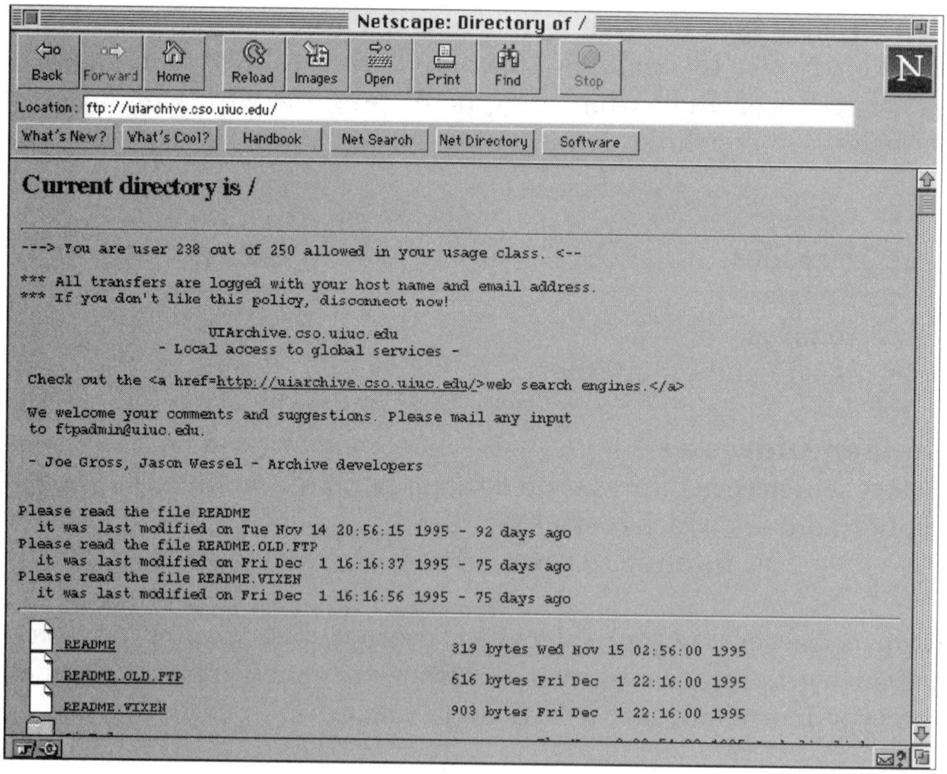

Notice that the FTP directory and content pages have minimal formatting. When possible, Netscape shows the type, size, date, and a short description of each file in a directory. The directory is presented as a list of links, each link preceded by a small icon indicating whether the link is a directory or a file. Clicking on a directory link brings you to another subdirectory.

Scroll down the list and notice the "README." files. These are text files with information about the FTP server. To read any of these text files, click once on the file's underlined name.

Figure 6.4
Hyperlinks to FTP resources using the Netscape browser.

README	319 bytes	Wed Nov 15 02:56:00 1995	
README.OLD.FTP	616 bytes	Fri Dec 1 22:16:00 1995	
README.VIXEN	903 bytes	Fri Dec 1 22:16:00 1995	
SimTel		Thu Nov 2 20:54:00 1995	symbolic link
bin/		Tue Jun 6 00:00:00 1995	Directory
du.out	1573 Kb	Tue Feb 13 18:45:00 1996	
etc/		Tue Jun 6 00:00:00 1995	Directory
index.html		Sun Oct 15 16:25:00 1995	Symbolic link
licensed/		Sun Dec 31 18:37:00 1995	Directory
local/		Thu Nov 23 02:11:00 1995	Directory
ls-lR.Z	3606 Kb	Tue Feb 13 18:23:00 1996	
pub/		Tue Feb 13 15:25:00 1996	Directory
usage.stats/		Fri Feb 2 20:18:00 1996	Directory
usr/		Tue Jun 6 00:00:00 1995	Directory

The icons that look like folders have an underlined name next to them followed by a slash (/). This indicates a link to a subdirectory. Follow this pathway to Project Gutenberg **/pub/etext/gutenberg** where each segment pub, etext, and gutenberg are displayed.

> **NOTE**
> One disadvantage of using a Web browser to access FTP sites is that the browser automatically logs you in as anonymous and uses your e-mail address as your password. Most FTP sites use this login for unregistered visitors. However, some FTP sites may require different login information. Consequently, you will need to use FTP software. Visit the software sites in the Expedition Experience to obtain free copies.

Figure 6.5
FTP directory for Project Gutenberg.

Current directory is /pub/etext/gutenberg

```
---> You are user 246 out of 250 allowed in your usage class. <--

*** All transfers are logged with your host name and email address.
*** If you don't like this policy, disconnect now!

                      UIArchive.cso.uiuc.edu
                - Local access to global services -

Check out the <a href=http://uiarchive.cso.uiuc.edu/>web search engines.</a>

We welcome your comments and suggestions. Please mail any input
to ftpadmin@uiuc.edu.

- Joe Gross, Jason Wessel - Archive developers


Please read the file README
  it was last modified on Tue Nov 14 20:56:15 1995 - 92 days ago
Please read the file README.OLD.FTP
  it was last modified on Fri Dec  1 16:16:37 1995 - 75 days ago
Please read the file README.VIXEN
  it was last modified on Fri Dec  1 16:16:56 1995 - 75 days ago

Up to higher level directory
```

.dir3_0.wmd	191 bytes	Sun Mar 20 00:00:00 1994
.hidden	11 bytes	Sun Mar 20 00:00:00 1994
0INDEX.GUT	44 Kb	Mon Oct 16 09:00:00 1995
INDEX100.GUT	9 Kb	Sun Aug 27 17:44:00 1995
INDEX200.GUT	7 Kb	Sun Jan 7 16:20:00 1996

Notice the hyperlinks that access text files, software, images, and other subdirectories. Here is an example of a text file that you can download from Project Gutenberg.

Figure 6.6
FTP text file.

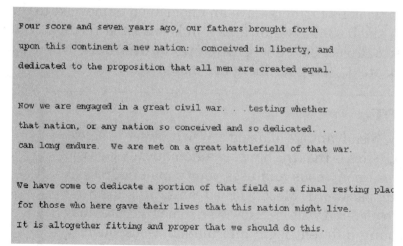

```
Four score and seven years ago, our fathers brought forth

upon this continent a new nation:  conceived in liberty, and

dedicated to the proposition that all men are created equal.


Now we are engaged in a great civil war. . .testing whether

that nation, or any nation so conceived and so dedicated. . .

can long endure.  We are met on a great battlefield of that war.


We have come to dedicate a portion of that field as a final resting plac

for those who here gave their lives that this nation might live.

It is altogether fitting and proper that we should do this.
```

Files And Programs For Downloading

Many large files and programs for downloading will be compressed and will have an extension added to the file name. The extension indicates the way the file was compressed and what helper application you will need to look at the file. If the name ends in **sit**, it is a compressed Macintosh file that will automatically decompress by clicking on the file after it has been downloaded to your hard drive.

This is an example of a file with a **sit** extension at the NASA site.

DiveLogStack.O.sit

To download a copy of a binary file (programs, images, sounds, and movies) click on the file or program. Netscape will then download a copy to your hard drive and look for the necessary helper application to launch the program.

Netscape also provides the option to upload a file to an FTP server. Upload files to the server by dragging and dropping from your desktop to the Netscape browser. You can also choose **Upload File** from the **File** menu.

To download a text file, follow these steps.

1. Open the file.
2. Click on Netscape's **File** menu. Select **Save As**.
3. Enter the location in which you want to save the file.
4. Select **text** under the **Forma**t option.
5. Click the **Save** button.

Telnet

Telnet is one of the oldest Internet tools that allows users to log on to another computer and run resident programs. Although telnet is not as visually interesting as the World Wide Web, it is essential to Internet travel. Telnet is a text-based environment requiring commands to navigate. Some telnet access sites automatically link you to Web pages. Many telnet sites, such as libraries, allow anyone to login without having a special account. Others, require users to have a valid account before accessing many of the resident programs. Basic instructions for using telnet can be found at these Web sites: **http://www.w3.org/ hypertext/WWW/FAQ/Bootstrap.html** or **http://www.web.com. com/~futures/telnet.html**

There are things you cannot do on the Web that telnet can do better. For example, when you telnet to a remote computer, frequently a mainframe supercomputer, you are working on another machine and are using that machine's speed and power. College students and business travelers dial a local Internet service provider and then telnet to their college or business accounts to get their e-mail. Telnet saves them the cost of a long distance phone call.

Telnet also provides direct access to Internet services not always available from your Internet provider. Many of these services are exciting and interesting. Some open doors to alternative learning environments.

Some of the Internet services available using telnet include

- databases (such as earthquake, weather, special collections)
- libraries (public, academic, medical, legal, and more)
- Free-Nets (noncommercial, community-based networks)
- interactive chats
- MOOs, MUDs, and
- bulletin boards.

Databases

Many of the databases that you access with telnet have the latest information on many topics like severe storms and weather conditions. Others, such as the Library of Congress, have archive collections.

Libraries

Telnet makes it possible to access libraries all around the world. Each library will vary on how much on-line help they make available to you.

Free-Nets

Free-nets provide networking services to a local community. Access to free-nets is achieved either at public libraries or by dialing in. To connect to a free-net, you will need to telnet.

Free-nets establish their own resources for users in their community and are usually designed around a model of an electronic town. For example, you may be able to discuss local issues with the mayor or stop at an electronic school to discuss educational issues. These local networks usually have bulletin boards, electronic mail, informational resources, and educational resources. Educational resources may have local projects for classrooms or may provide information on national or international projects. Free-nets also provide links to global educational resources. They help to make finding and using Internet resources more manageable for educators who frequently do not have the time to explore cyberspace for classroom resources.

You may use a free-net as a guest, but your access privileges may be limited. You will have to register to have full access privileges. Registration is free to people within the community. For those outside the community, there is usually a nominal registration fee. Today, there are more than 30 free-nets on-line in cities across the United States and Canada. You can also find a few in Europe and New Zealand.

Chats

Chats are programs that allow you to talk to many people at the same time from all over the world. Internet Relay Chat (IRC) is the most widely used program. Many Internet access providers make IRC available to new subscribers. Some World Wide Web sites will have chat rooms for interactive discussion of topics of interest. For example, Time Warner's Pathfinder Web site has a chat room for discussing news of the day. Wired magazine has a chat room open for discussion.

NASA has chat rooms for teachers and classrooms participating in on-line learning adventures.

MOO (Multi-User Shell, Object Oriented) & ***MUD*** (Multi-User Domain) MOOs and MUDs put visitors into a virtual space where they are able to navigate, communicate, and build virtual environments by using computer commands. Each of these environments uses a different type of software, but they are very similar in that users telnet to a remote computer to create, communicate, and navigate in a text-based environment. Some MOOs and MUDs offer alternative learning environments such as Diversity University; others, fantasy role-playing games. New identities are created and experimented with. A popular Internet cartoon captures the essence of these virtual worlds and of the Internet when it shows one dog at a computer stating, "On the Internet, no one knows that you're a dog."

MOOs are very similar to MUDs, but use a more sophisticated programming language than MUD. A MOO lets users build things in a simulated environment by creating objects that are linked to a parent object. A vast number of creations originating from this parent object can exit. MUDs and MOOs are interactive systems suited to the construction of text-based adventure games and conferencing systems. The most common use, however, is multi-participant, virtual reality adventure games with players from all over the world.

Bulletin Boards
Usenet newsgroups are examples of bulletin boards (BBS). BBSs are places where people with similar interests can exchange information and share their thoughts with others without being logged on at the same time. Additionally, users can upload and download files and make announcements.

Telnet Software
Netscape and most browsers do not support telnet. However, you can use Netscape to telnet if you have a telnet application program (a *client*) and tell Netscape where the program is located on your computer. When you type in a telnet address, Netscape launches the application. When you are connected to the telnet site, you will be in a text-based environment. There will not be hyperlinks for navigation. You will using computer commands.

NOTE

Telnet programs are usually included with your TCP/IP software from your Internet provider. If you do not have a telnet client program visit one of the Web software sites listed in the Expedition Experience in Chapter 4.

Configuring Netscape For Telnet

1. To find your telnet client, open the Netscape application.

2. Go to the **Options** menu and select **General Preferences.**

3. Go to the **Applications** panel.

Figure 6.7
Netscape **Applications** panel.

```
═══════════════ Preferences: General ═══════════════
┌──────────┬────────┬───────┬─────────┬────────┤ Applications ├────────────┐
│ Appearance │ Colors │ Fonts │ Helpers │ Images │            │ Languages │

  ┌─Supporting Applications────────────────────────────────────────────────┐
  │   Telnet Application :  Macintosh HD :APPLICAT...t2.6 :NCSA Telnet 2.6   [ Browse ]
  │   TN3270 Application :                                                   [ Browse ]
  │        View Source :  Macintosh H...:SimpleText    [ Browse ]  ☐ Use Netscape
  └────────────────────────────────────────────────────────────────────────┘

     Temporary Directory :  Macintosh HD :System Folder                     [ Browse ]




                                      [ Cancel ] [ Apply ] [ OK ]
```

4.. Click on the **Browse** button to find your telnet client.

Figure 6.8
The Browse dialog box.

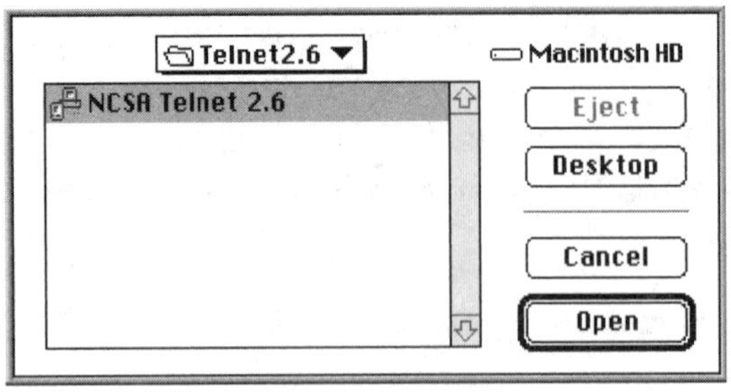

Netscape will now be able to launch the telnet client program when you enter a telnet URL.

GUIDED TOUR... Traveling To A Telnet Site

To visit a telnet site using Netscape, type in the URL information. The format will be

telnet://address

We will now visit a telnet site.

1. Type in this URL for the Smithsonian
   telnet://siris.si.edu/

Figure 6.9
Smithsonian Welcome screen.

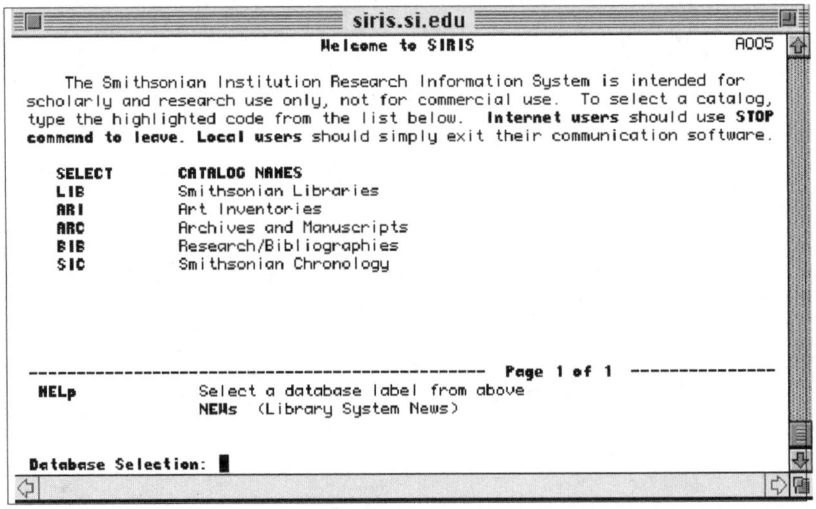

2. We will select the Art Inventories Catalog and type in the code **ARI** next to Database Selection.

Notice that you no longer have hyperlinks for navigation. Read all the information to find the command you must use for navigating at the site. This screen informs visitors to select the Smithsonian archive that they would like to visit.

Figure 6.10
Art Inventories Catalog, Smithsonian.

```
              WELCOME TO THE ART INVENTORIES CATALOG
The database, maintained by the National Museum of American Art, contains over
300,000 records describing American paintings and sculpture.  This information
is compiled from reports supplied by museums, historical societies, special
survey projects, public art programs, published catalogs, and private
collectors.  Reports are recorded as given and are not certified as accurate
or complete.  Inclusion of a painting or sculpture in the database does not
imply a recommendation of its aesthetic merit, historic significance, or
authenticity.
Copyright 1994 Smithsonian Institution.  Data may be used solely for non-
commercial study or research purposes.  Commercial use of information obtained
through the Inventories is prohibited without the express written consent of
the Smithsonian Institution.
For more information on the Art Inventories, press ENTER .
Type CHOOSE  to switch to other catalogs on SIRIS.
----------------------------------------------- + Page 1 of 4 -------------
STArt over         Enter search command                <F8>  FORward page
                   NEWs


NEXT COMMAND: █
```

3. Read the Welcome screen for information on what command to enter to continue your exploration. In this case, we press the ENTER key.

Figure 6.11
The Art Inventories Catalog.

```
                                                      ART INVENTORIES
                                                        Introduction
-------------------------------------------------------------------------
                   THE ART INVENTORIES CATALOG
The Art Inventories database contains over 300,000 records from two ongoing
projects -- The Inventory of American Paintings Executed before 1914 and
the Inventory of American Sculpture.   You may limit your search to a
specific Inventory, or search both Inventories together.

To choose one of the inventory catalogs, type SET CAT .
To search both inventory catalogs together, use a command from list below.
             COMMAND:        TO SEARCH BY:
                 A=          Artist
                 T=          Title
                 S=          Subject
                 K=          Keyword
                 C=          Record number
For more information on searching commands, press ENTER.
----------------------------------------------- + Page 2 of 4 -------------
STArt over         Enter search command          <F8>  FORward page
                   NEWs                          <F7>  BACK page
```

4. We will search for information on Native Americans. The screen indicates to type in the command **K=name of keyword**. In this case we type *K=native americans.*

Figure 6.12
The result searching for native americans.

```
Search Request: K=NATIVE AMERICANS                    ART INVENTORIES
Search Results: 23 Entries Found                        Keyword Index
-----------------------------------------------------------------------
        DATE  TITLE:                                   AUTHOR:
    1   1993  Touching Souls <3-dimen>                 Kaufman, Mico
    2   1992  Intersect <3-dimen>                      Canneto, Stephen
    3   1992  River Scenes at the Tennessee Aq <3-dimen>  Nivola, Claire
    4   1989  Buffalo Dance <3-dimen>                  Goodacre, Glenna
    5   1988  Maui Pohaku Loa <3-dimen>                Toth, Peter
    6   1987  Prelude <3-dimen>                        Cunningham, Robert
    7   1985  The Immigrants <3-dimen>                 Hopen, W. D
    8   1985  The Future <3-dimen>                     Houser, Allan
    9   1982  Bodark Ark <3-dimen>                     Puryear, Martin
   10   1981  Trail of Tears <3-dimen>                 Toth, Peter
   11   1976  Native American <3-dimen>                Toth, Peter
   12   1973  Cherokee Chieftain <3-dimen>             Toth, Peter
   13   1957  Ten O'Clock Line Monument <3-dimen>      Hollis, Frederick L
   14   1935  Hoover Dam Elevator Tower Relief <3-dimen>  Hansen, Oskar J. W
-----------------------------------------------------------------------
                                         CONTINUED on next page  ----
STArt over          Type number to display record       <F8>  FORward page
HELp                MARk
OTHer options

NEXT COMMAND: █
```

5. To find information on the first title, type the number 1.

Figure 6.13
Information on Touching Souls.

```
Search Request: K=NATIVE AMERICANS                    ART INVENTORIES
ARTWORK -Record 1 of 23 Entries Found                     Brief View
-----------------------------------------------------------------------
ARTIST:      Kaufman, Mico, 1924-       , sculptor.
TITLE:       Touching Souls, (sculpture).
DATE:        Dedicated June 13, 1993.
MEDIUM:      Sculpture: bronze; Base: concrete.
DIMEN:       Sculpture: approx. H. 27 in. x W. 8 ft. 3 in.; Base: ranges
                from: H. 7 1/2 in. to H. 3 in. x Diam. 9 ft. 9 in.
OWNER (outdoor site):
             Tewksbury United Methodist Church, South Street, Tewksbury,
                Massachusetts 01876
-----------------------------------------------------------------------
FILE:               RECORD NUMBERS:          CATALOGED
Sculpture Inventory MA000015                 Circ. info not available
(Non-Circulating)


-----------------------------------------  Page 1 of 1  ---------------
STArt over          LONg view               <F6>  NEXt record
HELp                INDex
OTHer options       MARk

NEXT COMMAND: █
```

Notice you can type *LONG* for a longer descriptive passage.

GUIDED WALKS

Using Netscape For Gopher, FTP, And Telnet

GUIDED WALK 1
Connecting To Gopher

In this Guided Walk you will use Netscape to connect to a gopher server.

1. Use one of these three Netscape locations to enter URLs.

    *   The **Location** field
    *   Under the **File** menu, select **Open Location**
    *   The **Open** dialog box

2. Type in **gopher:cwis.usc.edu/**

Figure 6.14
The gopher server menu.

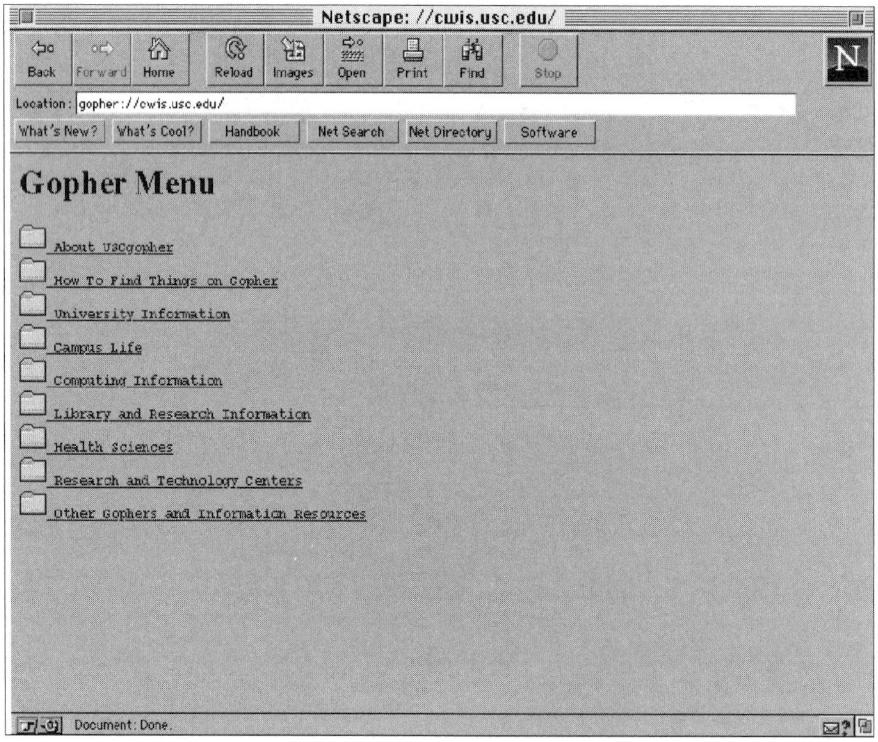

Notice the hyperlinks.

3. Click on **Other Gopher and Information Resources**.

Figure 6.15
The Other Gopher and Information Resources menu.

Gopher Menu

📁 GOPHER JEWELS Information and Help

📁 Community, Global and Environmental

📁 Education, Social Sciences, Arts & Humanities

📁 Economics, Business and Store Fronts

📁 Engineering and Industrial Applications

📁 Government

📁 Health, Medical, and Disability

📁 Internet and Computer Related Resources

📁 Law

📁 Library, Reference, and News

📁 Miscellaneous Items

📁 Natural Sciences including Mathematics

📁 Personal Development and Recreation

📁 Research, Technology Transfer and Grants Opportunities

Click on Gopher Jewels and EXPLORE.

For more gopher expeditions, see the Expedition Experience in this chapter.

GUIDED WALK 2
Transferring Files—FTP

In this Guided Walk you will use Netscape to visit a FTP site. Download any files that interest you.

1. Use one of these places to type-in the FTP information.

    *   The **Location** field
    *   Under the **File** menu, select **Open Location**
    *   The **Open** dialog box

2. Type in this URL **ftp://mrcnext.cso.uiuc.edu/**

Figure 6.16
The FTP screen.

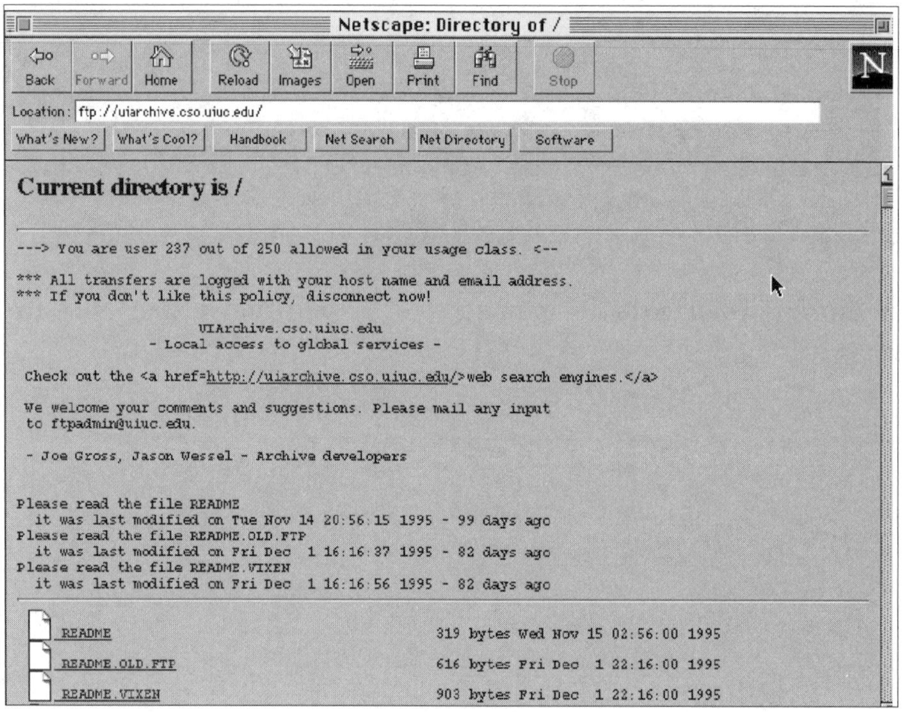

This screen has general information about this FTP site. The icons that look like folders and have underlined names next to them followed by slashes (/) indicate links to other subdirectories.

3. Scroll down and click on the directory **pub**/.

Figure 6.17
The /**pub** directory.

Current directory is /pub

Main directory tree:

X11   - The X-Windowing System
com   - mirrors of selected commercial sites
doc   - documents - rtfm, rfc's, etc.
etext   - electronic texts including project gutenberg
games   - nethack
gnu   - the GNU project
infosystems - www (mosaic and netscape), gopher
lang   - languages - perl (CPAN), python, tcl, smalltalk, elisp, java
math   - Math items - uiuc archives
packages   - mail, news, shells, etc..
security   - cert, coast, and wordlists
systems   - FreeBSD, linux, mac, pc, os2

check out the <a href=http://uiarchive.cso.uiuc.edu/>web search engines.</a>

Up to higher level directory

     .message   632 bytes Tue Feb 13 15:18:00 1996

     x11/   Thu Feb 1 15:31:00 1996 Directory

     com/   Sun Feb 18 10:57:00 1996 Directory

     doc/   Tue Nov 28 21:46:00 1995 Directory

     etext/   Fri Jun 30 00:00:00 1995 Directory

     games/   Fri Jan 12 06:17:00 1996 Directory

4. Next, select **etext**.

Figure 6.18
The /**pub**/**etext** directory.

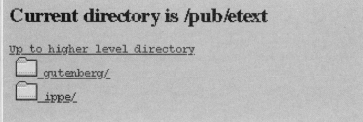

Current directory is /pub/etext

Up to higher level directory

     gutenberg/

     ippe/

5. Select **gutenberg.**

Figure 6.19
The gutenberg directory.

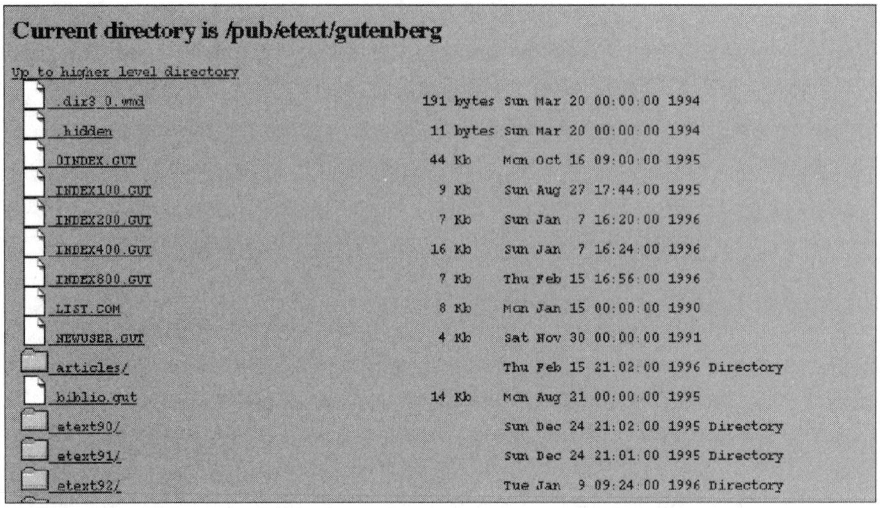

Current directory is /pub/etext/gutenberg

Up to higher level directory

.dir3_0.wmd	191 bytes	Sun Mar 20 00:00:00 1994
.hidden	11 bytes	Sun Mar 20 00:00:00 1994
0INDEX.GUT	44 Kb	Mon Oct 16 09:00:00 1995
INDEX100.GUT	9 Kb	Sun Aug 27 17:44:00 1995
INDEX200.GUT	7 Kb	Sun Jan 7 16:20:00 1996
INDEX400.GUT	16 Kb	Sun Jan 7 16:24:00 1996
INDEX800.GUT	7 Kb	Thu Feb 15 16:56:00 1996
LIST.COM	8 Kb	Mon Jan 15 00:00:00 1990
NEWUSER.GUT	4 Kb	Sat Nov 30 00:00:00 1991
articles/		Thu Feb 15 21:02:00 1996 Directory
biblio.gut	14 Kb	Mon Aug 21 00:00:00 1995
etext90/		Sun Dec 24 21:02:00 1995 Directory
etext91/		Sun Dec 24 21:01:00 1995 Directory
etext92/		Tue Jan 9 09:24:00 1996 Directory

6. To learn more about gutenberg, select **NEWUSER.GUT**.

7. Explore this FTP site. Practice downloading files. Download files by clicking once on the file that you wish to download to your hard drive.

Refer to Chapter 4 for additional information on compression and downloading multimedia files. For more FTP sites see the FTP Expedition in this chapter.

GUIDED WALK 3
Using Netscape To Telnet

In Guided Walks 3-7 you will use Netscape to telnet to the Smithsonian Institute, Free-Nets, a MOO called Diversity University, Bulletin Boards, and on-line, real-time chats.

In Guided Walk 3 you will telnet to the Smithsonian and explore the archived catalogs.

1. Use one of these places to type the telnet address.

    - The **Location** field
    - Under the **File** menu, select **Open Location**
    - The **Open** dialog box

> **NOTE**
>
> If you get a message that Netscape cannot find the telnet client program, refer to the telnet section in this chapter for information on how to configure Netscape to use telnet. If you do not have a telnet client program on your computer, visit one of the software sites listed Chapter 4 for a site to download a free copy.

2. Type in **telnet://siris.si.edu/**

Refer to the telnet section in this chapter for help in exploring and finding your way around this site.

> **NOTE**
>
> READ ALL THE INFORMATION CAREFULLY. Many of these telnet resources will provide you with all the information that you need to navigate and search for information.

3. Visit and explore the Smithsonian Libraries, Art Inventories, Archives and Manuscripts, Research/Bibliographies, or the Smithsonian Chronology.

GUIDED WALK 4
Visiting Free-Nets

As you travel Web sites you will find hyperlinks that connect you to telnet sites. In this Guided Walk you will first visit telnet sites from Web links. Then you will telnet directly to remote computers.

1. Use one of these places to type the FTP information.

    *   The **Location** field
    *   Under the **File** menu, select **Open Location**
    *   The **Open** dialog box

2. Type in this World Wide Web site URL for the International Free-Net/Community Net Listing.

    http://www.uwec.edu/info/freenets.html

3. Scroll down the page to Guest Access then to United States. Select the Free-Net in Arizona AzTeC.

4. Login as: **guest**
    Password: **visitor**

5. Read the screens and follow the commands for navigation.

6. Explore this Free-Net.

Notice that many of the resources are not available until you have become a registered user.

7. Next, explore one of these excellent Free-Nets: LA Free-Net, Big Sky Telegraph, or the Cleveland Free-Net. Follow the login instructions. Read screens for navigation directions.

Other Internet resources for Free-Nets:

gopher://info.asu.edu:70/11/other/freenets

http://freenet.victoria.bc.ca/freenets.html

8. Explore these excellent Free-Nets by using Netscape to telnet.

Big Sky Telegraph

To connect to Big Sky Telegraph,

1.	**telnet**	**bigsky.bigsky.dillon.mt.us**
2.	login:	**bbs**
3.	user ID:	*\<your e-mail address\>*

Cleveland Free-Net

This free-net is a very comprehensive and user-friendly telnet site. It contains an enormous number of historical documents and information related to the arts, sciences, medicine, education, and business. Although this free-net is an excellent resource for new Internet travelers, it is frequently very busy and difficult to connect with.

To connect to the Cleveland Free-Net,

1.	**telnet**	**freenet-in-a.cwru.edu**
2.	login:	**guest**
3.	user ID:	*\<your e-mail address\>*

LA Free-Net

This free-net has some good educational areas to explore. You will need to pay a $10 registration fee. Register on-line or by mail.

To connect to the LA free-net,

1.	**telnet**	**lafn.org**
2.	login:	**visitor**
3.	user ID:	*\<your e-mail address\>*

GUIDED WALK 5

Diversity University... A MOO Experience

In this Guided Walk you will visit Diversity University, a MOO-based cyberspace platform for experimentation with new and innovative approaches to learning. Diversity University is populated by educators and students from all over the world. Visit the virtual campus to learn more about this alternative learning environment.

1. Learn how to communicate, navigate, and create your identity in the MOO environment. For general information on Diversity University, Diversity commands, how to connect, or project descriptions, visit
   http://www.academic.marist.edu/duwww.htm

2. When you have a basic understanding on how to navigate, connect to Diversity University telnet to **moo.du.org:8888**

3. After reading the introductory material, type **connect guest.** The opening screens take you on a guided tour using some of the most common MOO commands. Use the Diversity MOO Commands to look around, speak to people, and move through the environment. If you have difficulty, type **help** at any time.

EXPLORE...ENJOY... Participate in this alternative learning environment and meet people from all over the world.

OTHER MOOs
To explore and learn about other MOOs visit these Web sites,
http://www.butterfly.net/~pyro/moo_page.html
http://www.bushnet.qld.edu.au/~jay/moo/
http://www.io.com/~combs/htmls/moo.html

One of the earliest and most popular MOOs is Lambda MOO. Stop by for a visit.
telnet://lambda.parc.xerox.com:8888/

MORE MOOs and MUDs
If you are interested in learning more about MOOs and MUDs use several search engines to research these multi-user simulated environments.

GUIDED WALK 6

Exploring Bulletin Boards

The best way to learn about Bulletin Boards (BBS) on the Internet is
to visit several Web sites that have links to BBSs.

1. Use one of these places to type the a Web address.

    - The **Location** field
    - Under the **File** menu, select **Open Location**
    - The **Open** dialog box

2. Type this URL for the BBS Showcase:
    http://www.versanet.com/bbsshow/part.html

    Explore this site and learn more about bulletin boards. Visit some
    of the bulletin board links at this site.

3. Visit this Web site for links to BBS sites on the Internet:
    http://www.augsburg.edu/~schwartz/ebbs.html

4. Visit this Web page for a Guide To BBS On The Internet.
    http://dkeep.com/sbi.htm

GUIDED WALK 7

Visiting Internet Coffee Houses...the CHAT

As you travel the Web, you will find that more and more sites provide opportunities to interact with others via on-line, real-time chats. Two excellent Web sites for on-line chats are Time Warner's Pathfinder and Wired magazine.

1. Use one of these places to type-in the URL for Pathfinder.

   - The **Location** field
   - Under the **File** menu, select **Open Location**
   - The **Open** dialog box

2. Type in this URL
   http://pathfinder.com/

   When you connect to Pathfinder, look for the **Chat** link.

3. Wired magazine **http://www.hotwired.com** has become one of the hottest magazines in America. It has won more than a dozen honors including a National Magazine Award. Their popular World Wide Web site, HotWired, is an experimental, esoteric form of journalism. Visit their site to experience state-of-the-art creative expression. Wired is one of the leaders in one of the fastest growing cultural movements—the digital revolution. You may need to register before you can chat and interact in Club Wired. There is no fee for registration and participation.

   You can also telnet directly to Club Wired using
   chat.hotwired.com.port 2428

   a. After you connect to HotWired, go to the **Piazza**.
   b. Next, go to **Club Wired**. Here you will find the on-line chat.
   c. Visit the **Toolkit** for Internet software including the telnet client program.

EXPEDITION EXPERIENCE

Gopher, FTP, Telnet

Exploring Gopher

Best Collection Of PC & MAC Software

The Pipeline site has one of the best collections of PC and Mac software.

gopher://gopher.pipeline.com/
directory: The Best Collections of PC and Mac Software

Civics And Government Archive

This site is maintained by Internet Wiretap and contains many excellent documents and resources. Many have been taken from different places; many are controversial. You will also find information on copyright, bills before Congress, historical documents, speeches and addresses, reports, treaties, NATO, and miscellaneous world documents.

gopher://wiretap.spies.com/
path: Government Docs/United Nations Resolutions

Department of Energy (DOE) Headquarters

This gopher server has general information on the DOE as well as links to other DOE and government gophers.

gopher://vm1.hqadmin.doe.gov/

Earthquake Data

This site contains information on past and recent earthquakes around the world.

gopher://gopher.stolaf.edu:70/
path: Internet Resources/Weather & Geography

Gardening Gophers

Whether you are interested in composting, alternatives to fertilizers and pesticides, or just love plants, you will want to check out these two excellent gopher sites.

gopher://gopher.nalusda.gov/

gopher://bluehen.ags.udel.edu/

Mother Gophers

Connect to the original gopher at the University of Minnesota. Here you will find links to computer information, discussion groups, fun and games, FTP sites, libraries, news, phone books, and other gopher and information servers.

gopher://gopher.micro.umn.edu:70/1
or
gopher://gopher.tc.umn.edu/

This excellent gopher site links you to other gopher resources, libraries and information access, and links to help you explore and find Internet resources.

gopher://liberty.uc.wlu.edu/

MUDs & MOOs

Use these gophers to access MUDs and MOOs. Select the MUD you wish to play in.

gopher://solaris.rz.tu-clausthal.de/
path: Student-Gopher/Liste derMUD-SERVER

or, **gopher://gopher.micro.umn.edu/**
path: Fun & Games/Games/MUDs

Pipeline

Pipeline is an Internet gateway in New York. Gopher links at this site include: resources for helping you to explore the Internet, on-line libraries, weather links, virtual shopping malls, arts and leisure resources, Smithsonian photos, and much more.

gopher://gopher.pipeline.com/

People of Color Environmental Groups Directory

This gopher server provides links to environmental groups such as Human Rights, PeaceNet-Peace, Social Justice, ConflictNet-Conflict Resolution, EcoNet-Environment, GlobalCommunications and more.

gopher://gopher.igc.apc.org:70/11/

Smithsonian Photos

A photographic collection can be found at this Smithsonian site.

gopher://gopher.pipeline.com/
path: Arts & Leisure/Smithsonian Photographs & Viewing Software

Subject Index

This directory is maintained by Rice University and contains links to Internet resources by subject matter.

gopher://riceinfo.rice.edu:70/11/Subject/

United Nations

To learn more about the United Nations, visit this gopher server.

gopher://gopher.un.org/

Virtual Space

Visit this site for information about MUDs and MOOs.

gopher://gopher.pipeline.com/
path: Arts and Leisure/Virtual Spaces (MUDs)

Weather

Some of the best links to weather information can be found at this Pipeline site including weather for all cities, ski reports, latest surface radar maps, access to computer model forecasts, and information on very bad weather.

gopher://gopher.pipeline.com/
path: Weather Everywhere

Yanoff's List

Scott Yanoff maintains a list of useful and interesting sites on the Net, sorted by subject.

gopher://gopher.uwm.edu/
path: Remote Information Services/Special Internet Connections

Exploring FTP

This section provides address information for FTP sites. The pathway to the resource is listed separately, but can be included in the site address. For example this address and path,

ftp://ftp.virginia.edu
path: pub/FTP.sites

becomes:

ftp://ftp.virginia.edu/pub/FTP.sites

You can either use the above address with the pathway included; or, if you have trouble accessing the resource directory when including the path in your address, first connect to the FTP site, then move to each directory individually.

NOTE
About Accessing FTP Sites

FTP sites allow a limited number of users to access file directories at one time. Some sites allow ten users at a time, others several hundred. It is frequently difficult to connect to an FTP site, and you may get a message that your connection is refused. If so, try again at a later time.

The best time to access the more popular sites is early in the morning, especially on a weekend. Sites in other countries on a different time zone

Berkeley Archive

Visit this site to find many interesting documents: Shakespeare, poetry, song lyrics, and much more.

ftp://ftp.ocf.berkeley.edu/
path: pub/library

Eudora Software

The current versions of the Eudora freeware for the Macintosh and Windows are available via ftp. To obtain freeware via ftp, login in to:

ftp://ftp.qualcom.com/

Login as *anonymous* and retrieve the application file from the **/quest/mac/eduora/** or **/quest/windows/eudora** directory.

FTP Primer

If you are interested in learning more about File Transfer Protocol, connect to this site for a document entitled *FTP Primer* that contains step-by-step instructions on how to FTP.

ftp://ftp.lightside.com/lightside/FTP_Primer/

FTP Sites

Travel to these sites and find a list of all the FTP sites on the Internet.

ftp://ftp.virginia.edu/pub/FTP.sites
or
ftp://ftp.virginia.edu/
path: pub/FTP.sites

ftp://rtfm.mit.edu/
path: pub/usenet/news.answers/ftp-list

History Archive

This site at Mississippi State contains historical documents and links to other historical databases.

ftp://msstate.edu/
path: pub/docs/history

Internet Phone

Internet Phone software allows you to make phone calls anywhere in the world for no charge by using your computer microphone and modem. The only charge is the cost of your monthly Internet account.

ftp://ftp.vocaltec.com/pub/iphone08.exe

Internet Relay Chat (IRC)

Visit this site to obtains the software needed for accessing IRC, a mult-user, multi-channel, chatting network.

ftp://cs-ftp.bu.edu/irc

MIT Media Lab

Visit the MIT Media Lab server to read papers and programs written by members of the MIT Media Lab.

ftp://cecelia.media.mit.edu/

Newsgroup List

This site has an updated listing of the currently active newsgroups.

ftp://rtfm.mit.edu/
path: pub/usenet/news.announce.newsgroups

Project Gutenberg

Project Gutenberg makes electronic books available. Visit this site to select your book.

ftp://mrcnext.cso.uiuc.edu/
path: pub/etext

NASA

Visit the Goddard Space Flight Center's FTP archive site. Here you will find great images of bodies in space and much more.

ftp://dftnic.gsfc.nasa.gov/
path: images/gifs/

Netscape Communication Corporation

For Netscape resources and links to the newest Netscape software, visit this site:

ftp://ftp.netscape.com/

For anonymous login for Netscape software use ftp2-ftp8. For example, **ftp://ftp2.netscape.com**

Software Archives

This site at Stanford makes personal computer software available.

ftp://sumex-aim.Stanford.edu/

Washington University has a large collection of freeware and shareware.

ftp://wuarchive.wustl.edu/

Weather Satellite Images

This site contains weather satellite images from all parts of the globe.

ftp://wuarchive.wustl.edu/
path: multimedia/images/wx

Exploring Telnet

Copyright Law

The Library of Congress Information Service lets you search current and past legislation (dating to 1982).

telnet://locis.loc.gov
Password: none needed

Current Events

Every year, the CIA publishes a Fact Book that is essentially an almanac of all the world's countries and international organizations, including such information as major products, type of government, and names of its leaders. It's available for searching through the University of Maryland Info Database.

telnet:// info.umd.edu

Environment

The U.S. Environmental Protection Agency maintains on-line databases of materials related to hazardous waste, the Clean Lakes program and cleanup efforts in New England. The agency plans eventually to include cleanup work in other regions, as well. The database is actually a computerized card catalog of EPA documents. You can look the documents up, but you'll still have to visit your regional EPA office to see them.

telnet:// epaibm.rtpnc.epa.gov
No password or user name is needed.

At the main menu, type: **public**

Fed World

Each year, the U.S. Federal Government spends more than $70 billion on scientific and technical research. The National Technical Information Service (NTIS) is tasked by Congress to help disseminate the vast amount of scientific and technical information along with other, nontechnical information. As a central point of connectivity, NTIS FedWorld offers access to thousands of files across a wide range of subject areas. You can find information from Environmental Protection to Small Business.

telnet:// fedworld.gov,
ftp://ftp.fedworld/
http://www.fedworld.gov/

Geography

The University of Michigan Geographic Name Server can provide basic information such as population, and the latitude and longitude of U.S. cities and many mountains, rivers, and other geographic features. No password or user name is needed. Type in the name of a city, a zip code, or a geographic feature and hit enter.

telnet:// martini.eecs.umich.edu 3000

Health

The U.S. Food and Drug Administration runs a database of health-information. You will be asked for your name and a password you want to use in the future. After that, type: **topics**

telnet:// fdabbs.fda.gov
Log in: **bbs**

Library of Congress

telnet://locis.loc.gov

Ski Conditions

telnet://wind.atmos.uah.edu:3000

Space

NASA Spacelink in Huntsville, Ala., provides all sorts of reports and data about NASA, its history and its various missions, past and present. You will find detailed reports on every single probe, satellite, and mission NASA has ever launched along with daily updates and lesson plans for teachers. When you connect, you'll be given an overview of the system and asked to register and choose a password.

telnet://spacelink.msfc.nasa.gov

The system maintains a large file library of GIF-format space graphics, but you cannot download these through telnet.

The NED-NASA/IPAC Extragalactic Database lists data on more than 100,000 galaxies, quasars, and other objects outside the Milky Way.

telnet:// ipac.caltech.edu/
Login: **ned**

Smithsonian Astrophysical Observatory in Cambridge, Mass.

telnet:// cfa204.harvard.edu/
Login: **einline**

Physics Department at the University of Massachusetts at Amherst runs a bulletin-board system that provides extensive conferences and document libraries related to space. Log on with your name and a password.

telnet://spacemet.phast.umass.edu/

Telnet Sites
Visit this Web site for links to interesting telnet sites including Library Catalogs:

http://www.germany.eu.net/books/eegtti/eeg_toc.html#SEC121

Weather

The University of Michigan's Department of Atmospheric, Oceanographic, and Space Sciences supplies weather forecasts for U.S. and foreign cities, along with skiing and hurricane reports.

telnet:// madlab.sprl.umich.edu 3000

Weather forecasts, severe weather, ski conditions:

telnet://wind.atmos.uah.edu:3000

Other Telnet Resources

Visit these Web sites for links to telnet sites.
http://www.nova.edu/Inter-Links/start.html
http://www.magna.com.au/bdgtti/bdg_92.html#SEC95

Bulletin Boards

SBI Links to Bulletin Boards **http://dkeep.com/sbi.htm**
Guide To Select BBSs on the Internet **http://dkeep.com/sbi.htm**

Chats

Time Warner's Pathfinder **http://www.pathfinder.com**
HotWired **http://www.hotwired.com/**
The Palace **http:www.thepalace.com/**
Globe **http://globe1.csuglab.cornell.edu/global/homepage.html**

Free-Nets

Community Computer Networks And Freenets
http://freenet.victoria.bc.ca/freenets.html

International Free-Net Community Listing
This page is a listing of Free-Nets and Community Nets around the
world. **http://www.uwec.edu/Info/Freenets/**

Gopher Links To Free-Nets **gopher://info.asu.edu:70/11/other/freenets**

MOOs and MUDs

http://www.butterfly.net/~pyro/moo_page.html
http://www.bushnet.qld.edu.au/~jay/moo/
http://www.io.com/~combs/htmls/moo.html

Diversity University
http://www.academic.marist.edu/duwww.htm
telnet://moo.du.org:8888

Lambda MOO **telnet://lambda.parc.xerox.com:8888/**

HtMUD (a graphical MUD) **http://www.elf.com/~phi/htmud/**

Hypertext MUD Lists provides links to MUDS all over the world.
http://www.eskimo.com/~tarp3/muds.html

Chapter Seven

BUSINESS ON THE NET

BUSINESS ON THE NET

The Internet is the fastest growing communications medium that we have ever experienced. Individuals and businesses—from Fortune 500 companies to small sole proprietorships—are establishing a presence on the Internet in the belief that cyberspace holds the potential for new profits, new customers, and a new way to conduct business. We have heard rumors that Internet advertising can lead to millions of dollars in revenue. In fact, many believe the Internet is about to become the hottest commercial property.

Despite all the Internet hype, there is one warning for those who think they may want to become netpreneurs.

Business on the Net is not easy.

In fact, many dollars are wasted on Internet advertising. Much of the advertising done on the Internet is of poor quality and attracts very little profitable business. It's safe to say that new business ventures on the Internet will probably not make a lot of money during their first six months.

So you ask, "Why should anyone consider establishing a business presence on the Internet?"

> The Internet is "a place you can't afford not to be right now. It's not so much that you're going to [profit] in the near term; rather, you'll lose money in the long term by not being there."
> Peter H. Lewis, Ziff Davis Publishing

> "If you're not an active Internet citizen by the mid-1990's, you're likely to be out of business by the year 2000."
> Patricia B. Seybold, Computerworld

Is Anyone Making Money on the Internet?

As this book goes to press, informative articles on Webonomics indicate that the groups making money on the Internet are

- popular Web sites that offer advertising,
- makers of Web server computers,
- Internet access providers, and
- advertising agencies that provide consulting services to set up Web sites.

The most popular Web sites such as TimeWarner's Pathfinder and Wired are charging between $30,000 and $10,000 for three months of advertising on their site, and the demand for advertising links continues to grow. However, the actual revenues generated from this advertising is much less than expected. In fact, marketers reveal an inside secret — prices published on advertising rate cards are seldom charged. Companies and organizations willing to pay such money for Web advertising want a trial period to see if there is a payoff for the money invested.

So why do companies continue to invest heavily in Internet sites and advertising? Data indicates that new sites are cropping up at the rate of one per minute. According to investment specialists Volpe, Welty & Co., the market for Internet services and software will grow 62.4 percent yearly from about $370 million in January of 1996 to about $5.8 billion at the decade's end. The company also estimates that by the year 2000, business-to-business commerce on the Internet will reach $50 billion and consumer transactions will surpass $200 billion.

This chapter provides

- steps to assist you in determining whether to put your business on-line,
- information on unique characteristics of the Internet as a new medium,
- Internet sites to visit to learn more about how businesses are using the Web,
- information on the new advertising paradigm,
- options for developing an online business site,
- guidelines for establishing an Internet business site.

Getting Started

Five steps provide valuable information to assist you in deciding whether or not to establish a business presence on the Internet.

1. Understand the Internet as a medium for communication, interactivity, and how the Internet is being used for information access and sharing.

2. Visit and analyze business sites. What products and services do they offer? How do they attract Web visitors? Are visitors their potential customers?

3. Learn about the new Internet advertising paradigm. How does advertising and communication differ on the Web from the traditional media?

4. Research Internet demographics. Learn about Web visitors. Who are the consumers? Are they the right consumers for your product? What is their income level? What age are they? Why are they on the Web? What are the buying patterns?

5. Learn about designing and maintaining a Web site. Do you have the time, money, and resources to design, develop, and continue to update a Web site?

STEP 1: Understand The Internet As A Medium For Communication, Interactivity, And Information Access

The Internet as a medium of communications is unique in that it attracts and quickly makes cyberaddicts of thousands of people of all ages all over the world. This new medium offers a unique experience that print, television, and radio can't deliver—interactivity and information not bound by the limits of time and space. The Internet offers a new form for creative expression. Most importantly, the Internet is FUN.

The Internet As A Medium For Communication

The Internet offers a low cost, globally accessible, and convenient way to communicate. Many individuals now prefer using electronic mail (e-mail) as their primary source of communication. Sending messages

generally requires little or no money. Messages are composed and answered quickly and at a time that is convenient to the sender and recipient. Hours of wasted phone time are eliminated. Electronic mail also enables users to access information on the Internet.

Internet communications take many forms. On-line users are drawn by the millions to interactive services where they can communicate with others: Usenet newsgroups, listserv mailing lists, electronic forums, on-line chats, bulletin boards, and multi-user simulated environments (MUDs and MOOs).

MUDs and MOOs are text-based networked communities residing on a computer connected to the Internet. One eighth grader in Massachusetts, describes it as a "text-based virtual world where you can build and explore rooms, objects, all sorts of places and meet interesting people from all around the world...[you] create your own places using object-oriented programming language learning as you go." Communication and interactions on MOOs and MUDs are free from age, sex, and ethnic stereotypes. Community norms call for sharing and for respecting others. One small child told me that what she most liked about her experience with the MUSE (Multi-User Simulated Environment) was that "on the Internet you do not have to be mean to have friends." A Native American student reported that in class he never felt comfortable speaking out, but on the MUSE he could not stop talking.

These communication environments become virtual communities where new relationships are formed and users find that they can interact and form virtual friendships without concern for race, creed, age, color, or sex. The ability to be whomever you would like to be opens new doors for many people to communicate.

The Internet As An Interactive Medium

Internet interactivity provides opportunities for new ways to communicate, entertain, and obtain feedback. In fact, the word interactivity is still being defined as new and creative forms of self-expression push and extend the traditional definition of interactivity.

Entertainment

Ask Internet users why they are drawn to the medium and they will answer without hesitation, "The Internet is fun." The Internet provides opportunities to take virtual field trips to other countries, view hypermedia travelogues, visit museums, art galleries, libraries, and botanical gardens all over the world. There are on-line images, video clips, and music in almost any area of interest. People seeking to learn about current events, for example, have links to news stories, on-line discussions, recent images and video clips, as well as opportunities to research more information on related topics.

Other entertaining interactive sites allow users to create their own electronic postcards, participate in a virtual archaeology dig, experience hands-on virtual museums, or create characters. Still others provide unlimited opportunities to express creative talents with interactive stories, games, and contests.

Feedback

Most Internet sites realize the importance of user feedback. Feedback options provide excellent ways to learn what visitors like or don't like about a site and what else they might like. Not only does feedback provide information on how to provide a successful and highly trafficked Web site, but perhaps even more importantly, users appreciate the opportunity to express their needs, likes, and desires for products and services.

Many sites have e-mail address links for additional information or for providing feedback. Built-in electronic mail options provide a low cost way for consumers to communicate with a seller or a company.

The Internet As A Medium For Information Access & Sharing

The Internet makes possible information access and sharing on a level never before experienced. Information can be made available at almost no cost to Internet travelers. Printing and postage costs vanish. No longer do businesses need to rent mailing lists to contact potential customers. They can now be reached through Internet discussion groups such as Usenet newsgroups, listserv mailing lists, and bulletin boards.

Internet advertising can be placed at a fraction of the cost of traditional methods, with the potential of reaching thousands more customers. Internet advertising allows a business to provide almost unlimited information to a new type of consumer who is searching for information. This new "wired" consumer is not just amassing quantities of information, but is also judging the value of a site on the quality of its content.

The World Wide Web offers capabilities to present information in new ways and in multiple formats. The Web's ability to easily incorporate and link graphics, sound and video files (hypermedia) have transformed the Internet into a medium that has the dynamic potential to be simultaneously entertaining, informative, and educational. Used creatively, hypermedia can be incorporated into an Internet site to attract thousands of daily visitors.

The most successful Internet businesses take advantage of hypermedia and provide information in a variety of formats. Net consumers are attracted to sites that provide creative, attractive, and relevant information presented using a variety of media. Such a site may include articles and chat rooms in which discussions occur; images, video clips, and audio; special guest appearances; invitations to submit personal stories or artwork; contests and prizes; fun and entertaining activities such as interactive stories or the capability to explore a Web graphic by pointing and clicking on objects within that graphic.

Most Internet activities are free, uncensored, and unedited. In fact, FREE is a vital element to success. Internet travelers keep returning to sites that provide free, interesting, and relevant information. Successful Internet sites find ways to change their content constantly in order to keep visitors returning. Freely available and worthwhile information is a most important ingredient in the Internet success formula. Surveys indicate that few Internet users are willing to pay to access Web information.

The best example of an information-providing industry that is adapting to the Internet are many newspapers and magazines. Although traditional subscriptions are not being replaced with on-line services, most large newspapers now have an Internet presence. Services vary, but usually include free access to some of their information. Others offer paid subscriptions to their on-line services for access to extended information and services (see Time Warner, San Jose "Mercury," and Wired sites later in this section.)

Many companies are now providing a freely available on-line newsletter. Electronic newsletters can be distributed almost without cost and have the potential for achieving widespread recognition and high volume site visits.

These new services help to illustrate the new advertising paradigm in which service is emphasized over product.

STEP 2: Visit And Analyze Internet Business Sites.

Listed below are a number of Web business sites. As you visit these sites, consider these questions

- Does this company provide a service or sell a product?
- Why would someone want to visit this site?
- Does the site offer something of value at not cost?
- Is it fun and entertaining? Why?
- How does this site use the Internet as a medium for communicating with their customers?
- How does their use of the Internet differ from the use of traditional media?
- What do you like most about it?
- What do you like least?
- Would you return to this site? Why?
- Is it attractive and/or appealing?
- What could be done to make this site more effective?

LINKS TO BUSINESS SITES

Listed below are Web addresses that link to some of the best business sites.

Commercial Sites Index

The Commercial Sites Index lists businesses that have set up home pages on the Web. Make this a scheduled visit to see how companies are using the Net for business.
http://www.directory.net/

Interesting Business Sites on the Web

This is a relatively small list of sites (less than 50) that cover most of the exciting business uses of the Web. The list is updated frequently, adding new and interesting sites while deleting others.
http://www.owi.com/netvalue/index.html

Internet Business Connection
An electronic storefront where you can browse for products and services through an alphabetical listing or by category.
http://www.charm.net/~ibc/

PR NEWSWIRE
PR Newswire has links to what they feel are some of the best and most important business sites.
http://www.prnewswire.com/cnoc/links.html
http://www.prnewswire.com/

The 25 Best Business Web Sites
Twenty-five business Web sites have been deemed the "best of the best." Each illustrates at least one of the more sophisticated uses of the Web, and they all have one thing in common—they do on the Web what they couldn't have accomplished in another medium.
http://techweb.cmp.com:2090/techweb/ia/13issue/13topsites.html

Thomas HO's Favorite Business Sites.
This very plain Web site is a must-visit guide to the best economic and business sites on the Internet.
http://www.engr.iupui.edu/~ho/interests/commmenu.html

PUBLISHING
Hot Wired
Visit this excellent hypermedia storefront that contains services, advertising, opportunities for advertising, special guest appearances, chat rooms, and much more. This site is an excellent example of the Internet's capabilities to deliver services and products.
http://www.hotwired.com/

New York Times
This site delivers highlights from the daily newspaper as well as articles on technology. You will need to download a copy of Adobe Acrobat reader (free) before you can read the Times on-line.
http://nytimesfax.com/index.html

NewsPage
NewsPage is one of the Web's leading sources of daily business news, with thousands of categorized news stories updated daily.
http://www.newspage.com/

San Jose "Mercury News"
The Mercury Center Web is the first complete daily newspaper on the World Wide Web. This service offers continually updated news coverage, the complete text of each day's final edition of the San Jose "Mercury News," including classified ads, and a variety of special features. **http://www.sjmercury.com/main.htm**

Time Warner
Pathfinder from Time Warner is an excellent Web site for discovering how an information-providing company pushes the capabilities of the new Internet medium. **http://www.pathfinder.com/**

Voyager
Voyager publishes some of the best laserdiscs and CDs. Visit this site to see a creative design using hypermedia. **http://www.voyagerco.com/**

Wall Street Journal
This on-line version of the Wall Street Journal has hyperlinks to money and investing updates, a variety of Journal offerings including headlines from today's paper, and the Wall Street Journal Classroom Edition—the Journal's award-winning educational program for secondary-school students and teachers. **http://www.wsj.com/**

FINANCIAL SERVICES
Fidelity Investment
Fidelity was one of the first financial services to establish a Web site believing that, given the right tools, individuals make their own best investment decisions. This World Wide Web server provides investors with information and assistance to make more informed choices. It challenges visitors to find out how their personalities impact their ability to save. They can also check out how others scored on the same questions. The site also includes a contest and games. **http://www.fid-inv.com/**

Bank of America
Buttons on this site offer users the opportunity to learn more about Bank of America, commercial services, personal finance, community, and capital markets. **http://www.bankamerica.com/**

RETAIL . . . The Virtual Shopping Malls
The London Mall (award winning)
http://www.micromedia.co.uk/default.htm

The Empire Mall
http://empiremall.com/

The Internet Plaza
http://plaza.xor.com/

The Internet Shopping Network (owned by cable television's Home
Shopping Network) **https://www.internet.net/**
Note... When you connect to this site, that you are connecting to a
secure server. Notice how your key icon on the bottom of the page
changes.

Branch Mall
http://branch.com/

iMall
http://www.imall.com/

The Online Shopping Center
http://www.shoputc.com/

OTHER BUSINESS SITES
Airlines On The Web
"Hello all. Welcome to the Airlines of the WEB page. I am a graduate
student at UC Berkeley's Haas School of Business studying the airline
industry for my dissertation..." Visit this award winning site of Marc-
David Seidel. **http://haas.berkeley.edu/~seidel/airline.html**

AT & T
This AT &T site ranked 5th in "Best of the Best Business Sites."
http://www.att.com/net/

CNN Interactive
This excellent site has links to U.S. news, world news, business,
weather, sports, politics, technology, and much more including search
options. **http://www.cnn.com/**

Entrepreneurial Edge Online
Visit this site to learn more about growing your business on-line. **http://www.edgeonline.com/**

Federal Express
FedEx provides a unique service from their site—tracking a FedEx package. **http://www.fedex.com/**

MCI
This site was voted as one of the top business sites. **http://www.internetmci.com/**

Relais & Chateaux
A well done Web site that provides links to world wide resorts. **http://www.calvacom.fr/relais/accueil.html**

Silicon Graphics
Surf this excellent site for a look at Silicon Graphics products, services, and entertainment. **http://www.sgi.com/**

Sony
The Sony site is an excellent example of how interactivity can be used on the Internet. It contains links to music, film, and electronics. Information can be found on musicians, their tour schedules, sound clips, record cover art, music videos, and special promotions, as well as information on Sony products. **http://www.sony.com/**

Southwest Airlines
Visit Southwest Airlines' Home Gate for an example of interactive graphics. **http://www.iflyswa.com/**

United Parcel Service
Learn more about how businesses provide useful services by visiting the United Parcel Service's interactive site. This site also helps you track your packages, calculate approximate costs for sending a package, and a form to help estimate how long it will take for your package to reach its destination. **http://www.ups.com/**

U.S. Postal Service
Need to find a zip code of your friend in Boston? Visit this Web site to find the zip+4code. This site is trying hard do save trees by providing services to those who prefer using e-mail to paper. **http://www.usps.gov/**

Zima Clearmalt
This site is an excellent example of how a business can use entertainment to entice visitors. Zima Clearmalt is a product of Coors Brewing Company. Find out who or what Zima is; join the Zima Fan Club (Tribe Z), or check out the story.
http://www.zima.com/zimag.html

Now that you have visited a few Web business sites, think and analyze the new advertising economy and new opportunities for publishing and making information available to customers. What new services can be provided using the Internet? How can you save your customer time and money?

STEP 3: Learn About The New Advertising Paradigm.

The Internet is a new frontier for exploration and discovery. There are no rules. Very few businesses have any idea of how to take advantage of the Internet as an advertising medium, of how to profit from the global marketplace, or how to avoid the dangers of the new emerging marketing paradigm. The Internet is substantially different from all other advertising media. The first mistake that businesses make when deciding to set up shop on the Internet is to approach advertising using traditional marketing strategies. The most common mistake made is to transfer advertising from conventional media to the Internet.

The first step in understanding the new emerging paradigm is to eliminate the word *advertising* from your thinking and vocabulary. Replace it with the words *customer services*. Think SERVICES before SALES and PRODUCT. Next, think carefully and creatively about how to use the unique capabilities of the Internet medium—interaction and communication—to provide useful services to your customers.

The success of your Internet business will depend on your ability

- to provide something of value,
- to be creative,
- to entertain,
- to provide a quality experience, and
- to get prospects and customers to come back.

273

STEP 4: Research Internet Demographics.

Learn more about Web visitors. Who are the users? What is their income level? Are they male or female? What are their buying patterns? What do they enjoy on the Web?

Current Web demographics taken from the Graphic, Visualization, & Usability Center's (GVU) 4th WWW User Surveys indicate that

- Web users are highly educated (67% have a college or professional degree).
- The overall average income is between $63,000 to $69,000.
- The average age is 31-35.
- Females continue to increase on the Web with gender proportions of 30% female to 70% male.
- Computer (29.1%) and educational (30.9%) occupations represent the majority of respondents.
- Slightly more respondents are married and have children.
- Users prefer using the Web for entertainment work and research.
- Shopping is the least commonly sited reason for using the Internet. However using the Web for collecting information about commercial products and services is very popular.
- On-line buying is more common for less expensive products.
- There is little on-line buying of apparel.
- Respondents are very concerned about on-line security for conducting financial transactions.
- One out of five users would not pay for access to World Wide Web sites.
- The majority of users who participated in the Survey indicate that they use their Web browser daily. Users in Europe spend slightly less time than those in the U.S.

Visit these Web sites to learn more about your audience.

http://etrg.findsvp.com/features/newinet.html

http://WWW.Stars.com/Vlib/Misc/Statistics.html

http://www-personal.umich.edu/~sgupta/hermes/survey3/

http://www.cc.gatech.edu/gvu/user_surveys/

STEP 5: Learn About Designing And Maintaining A Web site.

To learn about designing a Web site, read Chapter 8.

The Next Step...

If you are still interested in setting up shop on the Net, the next step is to learn more and to become smart about this new frontier called the Internet.

 Ask questions of yourself and others—what Web sites work best and why? What keeps a prospect/customer/user returning?

Continue to analyze the Internet medium as a new frontier for expression, interaction, communication, and entertainment. How can these unique properties be applied to customer support, services, and marketing?

Investigate ways to establish a business presence on the World Wide Web.

Work with others who understand the medium to help you design your customer services.

Financially profitable Internet business will belong to those individuals and companies that push the definition of interactivity and communication. These new netpreneurs will redefine marketing and what is meant by providing products and services to customers. Their businesses will be the Internet success stories of high profit products in a global market place.

Listed below are a few resources to assist your learning.

Listserv Mailing Lists
Internet Marketing Mailing List
To subscribe to this listserv
    1. Send an e-mail to: **listproc@einet.net**
    2. Leave the subject field blank.
    3. In the message field type: **subscribe inet-marketing <Name>**

TidBITS Mailing List
To subscribe to TidBITS
  1. Send an e-mail to: **listserv@ricevm1.rice.edu**
  2. Leave the subject field blank.
  3. In the message field type: **subscribe tidbits < Name>**

World Wide Web Sites

Entrepreneurial Edge Online
http://www.edgeonline.com

Entrepreneurs On The Web
http://sashimi.wwa.com/~notime/eotw/eotw.html

• •

What Are My Options For Setting Up Shop On The Internet?

There are several ways to establish a business presence on the Internet.

- Use a commercial on-line service such as America Online, CompuServe, Prodigy, or Microsoft Network (MSN).

- Establish a site with an Internet service provider,

- Set up shop on an established business site,

- Open shop in a virtual shopping mall,

- Work with an Internet marketing service,

- Use electronic mail.

Commercial On-line Services

An easy way to get started with a business site is to investigate the cost and advantages of using commercial on-line services such as America Online, CompuServe, Prodigy, or Microsoft Network. A presence on one of these sites will assure you visitors.

There are several ways to advertise with commercial on-line services. The three most common are classified advertisements, shopping malls, and display advertising. Classified advertisements are the least expensive and are similar to classified ads in daily newspapers. Listing your business in the Classified Ads area costs between $1 a line for one week to $15 a line for six months. Setting up shop in a virtual mall can cost as much as $10,000 to $20,000 plus a two percent commission to the service on each sale. Display advertising rates range from $27,000 to $55,000 a month. Rates depend on linking access points and the size of the display.

Advantages of commercial on-line services include

- Your site can be easily found,
- Advertising is more accepted on commercial online services,
- There are many accepted advertising options,
- Setting up shop can be easy.

Disadvantages of commercial on-line services include

- Setting up shop can be expensive,
- Commercial services typically take a cut of your profits,
- Subscribers to on-line commercial services are usually home computer users, not business owners,
- Only subscribers to your on-line commercial service can access your site,
- The number of individuals that can access your site is small by comparison to the entire Internet community.

Five years ago there were fewer than 1,000,000 subscribers to commercial on-line services. Today there are over 5,000,000 with predictions that this number will double in the next few years. Though these numbers appear large, the number of individuals with full Internet access is over 30,000,000! When deciding whether to use a commercial on-line service, consider the total number of potential customers that will have access to your business.

For more information on costs contact these commercial on-line services.

America Online:	(800) 827-6364	http://www.aol.com
CompuServe:	(800) 848-8990	http://www.compuserve.com
Prodigy:	(800) 776-3449	http://www.prodigy.com
Microsoft Network	(800) 426-9400	http://www.msn.com

Local Internet Providers

The second and perhaps the most popular solution for a small business in establishing a Web site is to work with a local Internet provider. As little as $20 a month can achieve Internet access from a local provider. Many providers make space available for your own home page. Many have services that assist in converting content to a Web document using the required HTML (Hypertext Markup Language). The cost for assistance in designing and developing a Web Home Page will vary. Fees range from $50-$75 per hour. The minimum costs to develop a few business Web pages will be between $1,000-$3000. There are also many free documents available on the Internet to assist you in learning HTML. See the Locator Map in Chapter 4 for these resources.

Established Internet Sites

One of the most prestigious and heavily trafficked business site on the Web is O'Reilly & Associates, Global Network Navigator. This site carries one of the highest price tags for an advertising link since its several million weekly visitors guarantee visibility to businesses. To check out this site, enter this URL: **http://gnn.com/**

Mecklermedia Corporation offers advertising opportunities with their Web site **http://www.mecklerweb.com/**

MecklerWeb feels that they are positioned to become the Internet Users' "First Stop on the Internet," where travelers find the very latest Internet news, tips, how-tos, product reviews, resources, directories, and expert commentary. The site has links to businesses, the Internet Mall, Net publishing, trade shows, a career web, and much more.

Shopping Malls

Visit a few of these virtual shopping malls to get a flavor of the products and services as well as information on how to set up shop.

Internet Marketing Services

Many companies can help create a business presence on the Internet. Their services include creating a Web home page, Web ads, and recommending an appropriate location for the Web page. To see an example of an Internet marketing service connect to the Downtown Anywhere site. **http://awa.com/** Services range from an entry into their Downtown Registry to a complete Internet Showroom. They will assist you in designing your message, its delivery, and in conducting your business on-line.

For information on businesses hosting Web directories connect to **http://www.directory.net/**

E-Mail

Some of the most effective sales and marketing can be done with electronic mail. Communication with potential customers costs no more than your monthly Internet access account.

Tips For Using E-Mail To Market Your Business

 Include your e-mail address in all brochures, ads, and letterheads.

 Create an e-mail signature that includes a few lines of information about your business.

 Participate in Internet discussion groups (listserv mailing lists, Usenet newsgroups, on-line chats) and interact with potential customers. Answer questions and assist others with finding information and resources. This will provide visibility for you and your business.

 Post a press release to an appropriate mailing list. Before posting, check to see if the list Archives contains FAQ (Frequently Asked Questions) to learn about acceptable use policies. When writing a press release, remember SERVICE over PRODUCT. Is there a way to tie in a service to what you are advertising? If the list has a moderator, send an e-mail containing your press release to see if it is appropriate.

- Provide on-line customer support. Respond to customers' questions, requests for information, and complaints.

- Create your own electronic discussion group or Usenet newsgroup. Mailing lists provide a way to distribute information to all subscribers on a regular basis.

- Collect names of potential customers from electronic discussion groups. Each posting to a discussion group has the return address of the sender. Use these e-mail addresses to create a database of names of prospective customers.

Guidelines For Creating An Internet Business Site

- Avoid traditional advertising strategies and techniques.
  Change your thinking to include "appropriate advertising" and "How to create value for customers?" Before thinking PRODUCT think SERVICE.

- Consider the Medium.
  Interactivity and information access are two characteristics that set the Internet apart from traditional advertising media. Investigate how successful businesses are taking advantage of the unique characteristics of the Internet. Visit business sites. Analyze what services they provide, how they provide these services, how they use interactivity and Internet tools, how they provide information, how they encourage information sharing, how they develop a relationship with their customers.

  After you have visited a number of sites, begin to consider what the Internet will allow you to do for your prospective customers.

- Provide something of value.
  Give something away that has a perceived value. Ask yourself, "What are my prospects' needs?" What information would they find useful and beneficial? Providing quality content will keep potential customers returning to your site.

Provide links that direct prospects and customers to useful services and relevant information at other Web sites.

⬛ **Make your site interesting and attractive.**
Internet users have total control over their travels. If a site is not well-organized, attractive, and appealing, then a point-and-click will quickly lose a prospect. Many sites take advantage of Netscape Navigator's backgrounds and make visually interesting and colorful pages. Web sites are highly competitive for appeal, entertainment, and content value. The quickest way to lose a visitor is to have a poorly organized, boring home page that is heavy with text.

Instead make your site interesting by providing information in a variety of formats: text, images, video, sound.

Create a dynamic, colorful, and unique graphic for your home page. Use this graphic on other pages to link back to your home page.

⬛ **Communicate with your prospects and customers.**
Think of ways you can communicate with potential buyers/users. How might the Internet do it cheaper, better, and more effectively?

Provide opportunities for developing improved interpersonal relationships with your prospects and customers. The new paradigm also includes establishing new and improved interconnections with your market.

Provide an e-mail address so visitors can contact you.
Ask for feedback about your site.

⬛ **Establish a virtual community.**
Internet marketing is also most effective in establishing a sense of community. Net users enjoy interacting, meeting new people, sharing their thoughts and feelings, or just chatting. Companies that use interactivity to establish communities with which they are identified will be successful.

⬛ **Provide entertainment that is fun and interesting.**

⬛ **Keep changing the content of your site to keep prospects and customers returning.**

Investigate ways in which potential customers can find your site. Investigate how to become listed in such Internet directories as Excite, Yahoo, InfoSeek, and the Magellan. Link to other sites. Trade links with other business sites.

Listed below are several resources that can help Net travelers find your site.

Internet Business Directory.

Your home page, and subsequent pages, will be indexed weekly by the Web Referral Service and be placed in the Internet Business Directory. The IBD serves as a "yellow pages" for businesses on the World Wide Web. **http://www.ar.com/**

Commercial Sites Index

You can use a special form to submit new listings, updates, and announcements to Open Market's Commercial Sites Index. This is a free service. **http://www.directory.net/dir/submit.cgi**

Downtown Anywhere

This Internet marketing service publishes a directory in which you can register your business site.**http://awa.com/**

Other Web pages for submitting your site

http://www.submit-it.com/

http://thehugelist.com/

http://www.webcom.com/~webcom/html/publicize.html

http://home.netscape.com/escapes/submit_new.html

Chapter Eight

DESIGNING A WEB SITE

Preparing To Become A Web Designer

The World Wide Web offers many opportunities and challenges for publicizing yourself to a global marketplace but before you can effectively take advantage of these new opportunities, you must first know as much as possible about the medium for which you are about to design. You would not think of building a house without first having a design blueprint. Before you can create the blueprint you must first understand what it is you want to build. The same holds true for building a Web site. You are not just creating a page, you are building and constructing a Web site. Therefore, it is critical that before you begin you learn as much as possible about

- the topic you are designing your Web site for,
- information technology—how to organize and present information,
- your audience,
- Internet demographics,
- multimedia capabilities of the Internet,
- effective Internet design and layout,
- Internet communication and interaction,
- Internet entertainment,
- the capabilities of your Web development tools, and
- the concept of QUALITY on the Internet.

Without initial analysis and a design blueprint, you and your Web site will look unprofessional. Users will very quickly leave your Web page in search of one with a more carefully designed layout and informative content.

In this chapter you will learn five steps for designing a Web site

- Step 1: Learn about quality Web sites
- Step 2: Analyze your information
- Step 3: Analyze your audience
- Step 4: Create a Web design blueprint
- Step 5: Build a quality Web site

Additionally, you will find information on
- where to find World Wide Web development tools, and
- about emerging trends for the Internet and why they are important to your Web site.

> **NOTE**
> It is beyond the scope and purpose of this book to provide information on Web development and using HTML or Java. However, resources are given for HTML documents online. There are also many excellent books on Java and Web programming.

STEP 1: Learn About Quality Web Sites

The best way to learn about effective Web design is to become an expert in the medium. Learn as much as possible about high QUALITY Web sites that are well-designed, informative, creative, and entertaining. The best way to acquire a better understanding of a quality site is to visit and analyze as many Web pages as possible.

Quality Web sites

- are visually appealing,
- have original content,
- are useful and informative,
- are easy to navigate,
- are interactive,
- draw upon, but are not limited to, age-old design principles.

Questions To Ask When Analyzing A Web Site
As you visit World Wide Web sites, analyze each site by asking the following questions

- What attracts me to this site? Why do I want to avoid this site?
- What is the value of this site?
- For who is this site designed?
- How is on-line communication different from print or traditional media?
- For what information will people pay money?
- Why would users return to this site?

- Does this site entertain?
- How does this site use the interactive capabilities of the Internet?
- What are the different types of interaction?
- Does the use of multimedia support the content?

Listed below are a number of Web sites to visit for analysis. Also refer to the sites in Chapter 7.

Cool Sites and Best Of The Web Lists

Awesome List
http://www.clark.net/pub/journalism/awesome.html

Cool Site of the Day
http://www.infi.net/cool.html

Cybertown's Site of the Week
http://www.cybertown.com/cybertown/spider.html

Justin's Links from the Underground
http://www.links.net/

Netscape's Cool Site List
http://home.netscape.com/home/whats-cool.html

PC Week Best of the Web
http://www.ziff.com/~pcweek/pcwbests.html

POINT'S Top Web Sites
http://www.pointcom.com/

Whole Internet Catalog
http://gnn.digital.com/gnn/wic/top.toc.html

Yahoo's Cool Links
http://www.yahoo.com/Entertainment/Cool_links/

Other Well-Designed, Interactive, and Innovative Sites

CNN Interactive
http://www.cnn.com/

Digital Planet
http://www.digiplanet.com/

Electronic Newsstand
http://www.enews.com/

SciFi Channel
http://www.scifi.com/

Total NY
http://www.TotalNY.com/

See also, *Whose Got It Right* (page 298.)

STEP 2: Analyze Your Information

A quality Web site provides original information, makes information easy to find, and has links to external information to support its topic. In your Internet travels you may have experienced frustration at not finding the information you need. Perhaps you had to connect to too many links or felt lost in your search for the content you were seeking. Or, you may have found that the information you found was useless, irrelevant, and shallow.

Therefore, the next step is to analyze your goals and the information you want to present. Answer the following questions

- What are your goals for this Web site?
- What information do you want to make available on my site? Are you dispensing information about your company or providing useful information for your customers? Or both?
- How will this information contribute to the site's value and usefulness for others?
- Are you an expert in your topic?
- Do you need to do more research to become an expert?
- Are there other Web sites that have similar information or related resources?

A clear understanding of your goals and your content are essential for creating a design blueprint for a quality World Wide Web site.

STEP 3: Analyze Your Audience

Knowing your audience and the demographics of the Internet is crucial to Web design and success. If Internet users are not interested in your topic then you will have few visitors and perhaps be wasting valuable time and money on Web design and development. For example, if a realtor believes that expensive homes can be sold on the Internet, the realtor first needs to see if Internet demographics support this type of customer. Are Internet users likely to use the Internet for finding homes? How might they use the Internet? How can the Web site provide a service to these customers that fit with their user profile? How can the realtor make this information more attractive and visible to any visitor?

Internet Demographics
In Chapter 7 you learned about how to find information on Internet demographics. Visit the following Web sites to keep up to date on the changing demographics of the Internet.

http://gnn.interpath.net/gnn/news/feature/inetdemo/web.size.html

http://etrg.findsvp.com/features/newinet.html

http://www.umich.edu/~sgupta/survey3/

http://turnpike.net/turnpike/demog.html

http://www.zilker.net/mids/mmq/index.html

STEP 4: Create A Design Blueprint

In Step 1 you identified your goals, information, or content that you wanted to present and other support resources on the Internet. You are now ready to create your Web design blueprint.

Step 4a. Organize your information into broad categories.
For example on my Web site **http://www.xplora.com/xplora/** I

identified the following categories after reviewing the content and information that I would like to put on my site

- About XPLORA (information about my company, products, and services)
- Internet Adventures Books
- Internet Adventures Newsletter (On-line examples of our newsletter)
- Kids Resources
- Internet For Families (information and resources for home education)
- Learning Adventures (educational resources and current classroom projects)
- Finding Information & Resources
- Business On the Net

Figure 8.1
The XPLORA Home Page.

Step 4b. Identify what information will be linked to each category.
For each of my categories, I identified what original content I had to
provide and what resources I was aware of on the Internet.

Step 4c. Determine hyperlinks.
One way to visualize and understand how your content and resources
will be linked is to use index cards. Each card is representative of a
Web page. Number the cards. For example, my link to *Internet For
Families* would be on Card #3. The next link would be Card #3a and
would have the following categories:

1. What is an electronic field trip?
2. Electronic field trips (links to other Internet resources)
3. Science adventures (links to other Internet resources)
4. How to plan a family vacation (links to Internet resources)
5. Parent resources
6. How to make an electronic field trip into a learning adventure

Figure 8.2
Subcategories for *Internet For Families.*

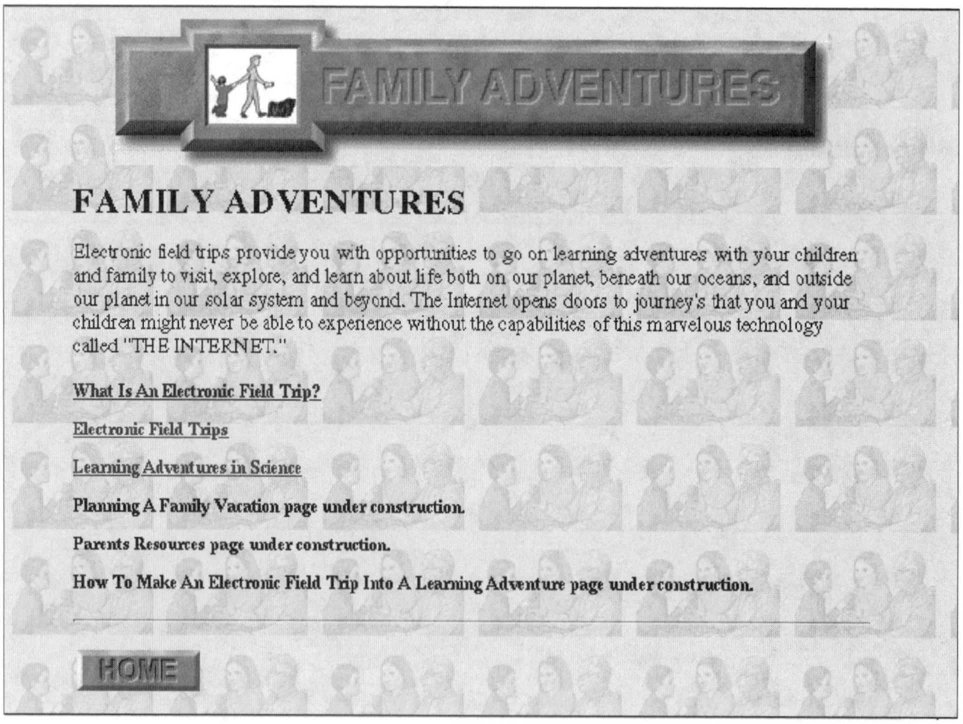

FAMILY ADVENTURES

Electronic field trips provide you with opportunities to go on learning adventures with your children and family to visit, explore, and learn about life both on our planet, beneath our oceans, and outside our planet in our solar system and beyond. The Internet opens doors to journey's that you and your children might never be able to experience without the capabilities of this marvelous technology called "THE INTERNET."

What Is An Electronic Field Trip?

Electronic Field Trips

Learning Adventures in Science

Planning A Family Vacation page under construction.

Parents Resources page under construction.

How To Make An Electronic Field Trip Into A Learning Adventure page under construction.

HOME

Next, I identified the Web sites for electronic field trips on Card 3a.1 My content for how to transform an electronic field trip into a learning adventure would be referenced on Card 3a.6. I continue to identify content or Internet resources for each hyperlink.

Figure 8.3
External Internet resources for **Electronic Field Trips**.

Step 4d. Review your proposed Web navigational design.
Lay out your index cards and ask yourself the following questions

- Do the categories best describe the type of information I am presenting?
- Does the content support the categories?
- Do the Internet resources support the categories?
- Will users be able to find the information easily?
- Can Internet visitors reach my content without using more than 3 links (3 screens)? (Content that you want your users to find should not be buried more than 3 screens deep.)

Step 4e. Determine navigational aids for your Web pages.
A visitor to your Web site should be able to recognize whether a link goes to one of your pages or leaves your site and goes to someone else's Web site. Consider the following for building consistency into your site

- The use of a signature graphic (masthead or logo) on each page
- The same color background on each page (Backgrounds may vary, but a color theme is followed throughout.)
- The use of navigational buttons on the bottom of the page: Back, Forward, Home, etc.
- Special graphical design for your hyperlink buttons

Figure 8.4
The signature graphic for XPLORA.

Figure 8.5
XPLORA Home Page navigational buttons.

Step 4f. Determine what graphics or images you will be using.
Do you have images to support your content? If so, make note of the image on your index card. If you do not have any images on hand, can you acquire some to make your site more visually interesting?

NOTE
Images should always support your text and not distract from the message.

Figure 8.6
Images to add visual interest to the content.

What is a rain forest?
There are two types of rain forests in the world: tropical and temperate. Tropical rain forests are hot, humid forests that grow in rainy areas near the equator. Some evergreen trees reach heights of 200 feet above the forest floor, branches intertwined to form a dense canopy that shades the forest. Few shrubs can grow here. Thick vines wrap around tree trunks and epiphytes (air plants) grow on high branches. Tropical rain forests receive between 100 and 400 inches of rainfall each year. The largest tropical rain forests are found in South America, Africa, Southeast Asia, Sumatra, and New Guinea. Smaller tropical rain forests are found in Central America and Australia.

Temperate rain forests grow in wet, higher-latitude regions, such as on the northwest coast of North America, in Chile, Tasmania, Australia, and New Zealand. These forests are homes to such deciduous trees as maples, oaks, and redwoods. There are fewer plant and animal species in temperate rain forests but their soils are made very rich by fallen, decomposing leaves. Enough light shines through to the forest floor to enable many shrubs and herbs to grow.

CLASSROOM CONNECTIONS
To allow students to participate in the shaping of the study, start the unit by creating a chart on the chalkboard or poster board. Divide the chart into three columns labeled: (1) What We Think We Know About Rain Forests; (2) What We Would Like to Know About Rain Forests; (3) What We've Learned About Rain Forests. Invite students to generate a list of items for the first column and record their responses on the chart. Don't be concerned if their "facts" are incorrect; students will have a chance to correct themselves as they do research. The second column allows students to take ownership of their own learning. What kinds of things do they want to know? Where do they think they should go to find out? What resources are available to them on the Internet? The third column should be added to throughout the unit, as students find answers to their questions.

To help bring closure to the study, be sure to revisit the chart at the end of the unit. Which facts in the first column weren't correct? What was the most surprising thing students learned in this unit? Which questions remain unanswered? Where might answers be found?

Consider the size of your images. Are your images going to download quickly when a visitor links to your site?

Step 4g. Analyze your use of other multimedia.
Are you considering using sound or video? What does the use of sound or video contribute to the value of your page? Will it only take up unnecessary space on the server? Should you wait before you include links to these types of media?

Step 4h. Determine the background for your Web pages.
When visiting and analyzing Web sites, you encountered many different types of backgrounds for Web pages. You also probably experienced that some downloaded quickly to your computer and others took more time. Were you frustrated at the time some fancy backgrounds took to download? What backgrounds added to the visual impact of a site? Which detracted?

Step 4i. Design each Web page.
Now you are ready to design each Web page. Review your content and external resources. Is there a theme? How will this theme be communicated on your Home Page? On hyperlinked pages?

As you prepare to design your pages consider the following

- Will you be using multiple windows or frames on a page?
- What text will you use on each page? What will be the color of the text? What size will the text be? Will the text be easy to read over the background?

Use your index cards and the information you have jotted down for information design.

WEB PAGE DESIGN GUIDELINES

Information Design Tips

- Become an expert in your topic. The more you know about your topic, the better you will be able to organize your information.

- Determine the major categories or divisions for your information and how each relate. From these categories, determine links and subsections.

- Provide an overview of your site on your home page. Think of the home page as a Table of Contents or orientation page.

- Include a date when your site was last updated.

Navigational Design Tips

- Be consistent with your text, design styles, and graphics. The more you experiment with variations in style, the more people become confused about your content.

- Develop a signature graphic for the title of each page.

- Provide a link back to your home page from each of your hyperlinked pages.

- Provide a back and forward button at the end of each page.

- Avoid presenting information more than 3 screens deep.

- Provide identification information on each page such as the name of your company, address, phone, and e-mail address.

- If you have a great deal of information on your site, consider using a search engine to assist visitors.

Visual Design Tips

- Consider using a graphic on your home page that will have links to your content and provide an overview of your site.

- Consider what images to use to support your content.

- Use open space. Avoid making pages cluttered and over crowded. These pages are difficult to read and are fatiguing.

- Consider using icons to identify your information categories.

- Avoid using boldface, all caps, or other text emphasis styles.

- You will probably be saving your images as either GIF or JPEG. Compare versions of each type of image to see which file format provides the highest quality image and downloads as quickly as possible.

Communication and Interaction Tips

- Provide a way that users can communicate with you such as an e-mail link and/or your address.

- Explore Web sites to learn about new and innovative ways to provide opportunities for your visitors to interact and communicate.

Tips On Providing External Links

- Provide a short annotation on each link.

- Organize the links. Divide long lists into categories. Consider using graphics as dividers.

- Check your links to be sure they are not inactive. Periodically check all links to be sure they have not changed or gone dead.

- Provide useful and valuable links. Assess whether they add value to your site.

STEP 5: Build A Quality Web site

One important step that is frequently overlooked is to beta test your site with inexperienced users. All designers believe that they are providing well-organized, easy to find, valuable information that is visually effective. The only way to evaluate a site is to have as many individuals as possible use your site. Observe them as they navigate and interact with your content. Do they appear confused over content organization or navigation to information? Are they responding to your content in the way you had anticipated? Ask them for their impressions. Based on the feedback from beta test, make changes and revisions.

Continue to improve and upgrade your site by asking Web visitors to provide you with feedback. Provide a link with your e-mail address at the bottom of your home page.

World Wide Web Development Tools

There are many excellent books on HTML programming. I highly recommend *World Wide Web Design Guide* by Stephen Wilson. This well-designed, informative, and easy to understand book provides excellent information and examples on how to design professional Web pages, HTML and formatting fundamentals, and important information on interactive environments and working with images, video, and sound.

There are also many documents available free on-line to assist you with learning HTML.

HTML pages can also be created using commercial authoring programs. These authoring tools help to ensure that you will be able to transform your Web design blueprint into an attractive Web page. While HTML is not complicated to learn, authoring programs save time and provide easy to use tools for building links to text, images, video, and sound files as well the latest hot design features. While HTML authoring tools are still in their infancy and still do not provide all the tools you will need for tables, background colors and images, they are worth investigating.

The following HTML authoring programs are recommended.

- PageMill by Adobe Inc. (800) 441-8657
- FrontPage by Microsoft Corp. (800) 426-9400
- Netscape Navigator Gold available at **http://home.netscape.com**

Other authoring programs install on top of your current version of Microsoft Word and provide HTML authoring tools to use with your Word documents.

- Internet Assistant by Microsoft Corp. (800) 426-9400
- WebAuthor by Quarterdeck Corp. (800) 683-6696

Emerging Trends For The Internet

Once you make a decision to create a Web presence, it is important to keep informed about new software tools such as JAVA, VRML (Virtual Reality Modeling Language), RealAudio, Shockwave, and Web 3D. Browser support for plug-ins, and filters offers new creative possibilities. Keeping up with changes in Web innovations is essential for sites that want to continue to attract visitors.

Sun Microsystem's Java and recent breakthroughs in VRML are changing the face of the Internet. To learn more about these exciting Web tools, visit the following sites.

Java **http://java.sun.com** brings motion and interaction to Web pages.

Experience Java applets at **http://www.gamelan.com**

Experience the excitement of sound on demand at National Public Radio's site **http://www.npr.org** or KPIG Radio **http://KPIG.com**

RealAudio provides immediate sound to a Web page **http://www.realaudio.com**

Welcome to Liquid Reality offers a new sensory experience of the virtual and the real at **http://www.dnx.com/lr**

Virtual Reality Modeling Language (VRML) is an ASCII-based language that describes three-dimensional worlds. For more information on VRML visit the VRML Architecture Group **http://vrml.wired.com/VAG/** and the VRML Repository **http://www.sdsc.edu/SDSC/Partners/vrml**

VRML's Multimedia Gulch is at **http://www.hyperion.com/planet9/vrsoma.htm**

Macromedia's ShockWave for Director allows you to author rich multimedia content at **http://www.macromedia.com/**

Who's Got It Right?

Visit these creative and visually interesting sites to learn about designing pages.

The Spot: **http://www.thespot.com/**

Vivid: **http://www.vivid.com/**

Eat: **http://www.eat.com/**

Downtown Digital: **http://www.dtd.com/**

HotHotHot: **http://www.hot.presence.com/g/p/H3/index.html**

ESPN Sports: **http://ESPNET.SportsZone.com/**

Pathfinder: **http://pathfinder.com/**

HotWired: **http://www.hotwired.com/**

The Electronic Zoo: **http://netvet.wustl.edu/e-zoo.htm**

NETIQUETTE

Emily Postnews Answers Your Questions On Netiquette

Author: Brad Templeton
Contributions by: Gene Spafford

NOTE: this is intended to be satirical. If you do not recognize it as such, consult a doctor or professional comedian. The recommendations in this article should recognized for what they are—admonitions about what NOT to do.

"Dear Emily Postnews"
Emily Postnews, foremost authority on proper net behaviour, gives her advice on how to act on the net.

Dear Miss Postnews: How long should my signature be? — **verbose@noisy**

Dear Verbose: Please try and make your signature as long as you can. It's much more important than your article, of course, so try to have more lines of signature than actual text.

Try to include a large graphic made of ASCII characters, plus lots of cute quotes and slogans. People will never tire of reading these pearls of wisdom again and again, and you will soon become personally associated with the joy each reader feels at seeing yet another delightful repeat of your signature.

Be sure as well to include a complete map of USENET with each signature, to show how anybody can get mail to you from any site in the world. Be sure to include Internet gateways as well. Also tell people on your own site how to mail to you. Give independent addresses for Internet, UUCP, and BITNET, even if they're all the same.
Aside from your reply address, include your full name, company, and organization. It's just common courtesy—after all, in some newsreaders people have to type an **entire** keystroke to go back to the top of your article to see this information in the header.

By all means include your phone number and street address in every single article. People are always responding to usenet articles with phone calls and letters. It would be silly to go to the extra trouble of including this information only in articles that need a response by conventional channels!

———

Dear Emily: Today I posted an article and forgot to include my signature. What should I do? — **forgetful@myvax**

Dear Forgetful: Rush to your terminal right away and post an article that says, "Oops, I forgot to post my signature with that last article. Here it is."

Since most people will have forgotten your earlier article, (particularly since it dared to be so boring as to not have a nice, juicy signature) this will remind them of it. Besides, people care much more about the signature anyway. See the previous letter for more important details.

Also, be sure to include your signature TWICE in each article. That way you're sure people will read it.

———

Dear Ms. Postnews: I couldn't get mail through to somebody on another site. What should I do? — **eager@beaver.dam**

Dear Eager: No problem, just post your message to a group that a lot of people read. Say, "This is for John Smith. I couldn't get mail through so I'm posting it. All others please ignore."

This way tens of thousands of people will spend a few seconds scanning over and ignoring your article, using up over 16 man-hours of their collective time, but you will be saved the terrible trouble of checking through Usenet maps or looking for alternate routes. Just think, if you couldn't distribute your message to 30,000 other computers, you might actually have to (gasp) call directory assistance for 60 cents, or even phone the person. This can cost as much as a few DOLLARS (!) for a 5 minute call!

And certainly it's better to spend 10 to 20 dollars of other people's money distributing the message than for you to have to waste $9 on an overnight letter, or even 29 cents on a stamp!

Don't forget. The world will end if your message doesn't get through, so post it as many places as you can.

Q: What about a test message?

A: It is important, when testing, to test the entire net. Never test merely a subnet distribution when the whole net can be done. Also put "please ignore" on your test messages, since we all know that everybody always skips a message with a line like that. Don't use a subject like "My sex is female but I demand to be addressed as male." because such articles are read in depth by all USEnauts.

Q: Somebody just posted that Roman Polanski directed Star Wars. What should I do?

A: Post the correct answer at once! We can't have people go on believing that! Very good of you to spot this. You'll probably be the only one to make the correction, so post as soon as you can. No time to lose, so certainly don't wait a day, or check to see if somebody else has made the correction.

And it's not good enough to send the message by mail. Since you're the only one who really knows that it was Francis Coppola, you have to inform the whole net right away!

Q: I saw a long article that I wish to rebut carefully, what should I do?

A: Include the entire text with your article, particularly the signature, and include your comments closely packed between the lines. Be sure to post, and not mail, even though your article looks like a reply to the original. Everybody **loves** to read those long point-by-point debates, especially when they evolve into name-calling and lots of "Is too!" — "Is not!" — "Is too, twizot!" exchanges.

Be sure to follow-up everything and never let another person get in the last word on a net debate. Why, if people let other people have the last word, then discussions would actually stop! Remember, other net readers aren't nearly as clever as you, and, if somebody posts something wrong, the readers can't possibly realize that on their own without your elucidations. If somebody gets insulting in their net postings, the best response is to get right down to their level and fire a return salvo. When I read one net person make an insulting attack on another, I always immediately take it as gospel unless a rebuttal is posted. It never makes me think less of the insulter, so it's your duty to respond.

Q: I cant spell worth a dam. I hope your going too tell me what to do.

A: Don't worry about how your articles look. Remember it's the message that counts, not the way it's presented. Ignore the fact that sloppy spelling in a purely written forum sends out the same silent messages that soiled clothing would when addressing an audience.

Q: How should I pick a subject for my articles?

A: Keep it short and meaningless. That way people will be forced to actually read your article to find out what's in it. This means a bigger audience for you, and we all know that's what the net is for. If you do a followup, be sure and keep the same subject, even if it's totally meaningless and not part of the same discussion. If you don't, you won't catch all the people who are looking for stuff on the original topic, and that means less audience for you.

Q: What sort of tone should I take in my article?

A: Be as outrageous as possible. If you don't say outlandish things and fill your article with libelous insults of net people, you may not stick out enough in the flood of articles to get a response. The more insane your posting looks, the more likely it is that you'll get lots of followups. The net is here, after all, so that you can get lots of attention.

If your article is polite, reasoned and to the point, you may only get mailed replies. Yuck!

Q: They just announced on the radio that the United States has invaded Iraq. Should I post?

A: Of course. The net can reach people in as few as 3 to 5 days. It's the perfect way to inform people about such news events long after the broadcast networks have covered them. As you are probably the only person to have heard the news on the radio, be sure to post as soon as you can.

Permission kindly granted from Brad Templeton and Gene Spafford to pring *Emily Postnews Answers Your Questions About Netiquette*. For the full version, visit this Web site: **http://www.clari.net/Brad/Emily.html**

References

Angell, D. (1996, March). The ins and outs of ISDN. *Internet World*, 78-82.

Bennahum, D. S. (1995, May). Domain street, U.S.A.. *NetGuide*, 51-56.

Bernstein, J. H. (1996, May). Casting your telnet. *NetGuide*, 87-88.

Braun, E. (1994). *The internet directory*. New York: Fawcett Columbine.

Butler, M. (1994). *How to use the internet*. Emeryville, CA: Ziff-Davis Press.

Conte, R. (1996, May). Guiding lights. *Internet World*, 41-44.

Dixon, P. (1995, May). Jobs on the web. *SKY*, 130-138.

Ellsworth, J. H., & Ellsworth, M.V., (1994). *The internet business book*. New York: John Wiley & Sons, Inc.

Leibs, S. (1995, June). Doing business on the net. *NetGuide*, 48-53.

Leshin, C. (1996). *Internet Adventures step-by-step guide to finding and using educational resources*. Boston: Allyn and Bacon.

Miller, D. (1994, October). The many faces of the internet. *Internet World*, 34-38.

O'Connell, G. M. (1995, May). A new pitch: Advertising on the world wide web is a whole new ball game. *Internet World*, 54-56.

Netscape Communication Corporation. (January/February, 1996). *Netscape Handbook*. [On-line]. Currently available by calling 1-415-528-2555 or online by selecting the Handbook button from within Netscape.

Richard, E. (April, 1995). Anatomy of the world wide web. *Internet World*, 28-30.

Resnick, R., & Taylor, D. (1994). *The internet business*. Indianapolis, IN: Sams Publishing.

Sachs, D., & Stair, H. (1996). *Hands-on Netscape, a tutorial for Windows users.* New Jersey: Prentice Hall.

Sanchez, R. (1994, November/December). Usenet culture. *Internet World,* 38-41.

Schwartz, E. I. (1996, February). Advertising webonomics 101. *Wired,* 74-82.

Signell, K. (1995, March). Upping the ante: The ins and outs of slip/ppp. *Internet World,* 58-60.

Strangelove, M. (1995, May). The walls come down. *Internet World,* 40-44.

Taylor, D. (1994, November/December). Usenet: Past, present, future. *Internet World,* 27-30.

Venditto, G. (1996, April). Dueling tools: IW labs test 6 HTML authoring programs. *Internet World,* 37-49.

Venditto, G. (1996, May). Search engine showdown. *Internet World,* 79-86.

Welz, G. (1995, May). A tour of ads online. *Internet World,* 48-50.

Wiggins, R. W. (1994, March). Files come in flavors. *Internet World,* 52-56.

Wiggins, R. W. (1994, April). Webolution: The evolution of the revolutionary world wide web. *Internet World,* 33-38.

Wilson, S. (1995). *World wide web design guide.* Indiana: Hayden Books.

Additional Resources

World Wide Web, gopher, and FTP sites were found using InfoSeek, YAHOO, Lycos, WebCrawler, Alta Vista, VERONICA, and Archie.

About the Author

Cynthia Leshin is an educational technologies specialist with her doctorate in educational technology from Arizona State University. Dr. Leshin has her own publishing, training, and consulting company. She has authored three books: *Internet Adventures — Step-By-Step Guide To Finding And Using Educational Resources*, *Netscape Adventures — Step-By-Step Guide To Netscape Navigator and the World Wide Web*, and *Instructional Design: Strategies and Tactics*. The last of these is being used in graduate programs. Her company, XPLORA, publishes the *Internet Adventures* quarterly newsletter to assist teachers with integrating the Internet into the curriculum. Additionally, she is currently writing discipline specific Internet books and Internet-based learning activities for Prentice Hall.

Dr. Leshin has taught computer literacy and Internet classes at Arizona State University West and Estrella Mountain Community College. She currently teaches Internet classes using distance learning technology for Educational Management Group, a Simon & Schuster company. The Internet serves as a tool for teaching and communicating with her students. Her World Wide Web site is a learning resource for students and is also used when making presentations.

Dr. Leshin consults with schools and businesses interested in connecting to the Internet. Her expertise in educational psychology and theories of learning provides her with a unique background for translating complicated technical information into an easy-to-use, easy-to-understand, practical learning resource.

Index

A

B

C

INDEX

INDEX